Repossessions
Selected Essays on the Irish Literary Heritage

Repossessions
Selected Essays on the Irish Literary Heritage

Seán Ó Tuama

CORK UNIVERSITY PRESS

First published in 1995 by
Cork University Press
University College
Cork
Ireland

British Library Cataloguing in Publication Data
A CIP catalogue record for this book is available from
the British Library.

ISBN 1 85918 044 2 hardcover
1 85918 045 0 paperback

Typeset by Tower Books of Ballincollig, Co. Cork
Printed by ColourBooks, Baldoyle, Co. Dublin

do mo chuid mac léinn

Contents

PART IV OCCASIONAL

Acknowledgements

I am very grateful to Dr Joan Keefe (Berkeley, California), to Dr Peter and Siobhán Denman (Maynooth), to Professor Colbert Kearney (UCC), to Dr Pádraigín Riggs (UCC), to Dr Breandán Ó Conchúir (UCC) and to Dr Helen Solterer (Duke University) for their generous help in the preparation of this book for publication. Special thanks go to the editor and staff of Cork University Press, for their assistance and constant encouragement.

Repossessions is dedicated to the generations of my students in the Irish Department, University College Cork, who discussed and dissected in seminar with me much of the poetry presented here in translation.

The translations of contemporary poetry used in this volume are mostly to be found in *Translation* (Volume XXII, 1989, Columbia University, NY); translations of seventeenth and eighteenth-century poetry used are mostly to be found in *An Duanaire, Poems of the Dispossessed* (Ó Tuama/ Kinsella, 1981). Having both these anthologies at hand should be of considerable help to readers.

Notes and Abbreviations

When translations of poem titles are given in italics, reference is being made to a published translation with that title. Translations when not attributed are by myself. The date of publication of the original material is appended at the end of each essay.

The publishers wish to acknowledge the source of material that has been published previously. Original sources are to be found at the back of the book with the notes to each chapter. Translators' names appear in the text with the poems, and these translations are also gratefully acknowledged.

AOR   *Dánta Aodhagáin Uí Rathaille*, ed. Dineen and O'Donoghue, 1909
D   *An Duanaire: Poems of the Dispossessed*, Ó Tuama and Kinsella, 1981
DD   *An Dealg Droighin*, N. Ní Dhomhnaill, 1981
DG   *Dánta Grádha*, T. Ó Rathile, 1984
KLC   *Kings, Lords, and Commons*, F. O'Connor, 1962
F   *Filí faoi Sceimhle*, S. Ó Tuama, 1978
FS   *Féar Suaithinseach*, N. Ní Dhomhnaill, 1984
G   *Duanaire Ghearóid Iarla*, G. Mac Niocaill, Studia Hibernica 1963
Grá   *An Grá in Amhráin na nDaoine*, S. Ó Tuama, 1960
H   *Nuala Ní Dhomhnaill, Selected Poems*, trans. M. Hartnett, 1988
ES   *Eireaball Spideoige*, Seán Ó Ríordáin, 1952
Ph   *Pharaoh's Daughter*, N. Ní Dhomhnaill, 1990
T   *Translation (Irish Issue)*, ed. S Ó Tuama, XXII, 1989
U   *An Grá i bhFilíocht na nUaisle*, S. Ó Tuama, 1988

Foreword

THIS COLLECTION OF essays on Irish/Gaelic literature is primarily for readers of poetry who have little or no knowledge of the Irish language. Consequently – unsatisfactory though it may be – translations into English of the original texts are used for the purpose of critical commentary. The quality and objectives of the English versions vary widely, making it particulary difficult to attempt close readings based on the translations alone. At the same time, given that a large number of Irish people do not read Irish with any facility, it is appropriate that they should be provided with some kind of analytic introduction in English to what is, after all, their own cultural heritage. No other way suggests itself of helping them to repossess, to some extent, their own literature.

Critical analysis of literature in Irish has as yet scarcely begun. When I, as a young university lecturer (c.1950), was given the task of teaching some simple literary texts in Modern Irish, neither I nor anybody known to me in the field had any inkling of how to deal critically with such material; there were virtually no critical essays extant at the level required, no training available at undergraduate or postgraduate level which would allow one to present writing in Irish as an aesthetic act. Decades were to pass before it became possible for me to speak with some confidence of the literary qualities of Irish traditional literature.

In more recent times progress has undoubtedly been made in the critical presentation of writing in Irish. Some valuable work has been done, in particular, on contemporary literature (1882–). Evaluation of Early Modern Irish (c.1200–1600) and seventeenth/eighteenth-century literature is still, however, quite rare. The work of scores – if not hundreds – of poets, including that of a substantial number of major figures e.g. Dáibhí Ó Bruadair (c.1625–1698), Eochaidh Ó hEodhasa (c.1600), awaits even the most basic critical presentation. Not only that, but the opus of most of these unexplored literary figures either remains unpublished – preserved only in manuscripts – or available only in unsatisfactory editions.

The greater part of my own academic work has been done through the medium of Irish and centres on seventeenth and eighteenth-century poetry, on Irish love-poetry throughout the ages, and on contemporary writing. The core of this present volume consists of short English language summaries of special studies I have published in these areas, along with some background material to put them in context. Included also is a selection of occasional English language essays on loosely related topics; most of these have been previously published in various books and journals and are reproduced here with minor emendations. As the book includes some general survey-type material as well as essays on specific topics, some repetition of critical commentary inevitably occurs. It was felt, however, that the most satisfactory solution to this editorial problem was to allow the original material to stand unaltered.

During the decades since 1950 academic critical theories have rapidly supplanted one another. Most of these theories proposed a special way of reading a text rather than of evaluating it or highlighting its unique qualities. Such approaches do not seem to have made a major impact on literary criticism in Ireland. Nonetheless some teachers and critics of contemporary Irish Gaelic literature (including myself) found elements of modern critical theory very helpful in their work. As a student of that splendid teacher of English literature, Daniel Corkery, I had long been made aware of the manner in which particular levels of style operated in a play,* a poem, or a prose fiction, and consequently found certain elements of the theories of the Russian Formalists in this regard of compelling interest in my own endeavours in teaching literature.

One of the pioneering critics of this century, Northrop Frye, held it impossible to teach literature as an academic discipline. In his *Anatomy of Criticism* (1973) he says: 'one learns about it in a certain way, but what is learned transitively is the criticism of literature'. That may be so in many university departments of literature but I am not at all convinced that it need be so. At the very least one can teach students how to work at *recognizing* good literature.

---

*As a practising dramatist, I found myself interested in particular in the complex relation between style and dramatic production. See, for instance, my comments on Synge's style, pp. 228-30 below.

Preferring them to develop a taste for literature rather than for criticism,
I have never attempted to teach literary theory to undergraduates. I have
always believed it necessary, however, to present a poem (initially at any
rate) as an independent stylistic construct, standing on its own, with no
need of biographical or socio-historical gloss. Once the poem's worth as
a unique utterance has been more or less established or agreed, presen-
ting it at a later stage in its historical or biographical context can certainly
deepen the reader's perception of its mood or insight – provided that he/she
is careful to recognize that there is no necessary one to one correlation
between the historical and biographical 'facts' and the 'data' which underlie
a genuinely creative piece of composition.*

The reaction of students to an unglossed poem read in seminar can often
be of the intuitive, though vague, kind. Set the task of identifying the specific
(as opposed to the general) mood or insight being developed throughout
the poem, and in particular, of pointing out what features of the diction/im-
agery/poetic stance helped (or hindered) such development, students find
themselves willy-nilly facing up to 'learning' literature through the medium
of stylistic analysis; checking out, in fact, the stylistic world created by
the author against their own initial perception of it. I find that students
who themselves write are invariably more skilled than others in under-
taking such an analysis of style.

Style in this context, however, does not necessarily connote for me fine
professional writing – rather the unique verbal transformation which oc-
curs when an artist of special sensibility endeavours to communicate
his/her individual insight. Very few poets in any country, in any genera-
tion, achieve substantial transformational power; genuine poets of a lesser
order are also, I believe, quite limited in numbers. This viewpoint, however,
need not be presented to students in a way which is likely to discourage
them from continuing to write verse themselves. To achieve good profes-
sional writing (including various kinds of concerned human reporting)
is an ideal to which a great number of people might legitimately aspire,
and could be an important act of self-revelation for many.

In coming to an appreciation, not alone of the aesthetic achievements
of major and minor traditional Gaelic poets, but also of the community
values and cultural data present in the vast professional Gaelic literary

---

*It has been clearly shown that some of the most acclaimed writers (e.g Tolstoy, Lor-
ca) have treated historical or biographical facts in a most cavalier fashion. See my *Cúirt,
Tuath agus Bruachbhaile*, pp. 191–92, n. 8.

output down through the ages,* students of literature, as well as readers of poetry in general, could well find their awareness of life and of themselves deepened immeasurably. *Repossessions* is designed to help the process forward.

Seán Ó Tuama
Cork, 1995

*I touch on shared community values in Irish literature in Gaelic, and in Irish literature in English, in a few of my essays. See, for instance, *Celebration of Place in Irish Writing*, pp. 248-66, below.

PART I

MODERN POETRY IN IRISH

1

Background

I RISH WAS THE language of the mass of the Irish people for some two thousand years up to the middle of the nineteenth century. Only in the second half of that century, following three hundred years of planned military, economic and cultural pressures, did English become the dominant vernacular of the country. By this time also, literature in English began to replace literature in Irish as the national literature of Ireland. The nineteenth century then is the century when literature in Irish, for the first time since recorded history, lost its status and dynamism.

Between the years c.1880 and 1921 a remarkable national resurgence took place. With the founding of an Irish Free State in 1921 the Irish language gained new status, and since that time the number of people who declare themselves to have a reasonable knowledge of Irish has grown considerably. There are now more than a million people in the Republic who claim to be able to read and/or speak Irish at a moderate level of competence. That figure of course, must greatly exaggerate the number of people who, in fact, do communicate - even sporadically - with other people through the medium of Irish. On the other hand, only a quarter of the population report themselves as having no knowledge of Irish. Moreover, the level of claimed Irish language competence is found uniformly throughout the greater part of the Republic. Even in Dublin, where in Joyce's time not more than a few thousand people would claim knowledge of Irish, the figure now stands at more than a quarter of a million.

Favourable statistics regarding competence, and still more favourable statistics regarding attitudinal support, are not good indicators of the

3

position of Irish as an every-day spoken language in the country as a whole. Indeed Irish is rarely heard as a normal spoken language, a language of daily routines, except in the minute Gaeltacht areas where the number of Irish speakers continues to decline: in fact the numbers have declined since 1921 at approximately the same rate as they declined in the nineteenth century under British rule. In these areas there are now no monoglot speakers; English as well as Irish is used in everyday affairs. A certain stabilization in the linguistic position in the Gaeltacht may have been achieved in recent years with the establishment of a vital community radio and a successful programme of industrialization. In the next twenty years or so – during which time the influence of a long promised Irish language television station could well be a determining factor – it will finally be revealed, one thinks, whether the last traditional Irish-speaking communities in Ireland are going to survive. As it is, the picture is bleak: there is probably no more than one to two per cent of the population of the of the Republic, some 30,000 to 60,000 people, speaking Irish as a community language today in the Gaeltacht areas.

Viewed against this general linguistic and cultural background, modern literature in Irish is quite a remarkable phenomenon; for so disadvantaged a language, the amount and quality of verse produced is astonishing. Rarely does any language – even the most flourishing – produce, within a generation or two, a significant concentration of poets with substantial creative talent. It is all the more surprising then that in this century so many talented poets are writing in a language that has been in danger of extinction since the middle of the nineteenth century. I would regard three of these poets, Máirtín Ó Direáin, Seán Ó Ríordáin and Nuala Ní Dhomhnaill, as having gifts of a very high order.

Máirtín Ó Direáin (1910–1988) is undoubtedly the stylist *par excellence* among modern Irish writers. From both the living language of the Gaeltacht and literary sources, he has forged an elegant and polished mode of speech. Everything he has written bears the seal of a master stylist. Ó Direáin was the first Irish poet to speak in a recognizable contemporary voice to the generation which emerged after the founding of the state. His early work was an innocent lyric celebration of traditional life and values: later on, a defiant bitterness – and a developing hard-edged style – takes over as he protests against how modern urban materialistic society has reneged on these values. At the same time his best poetry grows, either directly or indirectly, from his naïve vision of life in his native Aran Islands. There is a tendency towards sentimentality throughout his work, however, not only in his idealization of the lost paradise of his youth — a tendency common in the work of many artists – but in his idealization of the entire life of his Aran Islands. This prevents him from dealing at a deeper level with that world, or any other world; he has indeed been unable to take a major leap into the dark – into the dark of Aran, or the dark of his own psyche. As a result, his work as a whole lacks incisive insight and a certain substantiality. However, his opus includes a few of the most delicate and appealing lyrics in modern Irish.

On the other hand, Seán Ó Ríordáin (1916–1977) has agonized unendingly – sometimes even humorously – about his own personal dilemmas of faith and conscience. His entire work reflects his struggle to understand his own insecure feelings and the threatening world in which he finds himself. This gives his poetry an overwhelming sense of search; at times a restless and agonized search, sometimes a witty intellectual search. His most memorable work is a handful of beautifully crafted lyrics, full of unique imagery, where his deep sense of terror and isolation is recorded. These poems of sickness, death, loneliness and frustration bear an overwhelming taste of the dark abyss to which he fears he will be consigned. In the conflict between the poet's chaotic feelings and the rigid, dogmatic society in which he lived, we come on some of the most authentic insights available to us into post-war Ireland. In developing these insights, Ó Ríordáin has integrated in a new way fundamental aspects of European Catholic or post-Catholic sensibility with Irish tradition. His work – the greater part of which is not yet adequately translated – is not in any noticeable way influenced by Yeats or by any other Irish poet writing in English; of English poets, only the modern, consciously Christian writers, Hopkins and Eliot, have left their mark. He is best read with these and with some of the classic European poets: Baudelaire, Rilke, Ponge. Above all other writers of Irish, Ó Ríordáin has brought 'modern' literature in Irish into the mainstream 'modern' European tradition.

Nuala Ní Dhomhnaill (1952–   ) may still be at an exploratory stage of her development, but already she has produced an opus which confirms her as one of the major poets of this century. Her poetry published to date is evidence of an overflowing feminine nature; yet it is not in any deliberate way a plea for women's rights or a proclamation of the freedom of modern woman. Freedom for her is the absolute right to confront and express her own turbulent feminine psyche. Her need for the life of the senses – children and lovers, flora and fauna – is evident throughout her work. There is a rich diversity, an immediacy, and a daring honesty in all her verse. She explores folk-tales and mythological concepts in a remarkable effort to comprehend her own nature, which she finds both highly attractive and highly repellent. Although she does not have the same sense of style as Ó Direáin had, or Ó Ríordáin's skillful craftsmanship, her sweeping grasp of her own explosive misshapen world – life as it is, rather than as it was or could be – can be clearly seen in her poetry.

The first attempts to establish a 'modern' poetry in Irish were made at the end of the nineteenth century. Poets then, and for a long period after that, had one major obstacle to overcome that is no longer a problem for contemporary poets. After the disastrous decline of the language and literature for a hundred years prior to this no one knew with any certainty where or how to begin. There was no living tradition of literary poetry, nor any recognized masters to help nourish a contemporary voice. For a long time previously the only contemporary masters had been poets writing in English; the nearest living literary tradition in Irish was the debased tradition of the late eighteenth century. Pádraig Pearse clearly identified the problem as far back as 1905: 'the predicament of the poets has been that, until now, they have had only two models: the fettered, complicated, vacuous eighteenth century [Irish] model, and the English language model, which had itself colonised the spirit of poetry' (trans.).

Pearse was entirely correct, and was himself, perhaps, the only poet of his generation to escape, to some degree, both dangers. As a result he managed to fuse his own sensibility with contemporary feelings in a handful of short lyrics. Although his corpus of poetry is miniscule, no other poet among the pioneers of the literary revival at the beginning of the century could by any stretch of the imagination be called a modern poet.

Some sense of his contemporary world was also captured by L.S. Gogan, (1891–1979) a poet who, of all those who wrote in the period between the founding of the state and the Second World War, has received the least recognition. Gogan was unusual in expressing his own sophisticated, urban mind by drawing on the poetic tradition of the eighteenth century, that very tradition most other good poets avoided. This, and his work as a lexicographer, left its mark on his language, which was often eccentric and over-literary. However, even in an eighteenth century idiom, he could successfully set a personal love-encounter in a wood painted by Corot, or portray a common canal barge in a manner that shows the influence of Impressionism. Gogan is perhaps the first Irish-language poet for many hundreds of years to feel at home in the realm of the visual arts.

There is even stronger evidence from the work of the generation of poets which emerged during the second stage of the literary revival (1939–c.1970) that the poetic muse, however personal or private, tends to be linked closely with contemporary feeling. Ó Direáin's poetry speaks to us not only of his own personal longing for the old ways of life on Aran, but also of the longing of all of those of his contemporaries who were concerned about the devastation of an old-world culture. Ó Ríordáin's poetry is a mirror, not only for his own troubled spirit as he faces eternity, but also for the turbulent doubting of the whole post-war generation. Máire Mhac an tSaoi's (1922-) most celebrated poem *Ceathrúintí Mháire Ní Ógáin* (The Quatrains of Mary Hogan) is an account of an illicit love affair which is rooted in that same general turbulence. *Aifreann na Marbh* (Mass for the Dead) by Eoghan Ó Tuairisc (1919-1982) is a highly-skilled description by a multi-talented writer of the greatest day of shame for his contemporaries – 'the day of the blasphemy against the sun', when a nuclear bomb was dropped on Hiroshima.

Neither Pearse nor Gogan provided a model which the post-war generation of poets (1939-c.1970) could use to nourish their own contemporary voices. Most poets had to begin a personal search for a language and for verse forms that would be suitable for their stylistic needs. Folk-songs, loose accentual forms of medieval syllabic models, versions of incantatory 'keening' verse, and so on, were all tried. Free verse forms – often quite closely based on songs and quatrains prevalent in the Gaeltacht – seem to be the most common. Máirtín Ó Direáin and Seán Ó Ríordáin were the most successful in forging their own voice from all this experimentation, and consequently are the most imitated. At last masters were available to the younger Irish poets, masters from whom they could learn or against whom they could react.

Máire Mhac an tSaoi, undoubtedly a gifted writer, does not seem to have widely influenced the poets who came after her. Though she was not born in an Irish-speaking area, she made a more determined effort than any other poet to link her muse (and her metrics) to the living Gaeltacht verse tradition. From this emanates both an exceptional richness of diction and, at times, a certain sense of pastiche. One can see, however, in her best lyrics – lyrics that are often concerned with passing moments of love and companionship – that her passionate sensibility is most fruitful when she restrains her eloquence, cuts back on traditional flourishes.

Most of the poets writing in Irish today belong, one could say, to the third phase (*c.*1970-) of the literary revival. This generation deals (more than any previous generation) with the contemporary world, life as it is lived now in cities and towns throughout Ireland. As Irish spreads, particularly in the cities, the psychological barriers that existed not so long ago between Irish and English speakers, become less clear. Consequently, while many young poets appreciate the richness of the language of the Gaeltacht, they often prefer to create an idiom which reflects more closely their own daily experiences, even if that idiom tends to reflect the influence of English. Though some of them are concerned about the threat to the language, or the waning of the ancient culture, they ultimately are more committed to celebrating or expressing their own humanity. They tend to ignore dogma, or at least any authoritarian traditional mode of thinking; though the language in which they compose is that of a tiny minority, they wish to see themselves as normal Irish people partaking in a common culture at the end of the twentieth century. It is no wonder then, that they take an interest – sometimes over-selfconsciously – in many of the distinctive features of that culture from rock and roll to haiku, from valium to ecology.

It is not surprising either that in the age of feminism the voice of women poets is to be heard with more openness and assurance than ever before in Irish. Besides Nuala Ní Dhomhnaill, two of these – Biddy Jenkinson (1949–) and Áine Ní Ghlinn (1955–) – have a rare poetic integrity. They each express a completely individual sensibility in a manner that will ensure, I think, that their work will gain increased recognition in the future.

If one poet more than another can be identified with this new wave in Irish poetry, it is Michael Davitt (1950–). The poetry journal *Innti* which he and his friends founded in 1970 has deeply influenced the attitudes of young poets, as much as the magazine *Comhar* did for the previous generation. Not only that, but he has himself composed highly distinctive poetry (containing a strange amalgam of violence and tenderness), and has developed a poetic idiom with which Irish speakers, from modern suburban Ireland especially, can identify.

Many readers of poetry in Irish first discovered in *Innti*, not only Davitt and the female poets mentioned, but also the work of many other writers of quality, e.g. Michael Hartnett, Cathal Ó Searcaigh, Liam Ó Muirthile, Seán Ó Curraoin. Of these, special mention must be made of Michael Hartnett who has written both in English and Irish. His poetry in Irish exudes an intimate lyric magic; indeed his poetic voice is more lucid, more natural perhaps, in his Irish poems than in those in English (which suggests that he probably was wise to turn away from composition in English for a while). Despite the naturalness of the poetic voice he discovered when he turned from composition in English, and however compelling the new lyrical quality surfacing in his work, he often finds it difficult to achieve an over-all definitive structuring of his subject matter through the medium of Irish.

It appears that the new generation of poets found little difficulty as to where or how they would start writing poetry. The way had been cleared for them; so much so that the increase in the number of poets writing today in comparison to twenty years ago is quite striking. It has been calculated recently, for instance, that at least ninety-four original books of verse had been published in the ten years between 1975 and 1985. It is likely that not even half that number of books of verse was published in the previous seventy-five years of this century. It must be admitted that some of the work being published is not of a particularly high quality, but on the other hand it should also be noted that the general standard of writing has improved dramatically. A high standard of writing does not itself, of course, ensure poetic achievement. One cannot ignore the possibility that some of our writers of verse might express themselves more effectively were they to turn to prose. As it is however, the fact that so many fine poets are writing in Irish must be seen as a remarkable phenomenon, as is the way modern Irish writing can successfully draw on a two thousand-year-old literaty tradition to come to terms, in a unique manner, with modern sensibility.

[1991]

2

Seán Ó Ríordáin,
Modern Poet

THE POST-WAR GENERATION of writers in Irish has in general produced work of a much higher quality in general than did the writers of the first period of Gaelic resurgence (1882-1939). These writers are possibly the first writers in Irish since the early seventeenth century to be in touch quite naturally with contemporary Europe (including Great Britain). They had read, of course, their own traditional Gaelic literature – e.g., O'Rahilly, Merriman, learned medieval love poems, folk poetry; Eliot and Freud, Joyce and Yeats, Marx and Beckett, also left their mark. Consequently when they wrote, they in some sense wrote modern literature of a kind that their elders (with the possible exception of Pádraig Ó Conaire) could not have done.

Of our poets, Seán Ó Ríordáin seems to be more in the main classic European poetic traditon than most others who have written verse in Ireland in the last fifty years. He stamps his own individual Irish personality on a western European mood and metaphysic which has been making itself felt since the time of Baudelaire. One cannot say that any one modern poet has had a deep formative impact on his work; least of all Yeats or any other of the 'Anglo-Irish' poets. The influence of Eliot and Hopkins in particular is certainly to be felt on his earlier work: these poets had an enormous impact on writing in the English-speaking world during the forties and fifties when Ó Ríordáin was at his most productive. But Ó Ríordáin did not become a 'modern' poet because of these – or any other – literary influences. That he is a 'modern' poet is due in the main to his own psyche, his special sensibility and the circumstances of his life.

Ó Ríordáin was born in Ballyvourney, County Cork, in 1916. Irish at that time was ceasing to be the normal everyday medium of communication for most of the people of Ballyvourney. Though his father spoke Irish, English was the language of the home; Ó Ríordáin's mother had little or no Irish. On the other hand, Irish was traditionally the community's literary language; a large amount of verse mostly based on eighteenth and nineteenth-century models, was still being composed in the district. Consequently Irish was probably the richer and more flexible of the two languages spoken in the community.

Some few of Ó Ríordáin's neighbours, including his grandmother, spoke Irish as an everyday language. Going from his mother's house to his grandmother's, was for him in many ways a journey from one world to another. The pull of these two worlds is seen constantly in his verse; it is strongly linked with the basic feeling of insecurity which pervades his whole work. His poetic personality is one besieged by storms, darkness, lust, sickness, religious doubts; looking feverishly for certainties, denying them as soon as they are found. In short, there is a basic psychological instability which the conflict of two languages, indeed of two cultures, must have severely aggravated.

After his father's death, Ó Ríordáin's mother moved with her family to Inniscarra, close to Cork City. Seán was fifteen years of age at the time, and attended the North Monastery secondary school where classes were mainly given through the medium of Irish. When he left school he worked as a clerk in the Cork City Hall, where (he says) he encountered Eliot's 'hollow men, stuffed men' circulating endlessly with bundles of forms and documents in their possession. Their lives and thinking was conducted entirely through English, as was most of Cork's everyday life. As a consequence, Ó Ríordáin often felt that Irish did not adequately express the needs of his personality. Indeed, at an early stage he set himself to writing in English, showing in some unpublished verses that he could achieve a certain level of competence, as in a light-hearted piece beginning 'It is restful to sit in an orderly room/Where the tongs seem to follow the thought of the mat . . .'.[1]

What is interesting about this and others of his trial pieces in English is the evidence that Hopkins, with his philosophical tendency to see the 'haecceitas'/'inscape'/'essence' of things as the proper goal of poetry, had already left his mark on Ó Ríordáin. Equally interesting about these pieces is the very un-Hopkins-like display of whimsical and irreverent humour which later on Ó Ríordáin deployed even in his most agonized lyrics. Ó Ríordáin, following Hopkins, declares his 'love incontinent/For all things, strange, fantastic, odd'; but in other phrases that would have dismayed the stern English poet he saw these things as 'The crooked things of accident/The fumbles of our funny God'.[2]

In a poem from his second collection, *Brosna* (Kindling), Ó Ríordáin speaks of the Irish language 'he carries' being suckled by the 'foreign whore', English. The 'foreign whore', of course, did perform a very necessary service for him as for all our modern writers: she brought with her a great slice of contemporary life – and of contemporary confusion – which literature in Irish had missed out on in the previous few centuries. Post-Christian Europe, with its doubts, its moods, its attitudes, began to affect strongly the traditional Irish mind from the mid-1940s on; Ó Ríordáin's poetry is perhaps the artistic achievement which best mirrors this turmoil as felt by the 'plain people' of Ireland.

I

It was about the year 1945 that the poetry of Seán Ó Ríordáin began to attract attention. In that year he published *Adhlacadh Mo Mháthar* (My Mother's Burial). He was over twenty-eight at that time, and what little verse he had published was not particularly distinguished. His mother's death seems to have been crucial to his poetic development – it seems likely that it helped him overcome the linguistic and psychological difficulties which had previously hindered his writing. He rarely treats of people other than himself in his verse; and when he does it is merely to place them within his own philosophic framework which he was constantly developing. When he speaks of his mother, however, he speaks in a tone of unabashed tenderness; a tone which otherwise scarcely appears in his work.

Adhlacadh mo Mháthar surprised and astonished those whose reading in Irish had hitherto been confined to traditional literature. Baudelaire, in his day, is spoken of as having created a new 'frisson' in French poetry; Ó Ríordáin similarly, in his day, created a new 'frisson' in Gaelic-Irish literature with the publication of this poem. In the very first verse we are in a milieu which poetry in Irish had never previously entered:

> A June sun in an orchard,
> A rustling in the silk of afternoon,
> An ill tempered bee is droning,
> scream-ripping the covering of day.

The imagistic and linguistic texture of these lines was entirely new to readers of Irish at the time. They would have found the syntax of the last two lines (in the original) particularly strange, as they would the compound word *scread-stracadh*/scream-ripping – a type of device ('synaesthesia') which Baudelaire and his symbolist followers popularized.

Another fashionably 'modern' effect which Ó Ríordáin introduces towards the end of his poem is that of 'bathos', which T.S. Eliot used skillfully to achieve a note of hopelessness, of despair. Ó Ríordáin's technique here is not at all as impressive as Eliot's:

> Lame litte verses being written by me,
> I would like to catch a robin's tail,
> I would like to rout the spirit of those
> knee-brushers,
> I would like to journey sorrowfully to the
> day's end.
>
> (V. Iremonger, *T*, p. 40)

Even though Ó Ríordáin has here produced one of his more memorable lines – 'I would like to catch a robin's tail' – it looses its impact by being placed in the middle rather than at the end of the verse.

Despite an occasional lack of mastery such as this in his verse technique, and despite what appears sometimes to be an over-obvious intrusion of English influences, *Adhlacadh Mo Mháthar* still stands as a unique poetic achievement: it is the first work in Irish where modern imagistic techniques are used, and fused successfully with a more traditional dramatic/storytelling technique.

In the story he narrates of his mother's burial, the majority of his images emanate from three main 'effects' – the grave, the snow, a wandering robin. These images fuse together, cross-fertilize each other and all relate finally to his relationship with his mother. At one point, even his description of the snowed over graveyard becomes a description of his mother's qualities – her innocence, her devoutness, her motherliness:

> And June toppled backwards into Winter.
> The orchard became a white graveyard by a river.
> In the midst of the dumb whiteness all around me,
> The dark hole screamed loudly in the snow.
>
> The white of a young girl the day of her First Communion,
> The white of the holy wafer Sunday on the altar,
> The white of milk slowly issuing from the breasts:
> When they buried my mother – the white of the sward.
>
> My mind was screwing itself endeavouring
> To comprehend the interment to the full
> When through the white tranquility gently flew
> A robin, unconfused and unafraid.

It waited over the grave as though it knew
  That the reason why it came was unknown to all
Save the person who was waiting in the coffin
  And I was jealous of the unusual affinity.

The air of Heaven descended on that graveside.
  A marvellous holy joy possessed the bird.
I was outside the mystery, a layman,
  The grave before me in the distance.

My debauched soul was bathed in the waters of sorrow,
  A snow of purity fell on my heart.
Now I will bury in my heart so made clean
  The memory of the woman who carried me three seasons
    in her womb.

The gravediggers came with the rough noises of shovels
  And vigorously swept the clay into the grave.
I looked the other way, a man was brushing his knees.
  I looked at the priest, in his face was worldliness.

(V. Iremonger *T*, pp. 38-40)

The 'unusual affinity' between the robin and the dead person (a topic which has been noted in Irish folk-tales) marks the moment where he feels that his mother is lost to him irrevocably. And at the end when he says 'I would like to catch a robin's tail', one senses this to be an expression of his feeling of futility. He is looking for the unattainable; the live presence, the intimacy, the stability of his mother.

The struggle for stability – for some belief, or person, to give meaning to his life – is the focus of much of his work from this time on. He sheds gradually the stylistic and metrical awkwardnesses which are noticeable in his first major effort. His exuberant and inventive imagery remains his principal poetic quality but he manages to give it a more Irish, a more homely shape, as for instance in his long poem *Cnoc Melleri* (Mount Mellary) where he struggles with his doubts about Catholic dogma and its effects on the human personality. In this first section of the poem where the positive, sunny aspects of Mellary are dealt with, the quirky cartoonist side of the Ó Ríordáin imagination is to the fore:

Last night over Mellary the stormclouds came snarling
and sin's easy past had my memory tumoured:–
Those soft days when life bedded down in fine linen,
Though the itchings of lust were like fleas going
    through me.

A windgust of footsteps swept up through the dark,
At midnight the monks were making for chapel,
Giddiness, twirlings and heels in the air,
Oh their sandals were singing out happily.

In the dining-hall supper is served by a brother
(Silence applied on the mind like a poultice)
And he mouthing phrases holy and hollow –
Naive carry-on of a natural-born Christian.

A dollop of sunlight infiltrated itself
By means of a humpy-arched casement;
Then this same sun, assuming the guise of a monk,
Studiously started perusing some pages.

A book had engrossed this pale alien cleric
Of a sudden the clock gave a cough,
The monk made of sun was snuffed out in a second,
In mid-sentence his reading cut off.

(P. Denman)[3]

The sudden darts of nonchalant humour which now appear in *Cnoc Mellerí* and in other work at critical moments are usually evidence of his struggle to master the unknown, the authoritarian. A puckish defence against chaos.

Doubts about religion and morality, as well as chronic periods of sickness, had begun from the earliest stages to aggravate Ó Ríordáin's basic feelings of insecurity. Aspects of life in Mount Mellary did nothing to put him at ease (as this prose translation of some verses makes clear):

They went past one by one, a graveyard incessantly praying, and a dense cloud of the church's green mould fell sadly on the evening's cheek.

Death puts a frost over life here, the monks are his servants, he is the abbot they serve, on whose behalf they fast and abstain.

A boy walking like a weary old man, an insult to God's protection whoever would do such injustice to a boy would put a cowl over the sun.

(S. Dunne)[4]

The Mellary experience only served to further deepen his insecurity: 'a drowning man's grasp of Mellary is this strawrope of verses'.

Ó Ríordáin spent quite a deal of his early manhood in sanatoriums, and at that period had been, once or twice, possibly on the point of death. In one early poem *Oíche Nollaig na mBan (The Women's Christmas Night)* – long before the existential notion of cosmic absurdity became familiar to Irish people – he imagines death as a melodramatic stormy event in an absurd world:

> Last night – the Women's Christmas Night –
>   From the madhouse behind the moon
> There escaped a storm that had Samson's might
>   As it screamed through the sky like a loon.
> The grating gates were gaggling geese,
>   The river a bronchial bull,
> And my candle was doused with a splutter of grease
>   By wind that hit it full.
>
> I hope that self-same storm will come
>   The night that I am weak,
> From the dance of Life returning home
>   As the light of sin grows bleak,
> That the chilling screams will lash like whips
>   And the crazy cries will drown
> Both the sound of the silence as through me it slips
>   And the battery running down.
>
> (D. Marcus, *T*, p. 41)

Sin is here viewed as 'light', the valley of tears as a dance venue, the other world as a 'madhouse behind the moon'; a human being is merely a machine that runs down into eternal silence. *Oíche Nollaig na mBan* is possibly the first poem in the Irish language where the existence of eternity and of a supernatural creator is openly refuted.

When he did have a real encounter with death, however, Ó Ríordáin found it a matter of no great terror or melodrama, in fact, a rather over-rated event. He tells us of this experience in *An Bás* (Death), which is curiously reminiscent of the well-known *Because I could not stop for Death* by Emily Dickinson:

> Death stood beside me
> I agreed to go
> No tears, no cry,
> Just analysed
> Myself in wonder.
> I said
> 'So that was me,
> Whole and entire,
> Goodbye brother.'
>
> As I look back now
> At that time

> When death came panting
> To take me
> And I was forced to yield,
> I think I recognise
> The ecstasy of a woman
> Expecting her lover
> – Tho' I'm far from female.

The conversational style here, and, in particular the resigned, nonchalant tone of 'Goodbye brother', successfully punctures the authority of death. As does his acceptance of Death as lover, puncture the authority of Christ. In typical medieval mystic theology (in the work of John of the Cross, for instance, who was one of Ó Ríordáins favourite authors), Christ is generally regarded as the lover who, on the death of the saint/mystic, takes him to himself throughout eternity as 'bride'. In *An Bás* however, while the poet-mystic still remains as 'bride', his eternal lover is imagined to be not Christ but Death. Behind the humorous casual exterior eternity again gets short shrift: here we have another statement of Ó Ríordáin's feeling that death is the last end. But there is no frenzy, no hysteria. Ó Ríordáin's humour, as developed in this and other poems, can be a very refined poetic instrument indeed.

While one of Ó Ríordáin's personae grappled agonizingly with his sense of the abyss, another more rational persona of his was constructing a philosophic system which would act as a defence against the dark. This is particularly apparent in the later poems in his first collection *Eireaball Spideoige*. In long poems such as *Oileán agus Oileán eile* (An Island and another Island), and *Saoirse* (*Freedom*), he explores his need for personal freedom as well as for a belief in the authentic essential self concealed behind his various personae. He finally finds both he tells us – but only within set limits. In *Saoirse*, for instance, he declares that freedom for his essential self was to be found only within the bonds of religion, and of traditional thought and behaviour (such as he had encountered in the Gaeltacht):

> I'll descend mid other men,
> Becoming pedestrian again,
> Starting tonight.
> Give me slavery I beseech,
> Free from freedom's frantic screech
> And my plight.
> Let a chain and kennel bound
> The packed thoughts that snarl around
> My solitude.

Organised religion rather,
Temples where the people gather
At set hours.
Let me cultivate the people
Who have never practised freedom
Or solitude.
Let me listen to the cheapest
Petty cash of thought and easy
Current coin
Let me learn to love that set
Of men from whom you only get
What's second-hand.
With you I'll spend nights and days,
And be humble in my ways,
And be loyal to every phrase
Of platitude.
Aspirations grew within me,
Grew and grew beyond all limit
And all measure.
So I've fallen in love with limits,
With all things with temperance in them,
With the derived.
With rule and discipline and crowded churches.
With common nouns and well worn words and
With stated hours.
With all abbots, bells and servants,
With all simile unassertive,
With all shyness,
With mice and the measured, the flea and the
    diminutive,
With chapter and verse, and things as simple as
The A.B.C.
With the drudgery of exchanging greetings,
And the penance of card-playing evenings,
And exits and entries.
With the farmer guessing at what wind
Will blow in harvest with his mind
On his field of barley.
With common sense and old tradition,
And tact with tiresome fellow-Christians,
With the second-hand.
And I declare war now and ever
On freedom's fruits and all unfettered
Independence.

Ah disillusion yawns for
The giddy mind that's fallen
Where freedom's deeps are calling.
We find within those borders
No hills God made or ordered,
But ghost-hills of the thought-world.
Abstract or metaphoric,
Each hill is full of longings,
Like climbers pressing onwards
That never rest in objects
Fruition never comes there.
Freedom that wills no limit,
Hills of undefined ideal,
Desire with no 'Don'ts' in it,
Unwill their own fulfilment,
And never reach the real.

(C. Quinn, *T*, p. 43-44)

Anyone reading this poem would not be in the least surprised that Ó Ríordáin, having wrestled with his doubts for a long time, openly reverted to Rome. In a poem called *Teitheadh* (Escape), which reminds one a little of Verlaine's *Il pleure dans mon coeur comme il pleut sur la ville*, he tells us explicitly how he fled into a city church to avoid a downpour and 'the rain fell down in Rome'.

But a poet's deepest feelings do not always coincide with his philosophy, and some of Ó Ríordáin's verse in later collections continues to reveal a poet who cannot find rest or assurance in the institutions, ideas or conventions he has been persuading himself to accept. In his second volume *Brosna* (Kindling) (a slim collection which appeared in 1964, twelve years after the publication of *Eireaball Spideoige*), and in his third even slimmer collection *Línte Liombó* (Lines from Limbo), published eight years later again, it was obvious that his philosophic exploration in *Eireaball Spideoige* of how to deal with his uncertainties had not been deeply or emotionally satisfying.

II

In *Brosna*, one of the most-distinguished volumes of verse ever published in Ireland, 'chaos is come again'. On one hand we have here a group of poems which tell in semi-philosophic terms of the poet's bewildered and continuing quest for his essential self; on the other hand we have a series of turbulent lyrics emanating directly from his own overwhelming fear of the abyss.

Ó Ríordáin's diction and verse forms are now much more assured than previously; his imagery more pruned, more functional. His most memorable poems are not those concerned with the poet's intellectual efforts to come to terms with his own unstable personality, but those expressing his immediate emotional day-by-day experiences. It is helpful to look more closely at a few of the more revealing of these (of which translations are available).

Underlying a significant part of Ó Ríordáins work, one senses a deepseated terror of an evil autonomous dark world 'outside', which is set on stifling him. In *Claustrophobia* this threat is felt in a very tangible corporeal fashion: the poet's defective lung is being besieged by the hostile powers of darkness:

> Beside the wine
> There is a candle and terror,
> The image of my Lord
> Seems to have no power,
> The rest of the night
> Is like crowds without,
> Night reigns
> Outside the window;
> If my candle goes out
> In spite of me now
> Night will leap
> Right into my lung,
> My mind will be overcome
> And terror created for me,
> I shall be turned into night,
> To be a living darkness:
>> But if my candle lives on
>> For one night alone
>> I shall be a republic of light
>> Till daylight comes.

(J. Gleasure, *T*, p. 47)

The scenario created for us in the first four lines – a candle, a statue of the Lord, wine, terror – would be widely familiar. They evoke the bleakness of an altar on which a sacrifice is about to be offered, and it is clear that the poet feels that he himself is likely to be the sacrificial victim. The Lord – or His image – does not seem to hold out much comfort to him in his battle against the forces of night gathered outside his window. These are seen as a fascist government* ready to put him down,

*The phrase 'Rialtas na hoíche' / 'The Government of night', is used in the original.

to puncture his lung. (The terror of suffocation, however, rather than that of claustrophobia is, I think, the paramount feeling in the nervous, breathless lines of the original Irish.)

Having re-created for us the immediacy of his particular terror, Ó Ríordáin focuses unexpectedly on the reassurance provided by his lighted candle. If it lasts through the night, he shall be (he remarks, one thinks, with a wry Beckettian smile) 'a republic of light until daylight comes'. The conjunction of 'light' and 'republic' is peculiarly apt in Ireland. The word 'republic' speaks of freedom, independence, of lone stands against tyrannical government. But in this instance all the poet can hope for is that his 'republic of light' will last until morning. The temporary nature of the hoped for relief only serves to underline the permanent nature of the threat. Ó Ríordáin must have frequently felt during his life that the best he could hope for was survival until morning.

Na Leamhain (*The Moths*) is a poem of disturbing mesmeric quality, not yielding easily to interpretation. The main scenario is established for us once again in the first four lines:

> Whirr of a fragile moth, a page turning,
> A spoiling of tiny wings,
> A night in Autumn in the bedroom,
> Torment of a fragile thing.
>
> Another night in a dream I saw
> A pair of great moth-wings,
> They were as wide as wings of angels
> And as a woman fragile things.
>
> It was my care to lay a hand on them
> Lest they go straying through the night;
> To possess them in the best of sanctuaries
> And bring them to the fullness of delight.
>
> But I spilled all the blessed dust
> That on each wing was poured,
> And I knew then that I was left without
>   numbers,
> The numbers of manliness for ever-more.
>
> And the ten numbers strode out of the error,
> Their authority still greater than before,
> And a sound was heard of races dealing in
>   numbers,
> And all were heard save me alone.

Whirr of a fragile moth, a page turning,
The diaphanous in ruins,
A night in Autumn and the moths are flying,
Great my heed on their little bruit.

(E. Ní Loinn, *T*, p. 48)

The *dramatis personae* - moth and poet - are subtly introduced, and iden-
tified with each other, through the sounds they make as they quest for
the light; the poet's 'turning of a page' ('iompó leathanaigh'), delicately
and impressionistically echoes moth-sound. In the first verse the moth
- prey to some minor torment - bruises its fragile wings; in the last verse
these wings are totally ruptured. Meanwhile in the body of the poem the
poet tells us of a dream he had on another occasion when he imagined
he had done irrevocable damage to a pair of mothwings which had been
entrusted to his care.

The image of mothwings would seem then to be the basic image from
which the poem evolves. It was the poet's business 'to possess them' and
'to bring them to full delight'. However he 'spilled the blessed powder that
was spread on every wing', leaving him with the realization that he was
'without the numbers of virility forever'. Then suddenly the ten digits stalk
unaccountably and authoritively through his dream: multitudes of peo-
ple, he felt - except himself - were dealing with these numbers.

Much of the imagery as it develops seems to have sexual connotations,
yet it can scarcely be maintained that the main image, a 'pair of mothw-
ings', is a representative image for any special sexual function or behaviour.
It is more likely - though here one may be accused of making use of extra-
textual information - that Ó Ríordáin perceived the mothwings as having
an analogous function to a pair of human lungs in maintaining mobility
and general health. A damaged mothwing, just like a damaged human lung,
was a clear threat to continuing health and life. For the poet, the primary
consequence of severely damaged health (as one divines it from this par-
ticular poem with its sexual undertones) is the isolation and frustration
which the absence of normal sexual activity brings about.

In the last verse the moth, whose bruised wings led to the poet's dream,
finally ruptures its membranes. It becomes the fatally wounded one amongst
a multitude of fluttering moths - not unlike what the poet imagines he
has become (or may become?) amongst his virile fellow human beings.
The poem which began as a simple identification of moth and human
sound in a bedroom on an autumn night points finally at a distressing
personal tragedy.

Fiabhras (*Fever*) brings us most perceptively through all the steps of a
debilitating fever:

The slow climb out of the bed
From the wet heat of its valley
To where its mountains step off into nothing . . .
So far to the floor now
Though perhaps, there is, somewhere
A long way off, a world that still works.

We are in a region of sheets here –
The thought of a chair in this place!
So hard now to believe
Sunlight back in the other world
Where we stood once high as a window.

The frame has dissolved and
His image is rising out of the wall –
No quarter there anymore:
Wraiths ring me now,
I think the world is melting . . .

A region is growing out of the sky,
There's a neighbourhood resting on my finger-tip –
So easy to pick off a steeple!
There are cows on the road to the north,
But the cows of eternity are still making noise.

(R. Ryan, *T*, p. 46)

What we have here is the geography of a fever. The fever is represented as gradually distorting all identifiable landmarks. Valleys, mountains, plains, roads, take on new dimensions; eternity, pressing down on the poet, is palpable.

In the first verse one senses the lucidity of a child not yet overwhelmed by illness: 'so far to the floor now'. In the second verse, where the poet speaks in the plural, only a little memory remains of childhood days: 'we once stood high as a window'. (The use of the plural may indicate the feeling, frequently reported, of a barely conscious self observing a separate sick self in the one body.) In the third and fourth verses not alone do the ordinary dimensions disappear but the whole world begins to melt. The picture on the wall swells up (a nightmare image of a kind one encounters in the work of Salvador Dali or Max Ernst); the frame dissolves. The living landscape and the landscape of eternity are telescoped into each other. The poet is clearly at the climax of his fever.

In the second last line of the poem, however, we encounter the first normally-focused observation in the poem: 'There are cows on the road to the north'. The poet is again in a world the dimensions of which he recognizes, and this is most likely a sign of recuperation. But (no matter how one translates or interprets the obscure last line of the original) the poet seems unsure whether or not eternity still threatens.

Reo (*Frozen*) is a poem of ten lines, in which Ó Ríordáin consciously or unconsciously reverses and transforms one of the oldest European love-formulas, that of the poet walking out one leafy summer morning and meeting a fair lady. Here it is a winter's morning, frost in the air, the boughs bare and he encounters not love but death. The frozen abrasive feeling of a handkerchief he touches on a bush is finally identified as a similar feeling – long forgotten, one feels – to that felt by him when he kissed a woman of his kindred 'and she in the coffin, frozen, stretched'. This is quite probably another lament for his mother, beautiful, unique, and absolutely in the Irish as well as in the European literary tradition:

> On a frosty morning I went out
> And a handkerchief faced me on a bush.
> I reach to put it in my pocket
> But it slid from me for it was frozen
> No living cloth jumped from my grasp
> But a thing that died last night on a bush,
> And I went searching in my mind
> Till I found its real equivalent:
> The day I kissed a woman of my kindred
> And she in the coffin, frozen, stretched.

> (V. Iremonger, *T*, p. 40)

Most of the verse in *Brosna*, and especially the verse discussed here, shows a master-craftsman at work. The jingling verse forms – often based on popular song in the Irish language – which cause some awkward moments in the longer poems of his first volume have now been abandoned. Ó Ríordáin finally manages, with ease, to merge modern feeling and imagery with traditional verse forms and structures. *Claustrophobia* and *Reo*, for instance, elegantly echo the metrical forms of classic Irish folksongs; *Claustrophobia*, *Fiabhras* and *Na Leamhain* clearly avail of a type of the traditional dramatic lyric developed by Aogán Ó Rathaille.

III

A cursory reading of some of Ó Ríordáin's poetry available in translation gives little idea of the complexities of feeling and thought underlying the whole opus. While he is in some ways a highly traditional Irish poet – influenced strongly by major literary poets such as Haicéad and Ó Rathaille, as well as by anonymous folk poets – he is also very much in the European tradition of 'modern poetry'. One of the most profitable ways, perhaps, of appreciating his work is to place it within its broad European framework.

The term 'modern poetry' is used here to describe in general the classic western European poetic movement from about the time of Baudelaire and Rimbaud, down (let us say), to the Ó Ríordáin era. Various aspects of this movement – some of them apparently contradictory – have been described in detail by literary critics and commentators, but for my purposes here I would like to point to what may well be a common philosophic insight at the base of this complex international movement which left its mark on various cultures from Great Britain to the Americas.

'A revolution in the imagery of poetry', says Edmund Wilson, 'is a revolution in metaphysics'.[5] Indeed it is virtually inconceivable that a broad international movement in poetry or art can take place without its being rooted in a new feeling about the meaning and conduct of life – reflecting a new sensibility. It has been rightly noted that at about the middle of the nineteenth century a deep distrust of reason as a guide to truth began to make itself felt in Western Europe. Baudelaire and Rimbaud in particular were virulent in their attack on the rational, dogma-making element in the human being. Of course poets, Romantic poets in particular, have always depended more on the truth of imagination than of reason, but in this instance a concerted positive attack was mounted, as never before, on the idea of rational man. The deeper purpose of this was, it seems, to release in greater measure the intuitive forces of the mind; to journey 'au-delà du possible, au-delà du connu' (Baudelaire); to discover moments 'in and out of time' (Eliot). Intuition was to replace reason and, ironically, with the concurrence of philosophers and social scientists, the concept of 'intuition' became a rigid rational dogma in its own right. Bergson (1859-1941), for instance, held that intuition was our most sensitive guide to the discovery of truth; Husserl (1854-1938) and his school of phenomenology – which deeply influenced Sartre – declared (as I understand it) that the essence of things can be discovered through the power of intuition.[6] Freud began to investigate the concept of a non-rational subconscious. Amongst the poets, the French symbolists in particular worked on imagistic techniques designed to help the poet release his intuitive perceptions, without hindrance from the rational mind made rigid by centuries of dogmatic philosophic thought (and indeed by formal, highly-structured verse forms). These imagistic techniques have influenced most major European poets down to the middle of the twentieth century, and Ó Ríordáin, as we saw, is no exception. One of the consequences of all this is that the classic modern poet has reverted, to some extent, to his age-old function as mage or druid. He feels that his intuitive use of word-images are the only certain good. In most of his poetry Ó Ríordáin unhesitatingly accepts this role of poet as intuitive seer, one whose sporadic insights puts him directly, as he says himself, 'in step with God'. And the traditional Irish view of poet as magician undoubtedly makes it easier for him to adopt this position.

It is noteworthy, however, that a great number of poets of the 'modern' movement do not seem to be overtly concerned with the grandiose concepts of the romantics, but with *things* – commonplace everyday things and happenings. It is as if they wished to experience anew man's first interaction with the material world without the intrusion of dogma or philosophy; to observe things as if we were the first generation on this planet. While Husserl and the phenomenologists were engaged in a most minute description of the most inconsequential events and things, Rilke was declaring that his poetry did not represent his own feelings but 'things he had felt'.[7] Joyce later made a similar remark about his own prose epiphanies,[8] and of course the whole of *Ulysses* is a celebration of the commonplace. Many major poets down to our own day have joined in this celebration of the commonplace.

One of the most notable of these in this century has been, perhaps, the French poet Francis Ponge who has said that poetry begins with things rather than with ideas. Thus the great bulk of his poems[9] bears mundane titles such as 'A glass of water', 'The pleasure of opening a door', 'An unfinished ode to mud', etc. Any of these could be the title of an Ó Ríordáin poem. The homely, daily event is central to Ó Ríordáin's work also. He writes of a blind man combing his hair, of himself smoking his pipe (a topic which had already been famously treated by Baudelaire and Mallarmé), of a man looking into the eyes of a horse, of sending his dog to the dogs' home, of putting the cat out at night and, fittingly enough, his most popular anthology piece is called *Cúl an Tí* (The Back of the House).

Concern with things should be understood, of course, as a concern with their essential rather than their accidental qualities. Yeats emphasized that it was the poet's business to fill the mind 'with the essences of things rather than with things'.[10] Rilke, Hopkins and many others of our major 'modern' poets have all made similar statements; indeed since Baudelaire's *Correspondences* it has been widely accepted both by literary figures and by the reading public that the poet has within him the power to identify with the essence of things, happenings, animals, other people.

It seems probable, however, that poets in general (and indeed philosophers such as Husserl) tended to equate an idea of the poetic essence of things with the philosopher's idea of a perennial immutable essence (an idea which can be traced back through Aquinas, Scotus and other medieval scholastics to Plato and Aristotle). Rilke, of whom it was said '[he] taught us to "see" essences',[11] finally dissented from this viewpoint: he saw the poet as celebrating the 'fleeting' quality rather than the enduring essence of things.

Ó Ríordáin, however, like many poets down to the Existentialist period, tends to accept in general the idea of the poet's gift – and indeed the gift of other special people – to identify with the enduring essence of things. He considerably extends and refines the idea in the foreword to *Eireaball Spideoige* and throughout much of his opus. In his poetry the *locus classicus* for his basic belief is to be found at an early stage in his throwaway, lighthearted poem, *Malairt* (Exchange), where sympathetic man and gloomy horse exchange eyes:

'Come here' said Turnbull, 'and see the sorrow
In the horse's eyes,
If you had his big hooves under you there'd be sorrow
In your eyes too,'

And 'twas clear that he well understood the sorrow
In the horse's eye –
Had considered it until he had plumbed the very marrow
Of the horse's mind.

I gave a look at the horse to see the sorrow
Standing up in his eyes,
I saw Turnbull's eyes tracking me like an arrow
From the horse's skull.

I gave Turnbull a look that was mean and narrow
And I saw in his head
Those everbig eyes that were dumb with sorrow –
The horse's eyes.

(D. Marcus, *T*, p. 42)

This, and other work by Ó Ríordáin, bears an uncanny resemblance to poems by Baudelaire (whom he is very unlikely to have read at that time). In Baudelaire's *Le Chat*,[12] for instance, the poet having looked so long into the eyes of his cat, feels them staring at him when he meditates within himself:

Quand mes yeux, vers ce chat que j'aime
Tirés comme par un aimant,
Se retournent docilement
Et que je regards en moi-même,

Je vois avec étonnement
Le feu de ses prunelles pâles,
Clairs fanaux, vivantes opales,
Qui me contemplent fixement.

There are, possibly, many different ways of explaining the pursuit, both
conscious and intuitive, of things and their essences in modern poetry.
One of the fundamental reasons, however, must surely be the overwhelming
need of the poet - through deep sympathetic contact with things and people
external to himself - to come to terms with his own essence, his own self.
'There can be no man' says a modern psychiatrist, 'unless there are two
men in communication.'[13] 'No one', says Ó Ríordáin, 'can taste his own
taste.' Ó Ríordáin, as we have seen, is deeply concerned with the number
of shifting personae contained within his own personality: his public versus
his private self; his Victorian Catholic and his traditional native self; his
English-speaking and Irish-speaking self; etc. By strengthening his intui-
tions about the essences of things and creatures external to himself, he
clearly hopes to discover the essence of his own self; to discover, in fact,
if he himself has an essence which is stable, immutable and eternal. The
poet who feels himself to have a stable unchanging personal essence will,
of course, intuitively feel the existence of a stable creator who has taken
the personal decision to create this particular essence. On the other hand,
an artist such as Beckett who feels that man consists of accidental strata
of changing selves moulded by history, geography, society, personal deci-
sions, etc., cannot intuitively feel the existence of anything other than an
unstable impersonal creator - the void. In this sense much of the greatest
modern poetry, in its pursuit of things and their essences, is ultimately
a spiritual poetry endeavouring to discover the nature of creation. Ó
Ríordáin may be one of the last authentic poets in the main tradition.
On the one hand he has the undeniable poetic ability to create in artistic
form the 'essence'/'haecceitas'/'taste' of a fever, a kiss, a burial; on the
other hand he displays an impressive intellectual ability in his meta-
physical poems to relate his poetic gift to a comprehensive philosophical
system.

It would be wrong, I think, to believe that Ó Ríordáin has deliberately
fashioned his philosophic system by consciously adopting the underly-
ing concepts of the modern poetic movement, or by following the precepts
of any one poet or writer. Ó Ríordáin had certainly read widely in poetry
and prose by the early forties: Yeats, Hopkins, Ibsen, Tolstoy, Chekov, Strind-
berg, Turgenev. Of these Hopkins and Ibsen seem to have been most directly
influential,[14] but generally speaking Ó Ríordáin feels and thinks as he
does because of his own psychological make-up.

From his beginnings it seems apparent from his verse that he was deeply troubled by what psychologists have called 'ontological insecurity/fear of engulfment'. Such a person according to R. D. Laing 'is forced into a continuous struggle to maintain a sense of his own being. . . . The total self, the "embodied self", faced with disadvantageous conditions, may split into two parts, a disembodied "inner self" felt by the person to be the real part of himself, and "a false self" embodied but dead and futile, which puts up a front of conformity to the world.'[15]

Ó Ríordáin's work from early times is obsessed with the notion of his true self and false self. He undoubtedly encountered this concept in Yeats and in other writers: the idea of 'essential self' as well as 'essence' was everywhere in the air. But for Ó Ríordáin this was no mere literary theme to deploy: it was an integral part of his fundamental sensibility, and in his opus a series of contradictory sets of concepts continue to flow directly from his obsession: self/anti-self; inside/outside; light (candle)/darkness (wind); eternity/death; freedom/bondage; truth/falsehood; Irish/English etc. One cannot help feeling that in some of his later poems like *Rian na gCos* (Footmarks) he is on the verge of becoming a victim of split personality.* Here he is clearly plagued by the feeling - which we all recognize in ourselves in a minor form - that one's nature consists of strata of changing selves: 'is mó mé i mise amháin' ('there is many a me in one myself'). Even the simple act of travelling from one place to another can lead to a persona change: 'He walked with me that morning/We two on the one same path./Returning home it struck me/I saw his footmarks in the mud'.

Variants of this feeling occur everywhere in his verse. In *A Ghaeilge im Pheannsa* (O Irish in my Pen) he asks of his Irish language persona: 'Is it your words I use/when I commit sin?'. In *Daoine* (People) he affirms that having played through a number of false personae, one finally discovers the essential self ('an duine is dual'). In *Fill Arís* (Return Again),[16] one of the most elegantly crafted poems he has written, he argues - rather improbably - that his real self can only be realized in the Kerry Gaeltacht when he has shaken off the crippling effects of English civility, of Shelley, Keats and Shakespeare. He ignores the extent of what his 'real self' owes to English civility, how impossible it is for him to disencumber himself of Shelley, Keats and Shakespeare. But anyone who has felt the deep, though transitory, healing quality of a rural Gaeltacht district in summer will forgive him for overstating the case.

In the foreword to his first collection, *Eireaball Spideoige*, Ó Ríordáin argues that the real self reveals itself most faithfully in its 'authentic'

---

* 'Schizophrenia' - a term often incorrectly used in the past to describe 'split personality' - is the term I use in my original essay in Irish.

actions ('gníomh ionraic'). In this he seems to be closely following Hopkins (whom he quotes): 'what I do is me'. He pursues this notion actively in his verse, and in particular in the long poem *Oileán agus Oileán eile* (One Island and another Island) where he endeavours to understand the free 'authentic' act of St Finbarr who chose the misty, sombre island of Gougane Barra to live out a life of grim asceticism. One should be able, according to Ó Ríordáin to come into contact with the 'essence', the 'true self', of St Finbarr by empathizing with this basic act.

When the poet arrives at Gougane Barra, however, he finds himself beset by doubts about all this: even the 'Domine dilexi decorum domus tuae' of the Latin mass becomes an insipid Irish language jingle on his lips. The song of an unidentified bird – a creature acting authentically according to its own essence – encourages him, however, to pursue St Finbarr further; and he celebrates his regained certainty in one striking passage which, it has been pointed out, seems to echo lines and phrases from Ibsen's *Peer Gynt*, which was one of Ó Ríordáins bedside books and in which 'to be yourself' (despite the lure of a malignant world), is a central theme.[17] Nonetheless, Ó Ríordáin's metaphysical statement here, made with consummate grace and skill, is an accurate reflection of his own very individual feelings at the time:

> In the truth that is within the mind
> There is a place serene,
> An island hermitage where you must dwell
> And seek your inmost being,
> Tremble not when you with you
> Come face to face,
> Though the fire you are
> Consume you in its rage,
> For you are but a curse
> The world flung about,
> An aimless chattering
> That goes from mouth to mouth:
> Though first you came a shining prayer
> By God's Son spoken,
>
> With wordly love the you He made
> You've rent and broken,
> Still on your island
> You remained a prayer,
> Still quietly whispered
> On God's lips there,
> While you unheeding
> Danced the world's way.
>
> (M. Ó Ríordáin)[18]

After this, the poet now feels himself finally able to investigate St Finbarr's essential nature on the island of Gougane Barra where the saint – reputedly – chose to dwell. He looks for a symbol or a sign to guide him, and 'found it in the trees'.

There is a strange similarity between this approach and that of the Greek poet, George Seferis, who in his much acclaimed poem *The King of Asine*[19] tries to discover the nature of the king by investigating the ruins of his ancient fort in Nauplia:

> And the poet lingers looking at the stones, and asks
>   himself does there really exist
> among these ruined lines, edges, points, hollows and
>   curves, does there really exist
> here where one meets the path of rain, wind and rain
> does there exist the movement of the face, shape of
>   the tenderness
> of those who diminished so strangely in our lives. . . .

Seferis concludes that it is impossible to discover in any significant way 'the King of Asine/we have been searching so carefully on this acropolis/sometimes touching with our very fingers his very touch upon the stones'.

On the other hand, the wild gnarled trees on the island of Gougane Barra yield up their secret message to Ó Ríordáin. He discovers that the essential St Finbarr, having fought and overcome a corrupt world, is stamped everywhere on the trees The saint emerges as an old Irish Gandhi, emaciated, eccentric, misshapen. And, most importantly, the poet senses an air of freedom everywhere on the saint's island:

> The joy of freedom is in the shape of trees/and love of squinted
> eyes/desire for what is crooked and entangled/rejection of what is soft
> and linear.

Whether one finds the poet's quest in Gougane Barra a product of high imagination or of theoretical 'fancy' (as Coleridge understood the word) it is clear at any rate that in this central poem in his first collection he is willing to countenance what had previously appalled him in *Cnoc Melleri*: that one should be willing to have one's humanity 'iced over', subjected to a rigid philosophic or religious system, so as to ensure – within stringent limits – personal freedom. And as we saw, this in turn led him in *Saoirse* to affirm his adherence (for a while) to traditional beliefs and established religion.

IV

Ó Ríordáin – especially in his first two volumes, *Eireaball Spideoige* and *Brosna* – functions on what seems to be two contradictory levels. First of all he has a basic corpus of poems (including *Adhlacadh mo Mháthar, Oíche Nollaig na mBan, Claustrophobia, Fiabhras, Reo, Na Leamhain*) in which he manages to recreate in the starkest forms the characteristics of his terror, his loneliness, his isolation. He reveals himself as a solitary figure in an unstable world where storms blow, lights are quenched, darkness or sickness or death threatens. Then on another level he tries to wrestle intellectually with the abyss. In a series of philosophic or semi-philosophic poems the poet tries in rational terms to understand or explain, or even explain away, his feeling of abysmal insecurity. After the death of his mother, who seems to have been his sole human defence against the dark, we find him stitching together a philosophical system which has all the rigidity, the absolutism, the symmetry characteristic of systems of life and art which emanate from a deep-seated fear of the void.

I find most of his philosophic poems not at all as compelling as those which emanate directly from his own immediate turbulence. Poems such as *Oileán agus Oileán eile, Saoirse, Fill Arís* are indeed splendid, highly inventive pieces of writing which demonstrate Ó Ríordáin's ability to flesh out his theory in striking imagery and metaphor. I would single out *Fill Arís* in particular as a piece where the poet fully feels his own metaphysic. But in general these poems depend too much on an intellectual theory which many people will find difficult to accept or be moved by – a common problem with poetry which argues a philosophy or supplies definitive answers to the meaning of life. Many of his minor philosophic poems, in fact, end up as game-playing with cold abstract concepts. On the other hand, it must be said also that his philosophic concentration on 'essence' greatly enriches imagery and mood in splendid occasional poems such as *Cúl an Tí, An Gealt* (The Lunatic), *Siollabadh* (Syllable-ism), *Seachtain* (A Week). Even in his lightest verse, for instance in *An Lacha* (*The Duck*), his main thrust is to identify the 'essential' quality of his subject-matter:

> We all know about the Duck
>   absurd bird, damned by her
>   ill-luck
> from paces long and strong and
>   free
>   It is her fallen nature now to
>   be

An awkward stumbler that goes
  bumping all
  her way broken and
  unmetrical
rocking and rolling on her
  posterior,
  yet looking so determinedly
  superior
that marvelling at such courage
  you must say
  See how heroic couplets stalk
  this way,
Yet how obvious it is
  to the discerning
that the best she can do
  is vers libre.

(C. Quinn, *T*, p. 45)

Ó Ríordáin ceased to be a major creative force after the publication of his second book, *Brosna*, in 1964. *Línte Liombó* (Lines from Limbo) (1971) and *Tar éis mo Bháis* (After my Death) published posthumously in 1978, bear witness to a spent talent. The intelligence, the 'Parnassian', the quirks of mind and style remain the same; what is absent (with some minor exceptions) is the urgency to master new experience or the ability to plumb old experience to greater depth. These later volumes do indicate increasingly, however, that he now suspected (as Rilke had discovered) that the pursuit of a stable immutable self was an empty dream. Observing the lovely brown eyes of a woman he knew looking at him (it seems) from her son's head, he muses:

Is this all there is of eternity
that something of us lives on
becoming masculine and feminine
From the mother to the son?

(G. Fitzmaurice)[20]

In what probably was his last verse composition, *Clónna Uber alles*, he wonders aloud: 'Is this the way it is then -/ We will disappear like last year's snow, / But our clones will keep recurring . . . / Our equivalents, not us?'[21]

In the years 1964 to 1977 Ó Ríordáin's chief survival weapon was prose, not verse. During those years most of his energy was channelled into writing his bizarre prose satires *ad hominem*, and his fantasy/political pieces, for

The Irish Times. It is probable that the only relief available to him then from his debilitating ill-health, and his growing intimations of mortality, was that of savaging the only world he felt he would ever exist in, and which had done him irreparable physical and psychological harm. If so, his exchange of poetry for journalism is completely understandable in human terms. Only those who suffered the whiplash of his prose can really feel aggrieved.

Of his verse, one can say that the level and magnitude of Ó Ríordáin's poetic achievement in general is remarkable – especially when one considers that the language he is using might have been given up for dead fifty years before he began to write. Few, if any other Irish poets since Yeats have composed so many lyrics bearing, as Ó Ríordáin's best work does, the marks of high creative genius. In his more mature, elegantly crafted work, the blend of an arresting evolving image (often containing within itself a wisp of mercurial humour) with an essentially dramatic stance, is unique. Unique also, within the Irish tradition he inherited, is the unflinching manner in which he makes his personal anguish and frustrations the central matter of his poetic opus.

[1978]

3

'The Loving and Terrible Mother' in the Early Poetry of Nuala Ní Dhomhnaill

I N THE IRISH-LANGUAGE literary tradition attested work by women poets is quite rare. Given the absence of such a supportive literary tradition our modern women poets – and there are some of considerable merit – must find special encouragement in the emergence in Ireland of a staunch feminist movement (which in turn must owe a good deal to the traditional matriarchal influence, long discernible in Irish family life). In the case of Nuala Ní Dhomhnaill's early work, however, one does not come on any special agenda regarding women's rights or any assertion about what a woman's role should be. Her primary demand is, in fact, much more revolutionary: absolute freedom to confront unflinchingly her own deeply turbulent feminine nature; and to be able to act and speak unhindered out of the insights revealed.

No special recognition was accorded Nuala Ní Dhomhnaill's verse, as distinct from the verse written by some of her fellow students, during her period in University College, Cork (1969–1972). One can see with hindsight, however, that she had even at that point identified precisely what was to become the main explosive theme of her work. She had by then got to know the Turkish man whom she later married – a union which brought her into open opposition with her own family (and with her mother, it would appear, in particular). The signs of this conflict are already present in a short series of poems written by her while still a teenage undergraduate. In this work, Mór, one of the great Irish mythological mother figures, goddess of sovereignty and fertility, makes a significant appearance. In the poem *Donncha Dí's Testimony*, Nuala stresses the goddess's negative

features. Mór's partner, Donncha Dí, found her seductive to begin with
– full of the fertility of the sea – but when he awoke after a night of love,
he saw that 'sallow scales encrusted her/and rotten teeth from the
abyss/snarled at me and hissed' (*H*, p. 35). Donncha Dí flees to Northern
Ireland from the woman he perceives now to be an ugly hag (a variant
of the traditional tale in which the ugly hag is transformed into a beautiful
young woman). While this poem, being over-casually structured, makes
far less impact than its material might warrant, it signals clearly that
some major elements of the ugliness and cruelty in the feminine nature
(and accordingly, in her own nature as well) had shocked Ní Dhomh-
naill. She found herself staring into an abyss she had not foreseen or
understood.

Donncha Dí's Testimony (and a few other associated poems) was written
*c.*1972. Soon after she had gone to live in Turkey and seems not to have
resumed her verse compositions in any serious or continuous manner
until 1977. One suspects that the trauma she had suffered, and the in-
evitable depression which followed it, lay heavily on her heart (like 'an
animal', as she says herself), during her period of silence. Then in 1977,
she speaks suddenly and starkly from Turkey in a poem called *Máthair*
(*Mother*):

> You gave me a dress
> and then took it back from me.
> You gave me a horse
> which you sold in my absence.
> You gave me a harp
> and then asked me back for it.
> And you gave me life.
>
> At the miser's dinner-party
> every bite is counted.
>
> What would you say
> if I tore the dress
> if I drowned the horse
> if I broke the harp
> if I choked the strings
> the strings of life?
> Even if
> I walked off a cliff?
> I know your answer.

> With your medieval mind
> you'd announce me dead
> and on the medical reports
> you'd write the words
> 'ingrate, schizophrenic'.
>
> (M. Hartnett, *H*, p. 41)

Reading *Máthair* in 1977, one felt that a new and indomitable female voice was about to make its presence felt. (From the same period, incidentally, comes a poem called *Athair* (Father). Noting how in Ní Dhomhnaill's work in general men have neither real authority nor staunch heroic characteristics, one is not at all surprised that the portrait in this poem is that of a male figure who is a mere flickering hesitant shadow in the memory.)

Having given vent in *Máthair* (and *Athair*) to her 'primal screech'/'*scréach bhunaidh*', she did not for a time pursue what was to be her major theme. Instead she embarked on a series of poems of a woman's love for another woman (which may, of course, stem indirectly from her concerns about motherly love). The stark and dramatic honesty of *Máthair* gives way to a refined and remarkable near-traditional lyricism in, for instance, *Leaba Shíoda* (The Silken Bed) where the Lays of Solomon, as well as Irish folk-song, are a discernible influence. But it is her own image of a silk bed for lovers under wrestling trees which mainly gives the poem its individual dimension:

> I'd make a bed for you
> in Labysheedy
> in the tall grass
> under the wrestling trees
> where your skin
> would be silk upon silk
> in the darkness
> when the moths are coming down.
>
> Skin which glistens
> shining over your limbs
> like milk being poured
> from jugs at dinnertime;
> your hair is a herd of goats
> moving over rolling hills,
> hills that have high cliffs
> and two ravines.

And your damp lips
would be as sweet as sugar
at evening and we walking
by the riverside
with honeyed breezes
blowing over the Shannon
and the fuchsias bowing down to you
one by one.

The fuchsias bending low
their solemn heads in obeisance to the beauty
in front of them
I would pick a pair of flowers
as pendant earrings
to adorn you
like a bride in shining clothes.

O I'd made a bed for you
in Labysheedy,
in the twilight hour
with evening falling slow
and what a pleasure it would be
to have our limbs entwine
wrestling
while the moths are coming down.

(trans. author, *H*, pp. 155-57)

As love fades, in time this mood gives way to something very close to
her previous thwarted or embittered state of mind, finally ending in a kind
of submerged grief: 'The flies die-off/here in Ankara/and back in Lon-
don/the falling leaves pummel/your closed door.'[1]

Ní Dhomhnaill tends to speak a little obliquely in her lesbian poems in
general. In a sequence of dream poems which followed these she is very
oblique indeed; so oblique in fact, so completely true to the seeming non-
sequiturs of some dream images - as in *Turas Oíche* (Night Visit), *Aghaidh
an Photadóra* (The Potter's Face) and *Na Sceana Feola* (The Meat Knives)
- that a literary critic might be pardoned for not attempting any minute in-
terpretation of them. Apart from noting the strong presence of mothers and
daughters in them, one is tempted to say of them what John Berryman -
who was a major influence in her early work - said of his own Dream Songs:

These songs are not meant to be understood, you understand.
These are only meant to terrify and comfort.
Lilac was found in his hand.[2]

Despite the turbulence one senses under the surface in both the dream and lesbian sequences, only a very few of these poems reveal that the poet is yet able to shape her communication in an authoritative or successful manner. But it is clear that the psyche which is speaking to us is isolated, endangered, half-submerged.

It is from the time (1980) she returned to Ireland on a bursary from the Arts Council that Nuala Ní Dhomhnaill has attained the assurance of a major artist. The quality and diversity of the poems whe wrote in the Kerry Gaeltacht in her first year back home, is quite simply astonishing. Since then the floodgates have remained open and the stream of verse shows no sign of abating. It would appear that Nuala, digging deep into her resources, found a voice in the eighties to exorcise the trauma of the seventies.

In her 1980 corpus of poems, *An Dealg Droighin* (The Blackthorn Clasp), one senses an immense and pulsating feminine energy releasing and exercising itself. The sense of fertility is everywhere. The hills and valleys of Anatolia - with their abundance of trees, flowers and produce - had, quite likely, awakened in her a new sensitivity to her own ancestral district in County Kerry. She recognizes and ecstatically names flowers and plants, fish and worms, herbs and animals. She equates herself with natural phenomena - she is herself, for instance, the mouth of the Shannon welcoming the return of the salmon from abroad:

> The leap of the salmon
> in darkness,
> naked blade
> shield of silver.
> I am welcoming, full of nets,
> inveigling
> slippery with seaweed,
> quiet eddies
> and eel-tails.
>
> This fish
> is nothing but meat
> with very few bones
> and very few entrails;
> twenty pounds of muscle tautened,
> aimed
> at its nest in the mossy place.
>
> And I will sing a lullaby
> to my lover
> wave on wave,

> stave upon half-stave,
> my phosphorescence as bed-linen
>   under him,
> my favourite, whom I, from afar
>   have chosen.

(trans. author, H, p. 159)

In another striking poem, *Na Súile Uaine* (*The Green Eyes*), she celebrates an imagined primeval paradise where the natural loving female flourishes and where couples – all redheaded and freckled – are, for a time, full of innocent and rapturous life:

> Before the green eyes
> of the serpent
> gleamed
> in the wilderness
>
> there were long Andalusian dances
> combs of bone
> and dresses of taffeta
> making swishing sounds
> like leaves of cabbage
> before the green eyes gleamed.
>
> Before he looped
> the loop of the loop
> down the sweet-scented apple-branch
>
> there were jaunty hats
> with pheasant feathers
> blackthorn sticks
> with tops of ivory,
> veils of lace
> and shimmering dresses
> before he looped along the branch there.
>
> Before he took
> a bite of the apple
> there were buttons being opened
> one after another
> bodies being unclothed
> in night-shadows,
> every couple was red-haired
> and busily painting freckles

on each other
with shafts of sunlight
laughingly,
before he took a bite of the apple.

But now
the bite is bitten
the apple is eaten
the maggot begotten
our feet finally bathed
and we are lying
in the eternal darkness
where there is crying and wailing
and gnashing of teeth
in saeculorum.

(trans. author, *H*, pp. 149-51)

In *Venio ex Oriente*, her first poem on her return to Ireland, Nuala proclaims dramatically that while she brings with her eastern spices and Arabian perfumes, the tang of her native hills is still to be found on her body. Striving to anchor herself in Ireland again, she continues to link herself in a new way with the old ancestral townlands. She also seeks out the folk-tales and lore of the district, some of which she would have heard already in her youth. She has clearly been encouraged in all this by her Turkish experience; she finds, evidently, that the Irish mind, like the Turkish, chiefly expresses itself in the form of stories and imagery rather that in the form of intellectual concepts so favoured in western Europe. She spurns everything that is 'Roman' and 'intellectual', 'European' and 'mathematical'. In *I mBaile an tSléibhe*[3] local lore and imagery are woven inextricably and masterfully through the feelings of stability and continuity which her ancestral place provides for her.

While her insight into the scope of the benign nurturing woman (within herself principally) increased immeasurably during the crucial year of 1980, so also did her insight into the dark authoritarian side of her own nature. It appears sometimes that she derives pleasure from some of these negative aspects. She is much taken, for instance, by a grand-aunt of her own, a mettlesome independent woman, whose haughtiness and cantankerousness she feels she may have inherited herself:

She got an honours degree
in biology in Nineteen-four,
then went back to her homeland

At the butt of the hill,
its backside to the wind,
and stopped there all her days.

She never married.
No one around was good enough for her.
When her brother married,
his bride wasn't good enough for him,
in Elly's view, and
she sold their land.

She fought with her father.
She fought with her brother.
She fought with the P.P.
To her it was all wrong
that dues were read out aloud
in the middle of Mass.
She saw right well the cheek –
imposing on the poor
to pay the Church beyond their means
and leave their children hungry.
On that account, she'd sit
satisfied in her own pew,
hand on her blackthorn,
hat on her head,
awaiting the call from the altar,
'Elly Ní Dhomhnaill – nothing.'

The only one to visit her
was my father
– the family's pius Aeneas –
and when she went
she left him the house,
which we sold – too damp.
I promised to write to her,
but didn't.
Maybe letters I've written since
addressed themselves to that proud spirit,
who had no call to lie
with a man her match.

My own man was guarded
when he met me,
for fear of the same bad drop,
saying I was just like her,
a loner,
her sole heir

In olden times
there was venom in the withering wind
    from Binn na Gaoith
as our people were herded into Macha
    na Bó.

           (G. O'Brien, *Ph*, pp. 25-27)

She sees herself at other times as a sort of hag figure radiating dark magical powers; having suffered a miscarriage abroad, she will not visit the house of a friend on whose newly born baby she might cast her evil eye:

You embryo, moved in me –
I welcomed your emerging
I said I'd rear you carefully
in the manner of my new people –

under your pillow the holy book,
in your cot, bread and a needle:
your father's shirt as an eiderdown
at your head a brush for sweeping.

I was brimming
with happiness
until the dykes broke
and out was swept
a ten-weeks frog –
'the best-laid schemes . . .'

And now it's March
your birthday that never was –
and white ribbons of tide
remind me of baby-clothes,
an imbecile's tangled threads.

And I will not go to see
my best friend's new born child
because of the jealousy
that stares from my evil eye.

           (M. Hartnett, *H*, p. 51)

She is Eve/Temptation/Serpent in the poem *Manach* (Monk), while at other times she collapses suddenly back into inexplicable depression. One of her finest poems on this strong depressive side of her female nature is *An Mhaighdean Mhara* (*The Mermaid*), where the poet imagines herself to be a mermaid thrown on land, her magic cap (as in the old tale) hidden away by her captors. She is a strange creature in the wrong place. She is deprived of her fertile sea-life; Gestapo figures surround her, intent on disciplining her:

> 'Ebbtide' I said,
> 'the tide will have to turn
> and cover this waste of sand,
> pour over limpets on rocks
> over wrack drying waterless
> (ribbons like withered vellum)
> because the lugworms' faeces
> Makes me nauseous.'
>
> Floodtide ebbtide
> floodtide ebbtide
> rise and fall
> rise and fall
> the same again.
> Everything's so bad now
> it can't get worse
> but 'we have ways of making you talk'
> I hear in Gestapo accents
> (water goes down and down
> but no tide nears me).
>
> Though I've got a fish's tail
> I'm not unbeautiful:
> my hair is long and yellow
> and there's a shine from my scales
> you won't see on landlocked women.
> Their eyes are like the stones
> but look into these eyes of mine
> and you will see the sturgeon
> and you will see fine seals
> gambolling in my pupils.
>
> Not without pain
> have I landed:
> I broke
> the natural law.
> I swapped swimming

for walking on earth,
picking my steps
like a curlew.
Believe you me
it was love, not God,
who gave the order.

You left
and took my magic cap.
It's not as easy to get back
in the roof's rafters
as it was in the fable.
I dug to the subsoil
and saw no sign of it.
The tide also fails us
and a rat
gnaws at the very sun.

(M. Hartnett, *H*, p. 53-55)

II

So far I have presented in straightforward fashion what I consider to be the main developmental lines of Nuala Ní Dhomhnaill's first book (*An Dealg Droighin*, 1981), where she is recreating instinctively from her own life-experience the female/mother archetype in different guises. In her second book *Féar Suaithinseach* (Remarkable Grass) published in 1984, we find her dealing more consciously with her instinctual feelings; we find her, it seems deliberately, operating a Jungian agenda. In his comprehensive account of the attributes associated with the mother archetype Jung says:

> The qualities associated with it are maternal solicitude and sympathy; the magic authority of the female; any helpful instinct or impulse; all that is benign, all that cherishes and sustains, that fosters growth and fertility. The place of magic transformation and rebirth, together with the under-world and its inhabitants are presided over by the mother. On the negative side the mother archetype may connote anything secret hidden, dark; the abyss, the world of the dead, anything that devours, seduces and poisons, that is terrifying and inescapable like fate. All these attributes of the mother arthetype have been fully described and documented in my book *Symbols of Transformation*. There I formulated the ambivalence of these attributes as 'The Loving and the Terrible Mother'.[4]

In *Féar Suaithinseach* the attributes of 'the loving and terrible mother' are put under rigorous scrutiny. Ní Dhomhaill wrestles with the women within her in an effort to come to terms with them to accomodate them, to appease them. She ransacks the folklore archives in University College, Dublin, searching for tales which would throw light on various elements of her feminine nature. She becomes embroiled with hags and goddesses, and with the heroes and giants who follow in their train. It is clear that she believes, as E.G. Gose the author of *The World of the Irish Wonder Tale*[5] believes, that the cosmos portrayed in traditional tales may reveal unconscious elements of the human mind. Accordingly, her agenda in *Féar Suaithinseach* is to a large extent an intellectual one – indeed intellectual conviction may sometimes take over from instinct.

She pursues more openly now the 'terrible mother' within herself, and confronts herself in the terms of traditional imagery: 'I am as pale as a sow rooting in gardens/I swallow back my litter each seventh year/I have high knuckles, bristles, ears that curl/I am a headless body floating your way through the night'.[6] Again in traditional terms she tells of the masculine hero who succours the ugly hag, transforming her back to her original feminine shape: 'Then the hero will lop off the old hag's head/. . . and redeem you with a stroke of his magic wand'.[7]

Throughout *Féar Suaithinseach* the 'terrible mother' waits patiently the arrival of the man-hero who will succour her; who will 'redeem her bogland'. Sometimes this male hero is, as it were, concealed within her own nature;[8] but more frequently the hoped for hero is a named mythological figure. So the poet becomes Queen Medb or the Great Queen awaiting some Cú Chulainn of acceptable status. She even becomes the Sphinx waiting for Oedipus to transform her:

> It is destined
> you will be
> the finest living man
> I'll ever meet:
> that you will get the question right
> that you will make the question clear
> that you will have my form revealed
> so that I can, after an age,
> accost and judge my own face.
>
> (M. Hartnett, *H*, p. 103)

As I understand it, Jung suggests that a major attribute of the 'terrible mother' is her going underground ('into the abyss, the world of the dead'), putting herself at risk of destruction. 'The woman from the *lios*', says Nuala Ní Dhomhnaill, 'walked straight into my verse'[9] an occurrence which causes her to suffer 'perpetual darkness'. The fairy woman from the *lios* becomes her image, it appears, for an elemental force which causes depression and lures one towards self-destruction.

One of her poems which has received special public attention is significant in this regard. It is *Thar mo Chionn* (On My Behalf)[10] where reference is made to the gruesome experience of a young girl from Granard, County Longford, who died at a grotto, having given birth to a child unaided. I do not interpret this poem – as another commentator does[11] – as being in any important way a berating of the very Irish tendency to disclaim responsibility for certain moral or social attitudes in our society. I see the poem as a purely personal statement.

In *Thar mo Chionn* the fairy woman lures the poet underground and gives her a fairy child to nourish at the breast, but fails to persuade her to partake of the magic food proffered. Refusing the food – fearing, perhaps, it would leave her in perpetual depression – the poet manages to escape. Not so in the case of the young girl from Granard – she accedes completely to the forces of depression; dying, she takes the poet's place in the *lios*, nursing a fairy child at the breast. The poet's feelings are plain: 'there but for the grace of God, go I'.

This is not one of Nuala Ní Dhomhnaill's best poems; nor is it as compelling as some of the other poems on the same fairy-woman theme. A few of these have a strange, depressive, trance-like aura about them and one of them, at least, refers to her youthful conflict with her own family.

The poet's paramount concern is, of course, to triumph over the negative, including the depressive, elements of 'the terrible mother'. Unfortunately the male heroes occurring in her everyday life fail to succour her. The figure of the *Masculus Giganticus Hibernicus*, which she identifies as the typical Irish hero in the typical Irish pub, is a 'dangerous relic from the Iron Age' who would turn every 'garden to a trampled mess'.[12] Even the national mythological hero, Cú Chulainn, gets short shrift. The *Mór-Ríon* (Great Queen) reviles him quite nonchalantly: 'My womaness overwhelmed you/as you admitted after to a friend/over a mutual drink./Fear, certainly, of castration/fear of false teeth in my cunt/fear my jaws would grind you/like oats in a mill'.[13]

So the poet has no other choice but to keep on hoping for her own 'shining hero' who will manage to show her 'her own face'. Even in the last poem of *Féar Suaithinseach* she is still, in depressive mood, frantically pursuing in Turkey her hero/lover:

                    Telephone poles
        threaten me. Foretelling danger electric pylons stride
        bold on the plateau of Anatolia,
        seven-headed monsters, seven-horned and-tailed
        rushing towards me in seven league boots
        declaring war on this impertinence of mine –
        to come and rear my child within their bounds.
        Soon one, like ragwort, will uproot a tree
        and use it like a switch on us.

        And where is the shining knight
        who'll come to aid me . . .
        alas no small bird or bush I know.
        I am totally wretched: deprived
        of even the common archetypes.

                        (M. Hartnett, *Ph*, pp. 81-83)

The identity of the 'shining hero' who will show her her own visage poses a problem. I doubt, however, that one can resolve this on the evidence of her work in *Féar Suaithinseach* – except that it is clear that her ideal hero is not anyone of that boastful masculine ilk that has emerged in western Europe since the Iron Age! The overall mood of the book seems to suggest that the ugly bruised side of feminine nature is due to masculine oppression of female life since these early historic times – before which the Great Mother, fertile and benign (a figure which Nuala Ní Dhomhnaill seems to equate on a few occassions with a neutral bi-sexual giant), held sway.

Some scholars have indeed suggested that the *Great Mother* – rather than the male God or hero – was the highest object of reverence in many cultures in pre-historic times. James Hillman puts it thus:

> The Swiss scholar Bachofen suggested for the first time in his book *Mother Right*, published in 1861, the idea, embarrassing to the Swiss, that in every past society known, a matriarchy had preceded the present patriarchy. His evidence, drawn from Mediterranean sources, was massive. Just as every adult was once inside the mother, every society was once inside the Great Mother. In Greece this mother absorption lasted until maybe 2000 B.C. What we called masculine consciousness is a very recent creation.[14]

Whether or not Ní Dhomhnaill feels deeply that 'masculine consciousness' is a recent – and a passing – phase, she sometimes seems to be on the point of saying that the female cannot survive, feel free, until she resumes the role she once had when the Great Mother of fertility and sovereignty reigned and was revered, from Anatolia to Eamhain Macha. If so, what then of the 'shining hero'? Is he (she) simply someone who would yield sovereignty to the female, serve her, and still be an intrepid hero (heroine) and lover? It is doubtful if even the most radical member of the feminist movement would demand so much scope and power for herself and her fellow-women.

In a few of her later poems in *Féar Suaithinseach* Ní Dhomhnaill becomes somewhat ambivalent about the qualities of the Great Mother. The woman she confronts here is not the caring heroic mother – rather the mother of the nuclear dark: 'Virgin, mother, nurse, atomic bomb/you will suckle us on the pitchblack liquid of your breasts'.[15] And when she aggressively seeks out, in the manner of a traditional hero, her masculine lover, she finds herself, in reality, speeding inexorably towards the cave, the abyss, where the Great Mother dwells. This is splendidly envisaged in *An Rás* (*The Race*):

> Like a mad lion, like a wild bull, like one
> of the crazy pigs in the Fenian cycle
> or the hero leaping upon the giant
> with his fringe of swinging silk,
> I drive at high speed through
> the small midland towns of Ireland,
> catching up with the wind ahead
> while the wind behind me whirls and dies.
>
> Like a shaft from a bow, like a shot from a gun
> or a sparrow-hawk in a sparrow-throng
> on a March day, I scatter the road-signs,
> miles or kilometres what do I care.
> Nenagh, Roscrea, Mountmellick,
> I pass through them in a daze;
> they are only speed limits put there
> to hold me up on my way to you.
>
> Through mountain cleft, bogland and wet pasture
> I race impetuously from west to east –
> a headlong flight in your direction,
> a quick dash to be with you.
> The road rises and falls before me,
> the surface changing from grit to tar;
> I forget geography, all I know
> is the screech of brakes and the gleam of lights.

Suddenly, in the mirror, I catch sight of the sun
glowing red behind me on the horizon,
a vast blazing crimson sphere like the heart
of the Great Cow of the Smith-God
when she was milked through a sieve,
the blood dripping as in a holy picture.
Thrice red, it is so fierce it pierces
my own heart, and I catch my breath in pain.

I keep glancing anxiously at the dripping sun
while trying to watch the road ahead.
So Sleeping Beauty must have glanced
at her finger after the spindle
of the spinning-wheel had pricked her,
turning it round and round as if in a trance.
When Deirdre saw the calf's blood on the snow
did it ever dawn on her what the raven was?

Oh, I know it's to you that I'm driving,
my lovely man, the friend of my heart,
and the only things between us tonight
are the road-sign and the traffic-light;
but your impatience is like a stone
dripping upon us out of the sky;
and add to that our bad humour,
gaucherie, and the weight of my terrible pride.

Another great weight is descending upon us
if things turn out as predicted, a weight
greater by far than the globe of the sun
that bled in my mirror a while back;
and thou, dark mother, cave of wonders,
since it's to you that we spin on our violent course,
is it true what they say that your kiss is sweeter
than Spanish wine, Greek honey, or the golden mead
       of the Norse?

(D. Mahon, *Ph*, pp. 95-97)

This view of the Great Mother as the ultimate wasteland is another dimension of the poet's feelings which cannot be ignored, even if it directly contradicts her previous feelings. This is, no doubt, another manifestation of the negative depressive mood associated with the fairy woman from the *lios*.

There may be a measure of disagreement on the interpretation being offered here of the poet's use of archetypical figures in *Féar Suaithinseach*, but it is clear, at any rate, that she has built up for herself here a fairly structured psychological schema (of the kind mentioned) in support of her outraged sensibility. However, very few of the poems which revolve too consciously or closely about her 'primordial images' are, I feel, amongst her best. She has particular difficulty when she deals with her material in the form of stories or incidents. One senses that she has not the instinctive feel for the pace of a story, and consequently fails to make necessary excisions, or fails to handle her material adroitly, as a storyteller must. On a more general note, I find that she is sometimes limited in *Féar Suaithinseach* – in comparison with her work in *An Dealg Droighin* – by over-reliance on her own schema. Instead of releasing her imagination, it rather curbs it; she is caught more than one would like within the rigorous frame of a story, or an archetype.

Such is often the consequence for an artist who depends on a schema to provide him/her with psychological equilibrium. Ó Ríordáin is a case in point: his work is much more vibrant when he speaks directly out of his own emotional abyss instead of subjugating his feelings to the philosophic schema he cultivated in order to enable him to survive. 'C'est pourquoi,' says Valéry, 'il ne faut pas faire des systèmes. Un système est un arrêt. C'est un renoncement. Car un arrêt sur une idée est un arrêt sur un plan incliné, un faux équilibre.'[16]

It would be quite wrong, however, for a critic to suggest to a poet how he/she might set about cultivating his/her own vein of poetry. In Nuala Ní Dhomhnaill's case a rigorous schema may have been absolutely necessary as a temporary survival measure (as indeed it was for Valéry, despite his protestations). The direction she took in her second book may have been the only direction open to her, the only direction which would guarantee her both stability and emotional enrichment, whatever disadvantages might follow. In addition to that, it must be taken into account that her second book contains some seventy poems written, more or less, in the space of two years: many other poets would have been quite happy to have done as much in ten years.

There is an extraordinary diversity in *Féar Suaithinseach*, as well as great integrity and (strangely) good humour. There is also a willingness on the part of the poet to expose herself to emotional risk. The style she is cultivating is a complex original style (though firmly rooted in the Irish of West Kerry). Her verse is loosely structured, nonchalant, conversational sometimes, full of the tropes of folk-stories and children's rhymes. Occasionally she allows a certain blandness or coarseness (or the odd ungrammatical phrase) to creep in; one even feels from time to time that she has been over-indulgent in her use of folklore, too cavalier in her attitude to verse as craft. Yet despite such minor blemishes she has created a new world, a new sensibility, couched in an unmistakeable style.

There is a substantial number of poems in *Féar Suaithinseach* that a reader of modern poetry will find highly exciting; and some half a dozen of these are superb. Though she may not generally be able, as I have said previously, to fashion very good poems directly from material which is too closely linked with her pursuit of archetypes, at the same time her best poems would not have been possible were it not for the added dimension indirectly provided by her quest. Amongst these poems I would mention: *Ag Cothú Linbh,*[17] *Gaineamh Shúraic,*[18] *An Bhábóg Bhriste,*[19] *Aubade,*[20] *Sceimhle,*[21] *Dán do Mhelissa,*[22] *An Rás.*[23]

These poems, it may be noticed, all stem initially from the poet's personal feelings as nurturing/heroic mother or as depressed female, but she is now enabled to put her personal feelings in a wider framework. For instance in *Ag Cothú Linbh* (Feeding a Child), a poem full of beautiful traditional rhymes and flourishes, she sees her child beating her 'little fists on her breast' as she is 'grazing in giants' territory'. And complicating our understanding of her need of a 'shining hero' she concludes: 'And who are the primordial models/of the heroes and giants/if not you and I'. In this fashion her pursuit of archetypes gives a new shape and substance to a nurturing mother's lullaby.

And it is the loving mother *par excellence* who speaks out of her own anguished experience in *Dán do Mhelissa* (*Poem for Melissa*):

> My fair-haired child dancing in the dunes
> hair be-ribboned, gold rings on your fingers
> to you, yet only five or six years old,
> I grant you all on this delicate earth.
>
> The fledgeling bird out of the nest
> the iris seeding in the drain
> the green crab walking neatly sideways:
> they are yours to see, my daughter.
>
> The ox would gambol with the wolf
> the child would play with the serpent
> the lion would lie down with the lamb
> in the pasture world I would delicately grant.
>
> The garden gates forever wide open
> no flaming swords in hands of Cherubim
> no need for a fig-leaf apron here
> in the pristine world I would delicately give.

Oh white daughter here's your mother's word:
I will put in your hand the sun and the moon
I will stand my body between the millstones
in God's mills so you are not totally ground.

(M. Hartnett, H, pp. 137)

Jung says:

> We could therefore say that every mother contains her daughter in herself
> and every daughter her mother, and that every woman extends backwards
> into her mother and forwards into her daughter. . . . An experience of
> this kind gives the individual a place and a meaning in the life of the
> generations, so that all the unnecessary obstacles are cleared out of the
> way of the lifestream that is to flow through her. At the same time the
> individual is rescued from her isolations and restored to wholeness. *All
> ritual preoccupation with archetypes ultimately has this aim and this
> result.*[24]

As a consequence of her 'ritual preoccupation with archetypes' (including
her early less conscious intimations of them) Nuala Ní Dhomhnaill has
produced a corpus of poetry more remarkable and more vibrant, I feel,
than any work done by other Irish poets of her generation, either in the
English or Irish language. Since the publication of her poem *Máthair* in
1977 she has taken an enormous imaginative leap in the dark. Of other
modern poets in Irish only Seán Ó Ríordáin displays such creative courage.
Ó Ríordáin spent his life in pursuit of his own immortal essence – and
denied God in the process. Nuala Ní Dhomhnaill is in pursuit of the basic
female elements in herself – and has denied her own mother in the process.

To her lasting credit, however, it is clear that Nuala Ní Dhomhnaill is
finally more in confrontation with herself than with any other person.
The relentlessly open manner in which she faces up to her own nature
is a revelation and a triumph.

[1987]

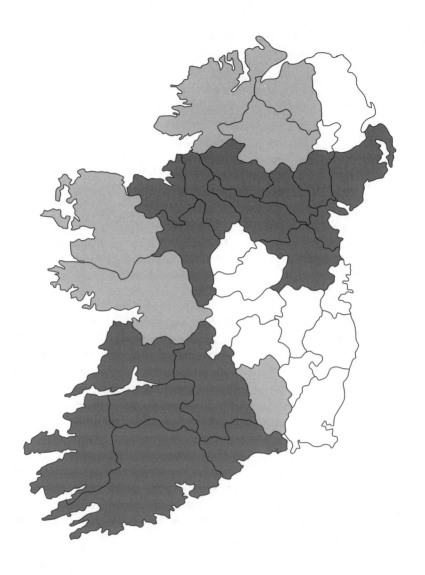

LITERARY POETRY PREDOMINANT

FOLK POETRY PREDOMINANT

A rough guide to the principal counties in which Irish language poets flourished between the early seventeenth and the mid-nineteenth century. The map does not indicate the varying degrees of poetic activity from county to county, or from district to district within each county.

PART II

SEVENTEENTH AND EIGHTEENTH-CENTURY POETRY

4

Background

THE YEAR 1601 IS A watershed in Irish history and literature. With the defeat of the Irish forces at Kinsale in that year the Elizabethan conquest of Ireland was assured. In the next hundred years some eighty-five per cent of Irish land was transferred into the hands of the new English colonists and the old Irish aristocratic order disappeared. The traditional system of poetic patronage disappeared also, with traumatic consequences for literature in Irish.

During the bardic period, from 1200 to 1600 approximately, noble Irish families, of whom there were many hundreds, had maintained hereditary poets with great honour and ceremony, and there was intense (if mixed) poetic activity. Judged only by what has been preserved in the family poem-books, bardic verse would seem to have consisted almost entirely of formal eulogy and elegy in difficult syllabic metres. But it is likely that the Irish aristocracy encouraged a wider range of verse than this. Otherwise it is hard to account for the corpus of delightful non-formal syllabic verse which survived from the same period, or for the sudden emergence of other types of verse, apparently fully-fledged, in the era after Kinsale: learned accentual verse, sophisticated folk poetry, lays and lyrics of the Fianna.

Accentual verse: Before the seventeenth century the chracteristic forms of Irish professional verse were syllabic. In the early seventeenth century a new poetry appeared, in poems that were frequently a direct response to the social and political upheavals of the time. These poems had some conventions of thought and style in common with bardic poetry but were composed in 'new' accentual forms, ornate and highly wrought.

Of the major figures of the seventeenth century – Céitinn, Haicéad, Feiritéar, Ó Bruadair, Mac Cuarta, Ó Rathaille – only Ó Bruadair bore a name which might suggest a connection with the old hereditary bardic families. Yet all of them wrote in the new accentual metres with the assurance and elegance which belongs to an established tradition. It seems certain that an accentual poetry existed throughout the medieval period without being written down in the official family anthologies, and that it was only the undermining of the bardic order that allowed this poetry to reach a new prominence. Certainly, from the beginning of the seventeenth century, the prominence of accentual poetry is attested by the substantial amounts that begin to appear in the manuscripts.

Poetic function and status: Verse, during these centuries, had a wider function than it has today, being often used where we might consider prose more appropriate. For Haicéad and Ó Bruadair, both lyricists of great intellectual energy and skill, verse was a natural vehicle not alone for evoking mood or passion, but also for social, historical and other rational discourse. After the seventeenth century the assurance of this discourse waned, as did the general quality of the poetry itself; the native institutions which had hitherto supported Gaelic poetry – the whole educational, legal, religious and economic continuum – virtually disappeared. Even in Ó Rathaille's poetry the hard intellectual quality of the earlier seventeenth-century poetry is missing. What Ó Rathaille's work lacks in intellect, however, is more than compensated for by the turbulent moods which underlie it. The half-dozen or so lyrics of high quality which he shaped out of his own personal chaos make him perhaps the greatest of Irish poets, writing in Irish or English, between the seventeenth century and the twentieth.

Even though the poets suffered increasingly the loss of their traditional status and privileges, traces of the great honour once accorded them survived for a time. In the socially important matter of hospitality, for example, poets were more readily provided for than others. Also, people still feared the satiric whip of their verse, or (after the battle of the Boyne in 1690) took refuge in their optimistic visions of a Stuart saviour who would return to undo the English conquest. But more and more of these poets, isolated within a political and social system which was both alien and repressive, died in despair or abject poverty, many refusing to consider seriously any way of life but that of the poet-scholar. The prospect of earning a living by manual labour could be regarded with wry humour by even a late eighteenth-century semi-professional like Eoghan Rua Ó Súilleabháin.[1]

Scholarly semi-professionals still subsisted in large numbers during the eighteenth and early nineteenth centuries in rural communities. On occasions throughout the year, in places where literary traditions were strongest, they gathered together in 'courts of poetry', recited their compositions, exchanged manuscripts, and engaged in extempore repartee in verse. As time, and the conquest, proceeded, it is their voices that more and more emerge as the voice of their community.*

After the battle of Culloden in 1745, and the defeat of Prince Charles Stuart (the last royal figure seen by the Irish as a potential saviour), Irish political verse grew out of touch with reality. It remains technically, however, a highly accomplished body of verse, meant (more often than not) to be sung to the great Irish airs of the period. Some of Eoghan Rua Ó Súilleabháin's *aisling* or vision poems, with all their extraordinary metrical virtuosity, live on into the present day in Irish-speaking communities in Munster as a type of highly-structured folk *lieder*.

The nineteenth century: During the nineteenth century the policies in-itiated in Tudor times for the elimination of the Irish language began to show dramatic success; by the end of the century the English language was the dominant vernacular of the Irish people. In this phase of the long tradition poetic activity retreated: the liveliest verse of the century was inspired not by large political or social issues but by local happenings in the residual Irish-speaking communities, mainly in the West of Ireland. Such communities used verse instinctively (and do so still) as the vehicle for heightened communication or for the celebration of the events of every-day life. There is, in fact, a remarkable abundance of Gaelic verse from the nineteenth century; though it is of minor artistic interest it could be argued that it has more vitality on the whole, and more reference to life as lived, than the bulk of nineteenth century Irish verse written in English. And sometimes a poet like Pádraig Ó hÉigeartaigh, an exile from South Kerry writing of his son's death in the Boston area in the first decade of the twentieth century, can marry his grief with traditional professional expertise in something of the manner of the distant masters of the seven-teenth and eighteenth centuries.[2]

---

*The classic source for an understanding of eighteenth-century Irish poetry is Daniel Corkery's *The Hidden Ireland* (1925), in which the author's chief concern is to highlight the poetry 'against the dark world that threw it up.' It has been argued that the eighteenth-century Gaelic world was not quite as dark as Corkery painted it, but it was quite dark enough to justify Corkery's astonishment at the flourishing of such a poetry in such a time.

The Poetry

Irish poetry of the seventeenth, eighteenth and nineteenth centuries is the poetry of a subject people. A great deal of it is political poetry or a response to social – and linguistic – injustice. The purely personal lyric voice is rarely heard, except in folk poetry, but there is no mistaking the strong personal feeling that attaches itself to public issues. And it is a kind of poetry that demands a listening rather than a reading audience.

Socio-political poetry: It is difficult today to comprehend the extent to which events after Kinsale violated the lives and sensibilities of the Irish people. The rape of the territories of Ireland, many of them with sacred and heroic associations rooted far back in pre-historic times, was profoundly felt. Certain poems of broad scope by Ó Bruadair, Haicéad and Ó Rathaille bear ample testimony to this. But the poets often fashioned their most successful poems out of the smaller material of daily human consequences. Some of the best socio-political poetry of the seventeenth and eighteenth centuries takes its subject from a reversal of relationships in the lives of the poets themselves: Ó Bruadair, in a few bitter lyrics,[3] rails against the new proletariat emerging in his time, wearing English clothes, aping English ways, yielding before an upstart's display of broken English, and respecting the native poet no longer – so that he is refused hospitality now by a mere servant girl;[4] a later poet, Mac Cuarta, is similarly appalled at the refusal of hospitality to himself and a fellow-poet;[5] Ó Rathaille's most agonized lyrics speak of fragile and unsettled ties with harassed patrons.[6] The quantity of such lyrics affirms that it is not a question of mere individual complaint but of the dispossession of an entire caste.

The 'aisling': Overtly political verse in this period found its highest expression in Ó Rathaille's *aisling*, or vision poems,[7] in which the poet encounters a vision-woman who foretells a Stuart redeemer. In lesser hands the genre becomes no more than a rigid formula, repeated with ever-decreasing intensity throughout the eighteenth century. But each of Ó Rathaille's *aislings* has a mood and a tone of its own, closely reflecting the changing political realities of the times. In *Mac an Cheannaí*,[8] probably his last poem in the vein, the political game is clearly lost, and hope dead. Poets who insisted on a redeemer after this time were lacking in a sense of political reality – and their achievement is of a lesser order – but they filled an undoubted social need by keeping some element of hope alive.

Occasional verse: There is, of course, much notable work in these centuries which has little or nothing to do with socio-political matters. Feiritéar, for instance, wrote fine poems of love and friendship addressed to men and women.[9] There is a whole class of elegant occasional poems in loose syllabic metres dating from the seventeenth century – love poems, satires, religious poems and others. These are transitional poems, echoes of the world before Kinsale, when love, learning, religion and human behaviour could be contemplated at leisure. They represent an older syllabic tradition surviving side by side with the more popular accentual verse.

Fine occasional poems in syllabic or accentual forms, or in a combination of both, continued to appear. MacCuarta's lyrics on the drowned blackbird and on the cuckoo are particularly fine examples,[10] as are Mac Giolla Ghunna's tragicomic elegy on a yellow bittern,[11] and Ó Rathaille's spirited account of a cock stolen from a priest.[12] In the late eighteenth century two supreme occasional poems stand out, *Caoineadh Airt Uí Laoghaire* and *Cúirt an Mheán Oíche*, the first a masterpiece in the lyric 'keening' tradition, the other a magnificently bawdy *jeu d'esprit*, half struggling with personal hurt.[13] But these owe more to the submerged popular tradition than to the high literary traditions so far discussed.

Folk poetry: Irish literature includes what is possibly the most distinguished body of folk poetry in western Europe. Written down in great quantities from the end of the eighteenth century onward, much of it must have been composed during the seventeenth and eighteenth centuries by anonymous poets and musicians. Many of the models on which this folk poetry was based – in particular the love poetry – are clearly those that were common in western European society from about 1100 to 1400. It is likely that some of these models came to Ireland in the wake of the Norman invasion in the late twelfth century, with the introduction of French literature and song. Later, English popular lyrics may have had an additional influence. Whatever their source, these foreign influences were assimilated and reshaped by the Irish folk poets with an assurance that is apparent even on a casual acquaintance. Verses are beautifully crafted in the native mode; impressionistic nature imagery, or metaphors from daily life, add the touch of magic or the jolt of reality. Frequently there is evidence of a strong sense of lyric or dramatic structure, a rarity in folk poetry. While the greatest poetic achievement is possibly in the genre of the love-lament of the abandoned girl,[14] an unusual feature compared with the folk poetry of other western European countries is the great number of men's love-songs.[15] The thematic material of these songs corresponds closely with that French and Provençal *chanson d'amour* of the thirteenth and fourteenth, both literary and semi-popular. These masculine love-songs are in fact a repository, in a folk or rural setting, of the medieval attitudes of courtly love.

Pre-Renaissance modes: From 1600 onward there was little direct contemporary European influence on Irish poetry. There are indications that Feiritéar may have been aware of Renaissance influences, as reflected in the English literature of his day, and the activities of exiled Irish priests and scholars (some of them fine poets in their own right)[16] may have helped to introduce common European political and religious themes. But none of this significantly affected the course or quality of Irish verse. Rather, the tradition as a whole became more isolated, adhering strongly to pre-Renaissance modes of thought and style. To such a degree, indeed, that some of the living conventions of Irish classic accentual verse of the seventeenth and eighteenth centuries can seem as alien to modern readers as the conventions of *Beowulf* – the use, for example, of periphrastic bardic chevilles as synonyms for Ireland or the use of standard heroic phraseology for contemporary figures or actions. Such modes of thought or phrase can become tiresome in the hands of mediocre poets, but a poet like Ó Rathaille could fuse them with basic feeling so that they too become a functioning element in his best poems.

In reading the work of the typical accentual poets of the seventeenth and eighteenth centuries (as also the work of the anonymous syllabic poets and folk poets) it would be a mistake to judge its imaginative quality primarily by criteria of imagery or metaphor. It is the dramatic or storytelling voice that is most frequently and effectively heard: a situation or story is postulated, imaginatively developed and resolved in the presence of a listening audience. One may find *en passant* a striking casual use of image or metaphor, but there is no conscious emphasis on this as there is in modern poetry. More congenial to modern ears is the poetry's freedom from the high Renaissance conventions of poetic diction and subject matter. Any subject, even the most commonplace, is an acceptable matter for poetry, and any word its instrument. There is a strong emotional involvement with place, in particular with family place or ancestral territory. And while much of the verse reaches a high level of eloquence there is a bluntness of attitude at its core that is essentially medieval, from the homeliness of MacAingil's Christmas hymn[17] to the comic crudeness of MacGabhráin's poem on the lover thrown by his horse.[18]

The quality of Irish poetry shows a considerable decline toward the end of the eighteenth century. More and more, poets like Eoghan Rua Ó Súilleabháin tended to cultivate technical excellence for its own sake.[19] But at its best, the poetry of the period achieved intense moments of grief or tenderness, homeliness or bitterness, such as were not often attained elsewhere in western Europe.

[1981]

5

Brian Merriman and his *Court*

THE EMERGENCE OF an uniquely talented poet such as Brian Merriman in County Clare in the second half of the eighteenth century was in many ways an unlikely event. The renowned Irish literary figures of the previous century and a half had without exception come from counties east of the Shannon, and given what we know of the Clare literary tradition one would not have held out great hopes for a remarkable work of literature to emerge there in the last decades of the eighteenth century. There had been of course a good deal of traditional poetic and learned activity in County Clare right down through the eighteenth and into the first half of the nineteenth century, but the quality of the verse composed by even early eighteenth-century Clare poets was generally pedestrian.

What we know about the author of the *Court* is very little indeed, and in some ways only helps to deepen the mystery about the provenance of the poem. He was born somewhere in County Clare (probably in Ennistymon) about 1749. It is generally accepted that he was of illegitimate birth – indeed the untraditional Irish name of Merriman may indicate that. It would appear that his mother married a travelling mason who reared Brian as his own son. Afterwards the family settled down in Feakle where Brian later taught school and cultivated a small farm assiduously (winning two prizes for his flax crops in 1797). In the year 1787 he married, had two daughters, transferred to Limerick city in 1802–03, where he continued to teach until he died suddenly in July 1805. Unusually for an Irish poet of the time, his death was noted in the local newspaper. He was referred to however, not as a poet but as a teacher of 'Mathematics, etc.'

This general picture gives us no clear idea of the personality or think-ing of Brian Merriman. We do not know what education he had, literary or otherwise. The two minor lyrics ascribed to him, apart from the *Court*, show no sign of special literary talent. He does not seem to have com-municated with other poets, or joined with them in their courts of poetry. Indeed in a wry comment in *The Midnight Court* he seems to refer to himself not as one who is a familiar of the poets but as one who is a familiar of the privileged gentry of the county.

The Midnight Court is undoubtedly one of the greatest comic works of literature, and certainly the greatest comic poem ever written in Ireland. Scores of copies of the original manuscript were made in the immediate years after its composition: it was read with avidity, discussed and fre-quently added to. But we know of no other Gaelic work similar to Merriman's poem in its overall structure.

The Midnight Court is, in fact, a *Court of Love* in the typical medieval western European mould. Literary parliaments, assemblies and courts were very much in vogue in western Europe between the twelfth and sixteenth centuries.[1] One finds courts of love in Provençal, French and Latin as ear-ly as the twelfth and thirteenth centuries. Later one comes on them in German, Italian and English. In English the genre is found in abundance from the time of Chaucer right down to Elizabethan times. Swift's *Cadenus and Vanessa* is one of the last to be written in English.

In Merriman's *Court* illegitimates are extolled, free love and the mar-riage of the Catholic clergy are advocated. Because of such ideas the poem has been looked on in the past as a work of the eighteenth-century Enlightenment, owing its inspiration to authors such as Rousseau, Voltaire and Swift. This view would scarcely be acceptable nowadays. Indeed it has been pointed out[2] that much of the thematic material in *The Midnight Court* is found already in that bawdy part of the courtly thirteenth-century *Roman de la Rose* which was added on to the original by Jean de Meung. The *Roman*, which in itself contains the influences of the court of love convention, was the literary bible of the Middle Ages; it was translated into other languages, and referred to incessantly in love-literature down to the end of the sixteenth century. It is extremely doubtful, however, if Brian Merriman would have read any part of the *Roman de la Rose* in either French or English. How then did a teacher of mathematics in Feakle, County Clare in the year 1780 become familiar with the medieval court of love conventions and manage to encapsulate in his poem the spirit of Jean de Meung, the man who (as Helen Waddell puts it) 'laid his not overclean hands upon the Rose'?

In attempting to find an answer to this problem one has to take into account that both the court of love conventions, and some of the basic thematic material used by Jean de Meung were common currency in various literary forms and works for some time before and for long centuries after the composition of the *Roman*, and could have been available to Brian Merriman in a variety of ways. His debt to the general European tradition is best understood by looking at the overall shape of the poem, and noting its affiliations with various medieval literary forms.

The Midnight Court may be said to consist formally of a prologue, three dramatic monologues, and an epilogue. In the prologue Brian Merriman tells us first of all of a typical court poet's summer morning's vision:

> By the brink of the river I'd often walk,
> on a meadow fresh, in the heavy dew,
> along the woods, in the mountain's heart,
> happy and brisk in the brightening dawn.
> My heart would lighten to see Loch Gréine,
> the land, the view, the sky horizon,
> the sweet and delightful set of the mountains
> looming their heads up over each other.
>
> (D, p. 221)

Later a woman appears and leads the poet to a splendid court where the fairy-goddess of Thomond, Aoibheall, supported by an assembly of women, is presiding over a love-debate. Elements of the literary apparatus of the prologue are found at random throughout medieval courts of love. The love-debate is common to all. The splendid court is frequent. The summer morning's vision in a nature setting appears in the *Roman de la Rose*, and in a host of other poems. The assembly of women – sometimes presided over by the goddess Venus – is a theme in several poems. (One of the earliest courts, the Latin *Council of Remiremont* from the twelfth century, was in fact an assembly of nuns.) Of special interest perhaps is the vision-woman who leads the poet to the place of assembly. W.A. Neilson tells us that 'the business of the cicerone in medieval allegory, especially in France, is usually given to a maiden.'[3] He then goes on to discuss some medieval instances in which such a woman takes on the appearance of an old woman or hag. 'Hag' is a mild description of the woman who appears in Merriman's opus:

> a frightful, fierce, fat, full-bummed female,
> thick-calved, bristling, bony and harsh,
> her height exact – if I guessed it right –
> six yards or seven, with something over.
>
> (D, p. 225)

The matter to be debated at court is why young men (like Merriman himself) were not getting married, thus leaving the women dissatisfied, and the country's population declining. The first person to take the witness stand is a young girl who in a long dramatic monologue complains of the lack of a husband. The young girl's *Complaincte* is a standard medieval popular form. There are examples of it to be found in traditional Irish literature which may have been composed before Merriman's time. Merriman's girl, however, makes her complaint very much in the extended burlesque tradition of the late sixteenth-century English or French ballad – and at the same time she speaks right out of the heart of the Irish eighteenth-century scene:

> I'm certainly always on display
> at every field where the game's fought hard,
> at dances, hurling, races, courting,
> bone-fires, gossip and dissipation,
> at fairs and markets and Sunday Mass –
> to see and be seen, and choose a man. . . .
> I never would settle me down to sleep
> without fruit in a sock beneath my ear;
> I found it no trouble to fast devoutly
> – a whole day I'd swallow no bite or sup:
> I'd rinse my shift against the stream
> for a whisper in dream from my future spouse. . . .
> But the point and purpose of my tale
> is I've done my best and I've still no man –
> hence, alas, my long recital!
> In the knot of years I am tangled tight,
> I am heading hard for my days of grey
> and I fear that I'll die without anyone asking. . . .

> (D, p. 227-29)

The second dramatic monologue is an old man's retort who points out to the court that the young girl's own poverty-stricken life and promiscuous habits are the cause of her trouble:

> It's a terrible scandal and show for the people
> that a wretch like yourself, without cattle or sheep,
> should have shoes with a buckle, a silken cloak
> and a pocket hanky a-flap on the breeze!

> (D, p. 231)

The old man goes on to tell how he himself was deceived in marriage
– a theme which got an airing in the *Roman de la Rose*, in a few courts
of love, and in many other medieval literary works:

> My total loss that I failed to choke
> on the night I was christened! – or before I lusted
> to bed with that woman who turned me grey
> and drove me wild, without friend or wits.
> Everyone old and young could tell me
> how game she was in the country pubs
> to drink and buy, as they beat the tables,
> and relax on her back for married or single. . . .
> In gruesome fact, she gave me a son
> (no sinew of mine) before its time:
> I'd a fireside family after one night!
>
> (*D*, p. 233)

There is an English ballad of the seventeenth century, *The Lass of Lynn's
new joy for finding a father for her child*, which tells of a situation very
reminiscent of the old man's plight.

In support of his plea that love should be free and marriage abolished
the old man finally embarks on a paean in praise of bastards. The message
of free love was of course the principal message preached in the second
part of *Roman de la Rose*, but the praise of bastards seems to surface prin-
cipally in Elizabethan times in England. Shakespeare's famous passage in
King Lear is a case in point. One contemporary of Shakespeare's had this
to say: 'It is so little feared that unless one hath had two or three bastardes
a peece, they esteeme no man.'[4]

An eighteenth-century poem by Richard Savage, *The Bastard*, published
in Dublin in 1728, may have been a part of Merriman's reading; but the
tone of Merriman's plea is very much the tone of English ballads of the
sixteenth and seventeenth-centuries:

> The dull offspring of the marriage bed
> What is it but a human piece of lead?
> a sottish lump, ingendered of all ills
> Begot like cats, against their father's wills!

Those of illegitimate birth, however, are thought to be of more sterling
quality:

> Hence spring the noble, fortunate and great
> Always begot in passion and in heat.[5]

This last line is echoed closely in Merriman's resounding couplet:

> . . . crobhaire crothadh go cothrom gan cháim é
> Le fonn na fola is le fothram na sláinte.
>
> (he is a stalwart, fully-fashioned without
> blemish/in the heat of the blood and the
> resonance of health.)

In the third monologue the young woman gives a harrowing commentary on the old man's performance as a husband to the young woman he married. The material here is typical of the bawdy medieval song type called *Chanson de la Malmariée*, which appears frequently in French, Italian, Scottish and indeed Irish popular literature. A Clare poet, Seán Ó hUaithnín, who preceded Brian Merriman by almost fifty years, had written such a song, but Merriman's extension of the theme leaves all his predecessors in the shade:

> It was gloomy doings, the nightly joy
> – oppression and burden, trouble and fright:
> legs of lead, and skinny shoulders,
> iron knees as cold as ice,
> shrunken feet by embers scorched,
> an old man's ailing, wasting body. . . .
> She'd never complain at a night of work
> but give a brave slasher as good as she got.
> She'd never refuse any time or place
> on bone of her back with her eyes shut tight,
> with never a balk or immoderate sulk
> nor attack like a cat, nor scrape nor scratch,
> but stretched her all like a sheaf beside him
> flank on flank, with her legs around him,
> coaxing his thoughts by easy stages,
> fingering down on him, mouth on mouth,
> putting her leg the far side of him often
> rubbing her brush from waist to knee,
> or snatching the blanket and quilt from his loins
> to fiddle and play with the juiceless lump.
> But useless to tickle or squeeze or rub
> or attack with her elbows, nails or heels
> – I'm ashamed to relate how she passed the night
> squeezing the sluggard, shuddering, sprawling,
> tossing her limbs and the bedding beneath her,

her teeth and her members all a-shiver,
not sleeping a wink till the dawn of day,
performing and tossing from side to side.

(*D*, pp. 239-41)

The young woman proceeds after this to plead that vigorous young men
– and well-fed priests in particular – should be drafted into marriage. The
advocacy of marriage for priests is somewhat unheralded in the poem,
and is, perhaps, a little surprising. A similar theme, however, is to be found
in a few medieval courts of love. In the *Council of Remiremont* the love
of a clergyman was deemed much more satisfying than the love of a clerk,
and any nun not acting according to this dictum was ordered to be
promptly excommunicated. Similarly a twelfth-century court called *Clerus
et Presbyter* – attended only by clergymen – decided that priests should
have concubines:

> Habebimus, clerici, duas concubinas . . .
> Si tandem leges implebimus divinas.[6]

They looked to the Pope to free them from the dire rules of celibacy as
indeed does the president of our *Midnight Court* in its concluding sec-
tion, the epilogue.

The typical Court of Love ends with judgement being given and statutes
being passed. A French poem, for instance, written by Christine de Pisan
in 1399 and translated into English by Thomas Hoccleve, reflects this con-
vention. It is decided here by the God of Love that in order to protect
womenfolk all villainous untrustworthy men should be seized, tied, and
roughly treated.

In *The Midnight Court* judgement is similarly passed, decrees proposed,
and the date noted. President Aoibheall's judgement, however, is unex-
pectedly on the conservative side. She would not advocate that the
institution of marriage be abandoned, but would allow rather unsatisfac-
tory provisions to enable young people to enjoy as much permissiveness
as possible – hoping old people would lend their names to the illegitimate
offspring. As for the matter of priests being permitted to marry, she counsels
patience in the hope that the Pope 'with full assent of a Council' would
in time remove the restrictions on marriage for the clergy. The only specific
decree she does propose is similar to that proposed in the poem by
Christine de Pisan: that all young men of marriageable age such as Mer-
riman himself, who had not taken wives unto themselves, should be seized,
tied, and severely punished.

It is reasonably clear then, whatever of the immediate provenance of

The Midnight Court, that it is throughout closely related to medieval and late-medieval conventions of thought and literary structure. The Court of Love apparatus is especially apparent in the prologue and epilogue. The love debate itself, carried out in the form of three burlesque dramatic monologues (which one does not normally associate with a Court of Love) has close affiliations with late medieval popular songs and ballads. Simpler models of one or two of these song types may have existed in Irish folksong for several centuries previous to this, but it is questionable whether the particular burlesque models of these which appear in *The Midnight Court* had been established in Irish for very long before Merriman's time. It is quite likely indeed that the matter and models that Merriman inherited and radically transformed in his poem belong more to the post-Elizabethan era in Ireland.[7]

The Midnight Court, in its conventions and themes, does, of course, emanate ultimately from a western European literary love-movement which began to make a profound impact on poetry in various languages as early as the twelfth century, and continued to do so, in different waves and guises until a new love poetry appeared in the Renaissance period. In my book *An Grá in Amhráin na nDaoine*, I make the case that Irish folk poetry was greatly influenced by this medieval movement which began to wield its influence in Ireland in the wake of the Anglo-Norman invasion (1169). My main thesis was that a great many of the types of Irish love-song be- ing sung in our Gaeltachtaí today were to be found in *troubadour* and *trouvère* literature of the twelfth and thirteenth centuries. This argument has frequently been misinterpreted as meaning that direct French influence on our folk song was unquestionably the dominant one. That is not necessarily so. Certainly, on the evidence available, it seems quite likely that in earlier medieval times (*c*.1200–1400) the French influence was greater than that of English, but it seems equally likely that in later periods (after 1500) English influence on both our folk poetry and literary love-poetry began to supplant that of French. Consequently it need not surprise us that many of the elements which constitute the structure of *The Midnight Court* should have made their way into traditional Irish literature in the post-Elizabethan era. English influence at that period was all pervasive. Indeed eighteenth-century Gaelic poets such as Eoghan Rua Ó Súilleabháin, Seán Ó Tuama, Aindrias Mac Craith could themselves write fluent – though execrable – verses in English. Two poets who lived for a time near Ennis and were contemporaries of Merriman, Seán Lloyd and Tomás Ó Míocháin, wrote some of their work in English. In fact in the year 1780, Lloyd publish- ed in Ennis a small book of prose in English called *A Short Tour, or an Impartial and Accurate Description of the County of Clare*.

Merriman, who spent most of his life in East Clare – where literary activity in Irish was minimal compared to West Clare – lived in an area and an environment which was much more susceptible to English influence than that of many other parts of Munster. The Irish language was receding rapidly there as it was in the area across the Shannon, North Tipperary, with which it was closely linked. The colonial gentry and the anglicized Irish gentry whom, we presume, Merriman numbered amongst his friends, would have been in constant touch with external commercial and cultural matters, not only in the nearby city of Limerick but in Dublin as well. At the same time it must be remembered that there was probably a high degree of bilinguality at all levels of society at this period in East Clare. Hely Dutton in his *Statistical Survey of County Clare* could still say of County Clare in general nearly thirty years after the composition of *The Midnight Court*: 'Almost all the better kind of people speak Irish to the country people.'

It is not at all easy, however, to envisage how the specific structural and thematic elements of the *Midnight Court* reached Brian Merriman in his East Clare *milieu*. The principal difficulty here is that (in terms of English literature) the Court of Love elements, as found in the prologue and epilogue, seem to belong to high literary tradition, whereas the monologues seem squarely in the late-medieval popular tradition. Did Brian Merriman then read some solemn English Court of Love and give his own comic Irish version of it, adding in the popular monologues (models for some of which might already have been assimilated into the Irish language by poets who preceded him)? Or did he in fact have as a model an English bawdy Court of Love containing, perhaps, burlesque elements of a kind already existing in the popular Irish literary tradition? Or, or, or . . . the permutations of the possibilities seem endless. But it must be noted that, despite the affiliations between the *Midnight Court* and the general thematic material of medieval courts of love, there is no single Court of Love we know of, which resembles it in any detail. The prologue and epilogue contain many Court of Love elements, for instance, which are not to be found in Swift's *Cadenus and Vanessa* – a work which has been suggested in the past as Merriman's model. If Merriman did, in fact, use a bawdy Court of Love in English as a complete or partial model for his *Midnight Court* it may have been a work such as the 'lost' *Court of Venus* which disappeared from circulation in England in the second half of the sixteenth century after Puritan Reformers had heaped 'universal opprobrium' on it because of its scandalous nature. There is a great deal of scholarly debate as to what this 'lost' *Court of Venus* really was,[8] but assuming it was in the traditional Court of Love form, it could possibly have been the starting point for Merriman's poem. It is not too extravagant to suggest that one of his friends amongst the gentry could have had such in his ancestral family library or could have picked it up in a bookshop in Dublin or Limerick. All that, however, remains a mere hypothesis.

II

The Midnight Court can, of course, be read with immense enjoyment and profit by a reader who has no knowledge whatever of its literary background and antecedents. It is a poem of gargantuan energy, moving clearly and pulsatingly along a simple storyline, with a beginning, a middle and an end. For a poem of over one thousand lines it has few *longueurs*. It is full of tumultuous bouts of great good humour, verbal dexterity and Rabelaisian ribaldry. It is a mammoth readable achievement with little need of gloss.

The literary critic does need to know, however, what exact conventions or thematic matter Merriman inherited, or grappled with, if he is to throw light on the poet's personal investment in his work. The originality of his new creation cannot be appreciated or put into focus until the nature of the old material is discovered.

It would be a help, then, in discussing Merriman's achievement to know whether he did or did not have an immediate model or models such as the 'lost' *Court of Venus*. At the same time, anyone who is familiar with the general literary background I have been describing, will be reasonably certain that all medieval themes and conventions as handled by Merriman were changed, transmuted utterly, and that a new demonic comic creation emerged which is absolutely eighteenth-century Irish. It says a great deal for the vigour and richness of the Irish literary tradition that, in a late eighteenth-century bilingual environment, it could still be manipulated so creatively and with such astonishing assimilating force. Material which remains conventional, inert, semi-abstract or solemn in medieval literature – material such as that of the young girl's complaint, the celibacy of the priests, the *chanson de la malmariée*, the vision-woman or cicerone, the natural splendour of the illegitimate child – is developed and extended into extraordinary new dimensions. Part of the poet's success here is due to the manner and verve with which he merges significant human detail, contemporary and other, with old themes. For instance, the girl's complaint is full of exact and fascinating references to Irish superstitions and behaviour at the time. Similarly the old man's diatribe against her contains precise observation of County Clare fashions in the second half of the eighteenth century. Again, the old man's description of the poor hovel the girl lived in is both more moving and more immediate than any social historian's – and yet somehow is not at odds with the comic vein of the poem:

> . . . the soot dripping wet and the rising damp,
> weeds appearing in great profusion
> and the signs of hens inscribed across it,

a weakened ridge and bending beams
and a brown downpour profusely falling . . .

(*D*, p. 233)

Even the often criticized conventional summer-morning opening of the poem has a good deal of human personal observation in it which saves it somewhat from being a tiresome old cliché.

Merriman's success was mainly due of course to his tumultuous, comic eloquence. It is virtually certain for instance that in no medieval text, lost or found, did the matter of clerical celibacy get the kind of virtuoso treatment it gets in *The Midnight Court*. The poet's eloquence could take different shapes as the requirements of the narrative or the dramatic monologues dictated. It is at its most effective when it flies into bawdy or bombast or vituperation; but (at the other end of the scale) it can also be quite effective in creating an animated conversational-type dramatic situation (as in the long section which portrays the gossips around the fireside dealing with the illegitimate child). Irish poetry has traditionally leaned towards the dramatic situational type of lyric structure; the bombastic vituperative vein has also been hugely cultivated. So in mentioning Merriman's stylistic achievements, one is also stressing that as a creative writer he is operating mainly within his own Gaelic literary tradition. The bombast, the adjectival rhetoric, may on occasion overshoot the mark. Generally speaking, however, it is an essential part of the outlandish quality of the poem.

The more one reads *The Midnight Court* – especially in the light of all the medieval themes and conventions which are found radically transformed in it – the more one is convinced that the poet is speaking of issues which are real to him; that a disturbing eighteenth-century revelation of some kind is taking place, or trying to take place. I have gone on record before this[9] as saying that the major defect of the poem is that it has no deep personal insights, or even interesting insights to offer on the problems broached (as one would expect in the works of the gifted comic writers from Aristophanes to Beckett). I should like to modify that view somewhat now and say that I feel the major defect of the poem is that the insights and feelings about love and marriage which abound in the poem are not brought to proper artistic definition. Yet behind all the comic alarms and excursions, behind the somewhat ramshackle old-fashioned structure, it must be noted that there is a certain deep sense of conviction and a consistency of feeling.

The *leitmotif* of the poem at all main stages seems to be that human beings must not allow their basic sexual vigour or instincts to become arid or conventionalized: the human animal must at all costs fulfil himself – whatever the rules or mores of society ordain at any given time. The young girl complains at the outset, for instance, of her own wasted years, and later complains of the wasted years of a woman-friend who was married off to an old man. She also complains of how the rules of obligatory celibacy lay waste the manhood of priests. The old man, despite his own experience – or more likely because of it? – appeals for an end to marriage, it being an institution which thwarts people (when they have to await the requirements of legal and ecclesiastical ordinances) from propagating 'as nature ordains'.

The idea of sex as vigour abounds in *The Midnight Court*; but there is no concept of sex as love, no feeling of sexual love being a spiritual or even a romantic force. The romantic concept of sexual love was developed inordinately in Western literature from the time of the troubadours, in literary *Courts of Love*, as well as in love-poetry in general. But as Johan Huizanga points out, a more archaic viewpoint co-existed with this concept during the middle-ages: 'We should picture to ourselves two layers of civilization superimposed, co-existing though contradictory. Side by side with the courtly style of literary and rather recent origin, the primitive forms of erotic life kept all their force. . . . [This] vision of never-ending lust implies no less than the screwed-up system of courtly love, an attempt to substitute for the reality the dream of a happier life. It is once more the aspiration towards the life sublime, but this time viewed from the animal side.'[10]

The archaic viewpoint prevailed very much in older rooted rural communities, and it is obviously the viewpoint of Merriman in this poem. Romantic love inside or outside marriage scarcely exists as far as this poem is concerned. Communion of mind or spirit is not entertained. If put to express the matter, Merriman (to judge by this poem) might easily have said that 'love' was a game or artifice invented by human beings to mask the preponderant animal vigour in their natures, which in his view was one of the greatest of human gifts.

Whatever Merriman might have felt or said on matters such as this, he didn't express it in his poem in any coherent way. The artistic indication of this is that the mounting feeling of indignation regarding the waste of our human animal potential peters out in the series of lukewarm conciliatory positions taken up in the final section of the poem. In Aoibheall's lack-lustre judgement, nothing insightful or memorable is proposed or felt. Frank O'Connor says: '. . . from the moment the Queen gets up to deliver judgement the poem falls away. Clearly this was intended to be the point at which Merriman would speak through her, and express his own convictions about life, but something went wrong!'[11] What most likely went wrong was that Merriman had no ready answers to offer about life. In this, of course, he was no different from some of the greatest of writers or artists. Unfortunately for him, however, the Court of Love traditional concluding structure demanded balanced rational answers of a kind a real poet cannot give. It is quite probable, then, that the Court of Love apparatus finally ended up for him more a hindrance than a help. Some more irrational or surrealistic type of concluding structure might have helped Merriman to reveal more climactically his dark, archaic feelings.

These feelings were obviously quite closely linked to the matter of his own illegitimate birth. Indeed the emotional climax of the poem as it stands is the old man's plea for bastards. One senses here more than anywhere else in the poem Merriman's personal statement as he struggles to deal in comic terms with a grievous personal hurt.

The ostensible reason for the whole love-debate is said by the vision-woman at the beginning to be the declining population of the country; but the pressing artistic reason most likely was the poet's need to dramatize and understand some profound inner disturbance emanating from the circumstances of his own birth. In this reading one is tempted to see the Court of Love structure used by the poet as a device by which he can put his own mother and (legal) father in the dock. For whether one looks on the young woman who speaks to the Court as Merriman's mother or not, she certainly presents the point of view of a (gadabout) girl who can't find a suitable mate (monologue I), and later (in monologue III), of a girl who, for whatever reason, is finally married off to an old man. And whether or not one looks on the old man who speaks to the Court as the travelling mason whom Merriman's mother married, he certainly presents the point of view of one who was harnessed in marriage to a young woman pregnant by some other man. President Aoibheall's judgement that young people should be able to couple freely, and old men ready to lend their names to illegitimates (and so preserve the institution of marriage) is in a sense then a validation of Merriman's situation as a child reared by a father not his own.

In trying to understand the hurt inflicted on Merriman by his illegitimacy it would probably be a mistake to think of illegitimacy as inevitably carrying the same type of slur in eighteenth-century Ireland as it did in nineteenth-century Ireland, especially in the post-Famine period. Merriman's feeling here must have been much nearer that of aristocratic Gaelic Ireland than of post-famine Victorian Ireland. Values and arrangements in matters connected with sex and marriage in aristocratic Gaelic Ireland remained to the end quite at odds with Christian teaching. Different types of marriage, divorce and so on, were allowed by the Brehon laws. Bishops and priests had wives ('concubines'). What is stigmatized as illegitimacy didn't exist as a concept – women were often proud to 'name' their sons after their aristocratic lovers and requisite arrangements were made it seems for their future. All this reflects the values of the Irish 'heroic' (pagan) society which prevailed by and large against the assaults of Christianity right up at least to the first half of the seventeenth century. One cannot see Brian Merriman in the year 1780 in County Clare being unaffected by such values. After all it was only a little over a hundred years before the date of Merriman's birth that the British Parliament (1634) passed an act forbidding polygamy amongst the Irish. And it was less than a hundred years before the date of Merriman's birth that an Irish poet reports (*c*.1655) that it was still the custom to be unchristianly flexible about matters of love and marriage: 'bean isteach is amach ag aoinfhear'.[12] Merriman may have been strongly influenced in the manner of his writing about these matters by *Court of Love* themes or Elizabethan ballads – he may even have been influenced by whatever he read or heard of the ideas of Rousseau and other writers of the age – but it seems virtually certain that the deeper feelings he is expressing throughout are the archaic feelings of his own traditional society. In fact it is expressly stated in *The Midnight Court* as a part of the old man's praise of bastards, that with the advent of free love an Irish heroic society would emerge again. Men would inherit the strength and body of a *Goll Mac Mórna*, says the old man, heroic vigour would burgeon anew in fruitfulness. 'It is', as Huizanga said, 'once more an aspiration towards the life sublime, but this time viewed from the animal side.'

English Common Law – with increasing aid from the Catholic Church – was engaged during the seventeenth and eighteenth centuries in combating both the ideals and the old practical arrangements regarding love and marriage in Gaelic Ireland. Under the growing power of English law, the legal position of an illegitimate in County Clare in 1750 would, of course, be a far cry from the relatively favoured position of the illegitimate in older times. Local lore has it that Merriman's natural father was a minor aristocrat, a gentleman ('duine uasal') called McNamara. In the old Irish dispensation Merriman might have been proudly calling himself McNamara (or whatever) and could have inherited land or been placed in a lucrative career. In the new dispensation his noble lineage was disparaged, and he ended up on a small farm of land with a travelling mason as a father and the career of a hedge-schoolmaster possibly the only one open to him. Was it the diminution of status and prospects for a person of his birth – rather than the strong social stigma later on attached to illegitimacy – which wounded Merriman? It is virtually certain, I think, that it was. Such diminution might also account for his courting of the local gentry rather than the poets. It also might explain what appears to be an irrelevant non-comic harangue against English law in the Prologue to the poem, where it is stated that remnants of the old aristocracy now 'have neither wealth nor freedom'.

There is one more matter worth mentioning in relation to Merriman's trauma: that is the possibility that the gentleman who was his natural father may have been a priest or seminarian. (It has to be stated immediately, however, that there seems to be no suggestion whatever in local lore, or otherwise, that this was so.)

A priest being married or engaging in sex would have been no novel idea to anyone with a knowledge of traditional (including eighteenth-century) life in Ireland. Indeed the young woman states in the poem that priests whom she calls 'mian ár gcroí' ('the desire of our hearts') were known for their philandering propensities, and that a number of their progeny existed bearing false names. I have no knowledge, however, that the question of marriage for priests was in any way a live issue in eighteenth-century Ireland; and except in the context of Merriman's natural father being a priest or seminarian can one make artistic or emotional sense of the elaborate and passionate plea made by the young girl (who I suggested may be expressing Merriman's mother's viewpoint) that priests should be allowed to marry, or understand the concern of Aoibheall when she assures the court that indeed they should, and would in time, be so allowed:

> . . . the time will come with the Council's sanction
> and the Pope applying his potent hand;
> a committee will sit on the country's ills
> and release to you all, under binding bonds,
> a torrent of blood, a storm of flesh,
> those ardent slashers – your heart's desire!

> (D, pp. 243-45)

Whatever further evidence does emerge in time about either Merriman's personal trauma or the literary background to his poem, it is reasonably clear I think that a prodigious creative comic energy was unleashed by him as he endeavoured to articulate his grievance within a framework yoked together from medieval bits and pieces. There may be no 'sense of the incommensurate' in the poem – as Daniel Corkery claimed – but there is certainly more than a hint of a somewhat uncomprehending hurt, trying confusedly, to reveal itself.

In the undistinguished epilogue, perhaps the liveliest sections are those which deal with Merriman's punishment because of his not being married. Despite the alarming fear which the poem attributes to him in the face of that punishment, he did not in fact marry for some nine years after the composition of *The Midnight Court*. He was then somewhere around his fiftieth year, which, even in County Clare, is nearer the average age of death than marriage.

[1981]

6

The Lament for
Art O'Leary

THERE IS GREAT difficulty in trying to make a clear-cut distinction between oral and written literature in the Irish tradition. Making such a distinction is not particularly helpful at any rate in the case of *Caoincadh Airt Uí Laoghaire*. Here a widespread and archaic folk-ritual is transformed into a remarkable literary utterance. Using the typical conventions of the popular Irish 'keen' (lament), the 'author', Eileen Dubh O'Connell, makes an extempore statement of grief for her husband Art O'Leary, murdered in 1773. Other relatives of the dead man also contribute their statements. Variants of all these have been handed down to us by oral transmission. Unusually for oral literature, the name of the 'author' of the lament, Eileen Dubh, is invariably mentioned. Indeed this keen had gained so much recognition in its own day that a Frenchman touring Ireland in the late eighteenth century (*c*.1790) referred to the recognition it had got as a poem which 'is praised above all others'.[1]

Today *The Lament for Art O'Leary* is one of the works of Irish literature most admired by littérateurs in Ireland. Large sections of the lament have been translated into English by Thomas Kinsella, John Montague, Frank O'Connor, Eilís Dillon, and Professor Kenneth Jackson. Peter Levi in his inaugural lecture as Professor of Poetry at Oxford (1984) says of the lament: 'I think it is the greatest poem written in these islands in the whole eighteenth century.'[2]

The popular folk-keen was central to the obsequies of the dead in Ireland, and to appreciate the provenance and nature of the *Lament for Art O'Leary* some understanding of traditional Irish death-rituals is necessary, especially the Irish wake. In all cultures people have found need for death-rituals, for funeral-games, of various kinds. The epic hero in ancient Irish sagas (as in Greek epics) was especially honoured: 'His tomb was built, his name written in Ogham, his funeral games carried out'. Whether the funeral games carried out in ancient times bear any relationship to the funeral games which survived in eighteenth and nineteenth-century Ireland is impossible for me to say. A description of Irish wakes from approximately the same period as *The Lament for Art O'Leary* gives a general idea of what these were like:

> These wakes are meetings of merriment and festivity to which they resort from far and near. The old people amuse themselves in smoking tobacco, drinking whiskey and telling stories in the room of the corpse, whilst the young men in the barn or some separate apartment exhibit feats of activity, or inspired by their sweethearts, dance away the night to the melodious *pleasing* of a bagpipe.[3]

Well down into the nineteenth century, those death-rituals were a source of scandal to well-meaning strangers (who chose, perhaps, not to scrutinize too closely their own ways of burying the dead). Between a hundred and two hundred so-called 'Wake-games' – or 'Wake-orgies' as Lady Wilde called them – were catalogued and described some years ago by Seán Ó Súilleabháin of the Folklore Commission in his book *Wake-games and Amusements*. The wake-games, though carried out in a nominally Christian community, were impeccably pagan. Despite that, however, they were not widely condemned until the nineteenth century when Irish priests and bishops began to be educated within the culturally hostile English educational system. The nature of many of these games had already been adverted to in the nineteenth century by a gentleman called (ironically enough) Mr Prim. He wrote of wakes in the Kilkenny area:

> The 'game' usually first performed was termed 'bout', and was joined in by men and women, who all acted a very obscene part which cannot be described. The next scene generally was termed 'Making the Ship', with its several parts of 'laying the keel', forming the 'stem and stern', and erecting the 'mast', the latter part of which was done by a female using a gesture and expression, proving beyond doubt that it was a relic of Pagan Rites. The 'Bull and the Cow' was another game strongly indicative of a Pagan origin, from circumstances too indelicate to be particularised.[4]

Such accounts, taken with various others of mock-marriges and other amusements at wakes, leave us in no doubt that part of the traditional death-ritual in Ireland was much concerned with life, with fertility, with gaiety, with challenging the authority of death. (Joyce's description of a 'funeral' in Ireland as a 'fun fer all' is not too wide of the mark.)

Emerging from all this lusty fun – and in sharp contrast to it – was the dirge of the keening woman or women. Here is a well-known nineteenth-century account of the setting by Mr and Mrs Samuel Hall:

> The women of the household range themselves at either side, and the keen at once commences. They rise with one accord, and, moving their bodies with a slow motion to and fro, their arms apart, they continue to keep up a heart-rending cry. This cry is interrupted for a while to give the ban caointhe (the leading keener), an opportunity of commencing. At the close of every stanza of the dirge, the cry is repeated, to fill up, as it were, the pause, and then dropped; the woman then again proceeds with the dirge, and so on to the close.
>
> The only interruption which this manner of conducting a wake suffers, is from the entrance of some relative of the deceased, who, living remote, or from some other cause, may not have been in at the commencement. In this case, the ban caointhe ceases, all the women rise and begin the cry, which is continued until the new-comer has cried enough. During the pauses of the women's wailing, the men, seated in groups by the fire, or in the corners of the room, are indulging in jokes, exchanging repartees, and bantering each other, some about their sweethearts, and some about their wives, or talking over the affairs of the day – prices and politics, priests and parsons, the all-engrossing subjects of Irish conversation.
>
> The keener is usually paid for her services – the charge varying from a crown to a pound, according to the circumstances of the employer. They –
>
>> 'live upon the dead,
>> By letting out their persons by the hour
>> To mimic sorrow when the heart's not sad.'
>
> It often happens, however, that the family has some friend or relation, rich in the gift of poetry; and who will for love of her kind give the unbought eulogy to the memory of the deceased. The Irish language, bold, forcible, and comprehensive, full of the most striking epithets and idiomatic beauties, is peculiarly adapted for either praise or satire – its blessings are singularly touching and expressive, and its curses wonderfully strong, bitter and biting. The rapidity and ease with which both are uttered, and epigrammatic force of each concluding stanza of the keen, generally bring tears to the eyes of the most indifferent spectator, or produce a state of terrible excitement. The dramatic effect of the scene is very powerful: the darkness of the death-chamber, illumined only by candles that glare upon the corpse, the manner of repetition or

acknowledgement that runs round when the keener gives out a sentence, the deep, yet suppressed sobs of the nearer relatives, and the stormy, uncontrollable cry of the widow or bereaved husband when allusion is made to the domestic virtues of the deceased - all heighten the effect of the keen; but in the open air, winding round some mountain pass, when a priest, or person greatly beloved and respected, is carried to the grave, and the keen swelled by a thousand voices, is borne upon the mountain echoes - it is then absolutely magnificent.[5]

Not alone is the woman's lament a thematic feature of Irish literature from the earliest times, but the historical evidence for the particular kind of women's keening described by the Halls goes back a long way. Cambrensis in the twelfth century, Spenser in the sixteenth century, and William Penn in the seventeenth century, are amongst those who refer to it. Spenser, like many others, considered the 'despairing outcries and immoderate wailings' as 'altogether heathenish'. In our own day Synge has given a magnificent description of keening on the Aran Islands, and has been greatly influenced by its rituals in his *Riders to the Sea*, particularly in the great last rhetorical utterances of Maurya. Amongst other writers strongly influenced in their work by the keening tradition, I would instance Liam O'Flaherty, Daniel Corkery, and Seán O'Casey (in *Juno and the Paycock*).

It remains to be said, however, that the type of women's keen we are talking about is not in any way specifically Irish. Such keening - unnoticed apparently by Spenser in his own day - was still going on in England and Scotland in the seventeenth and eighteenth centuries. In this present century keening rituals are still being carried out in Greece, Albania, Pakistan, Finland, Bulgaria, Hungary, former USSR, Lithuania, Latvia, etc. - indeed even in Italy and France.

Here is an account from a description of life in the southern Italian province of Lucania, in the years 1959-1960, by an American social worker, Ann Cornelisen:

My knock at the Widow Fascide's door was answered by the high eerie wails of formal mourning that swelled and shrilled ever faster to a crescendo of howls. . . . Every act, every gesture, every word is prescribed, and any deviation will rouse comment. The actual moment of death electrifies the mourners. They fling open the windows to let the dead man's spirit out and open the doors to invite people in; then settle down for the harrowing hours of the watch when the women chant, one singing the virtues of the dead man, the others wailing the chorus. They tear their hair, claw their faces, and weep until it seems they can mourn no more.[6]

Later on the author mentions an eighteenth-century quotation referring to

Calabria where 'women are hired to howl at burials'[7] – just as they were in Ireland.

Françoise Gilot, who wrote a book on her life with Picasso in Vallauris, on the Mediterranean, in the 1940–50s, tells of a woman who worked for her during that period, one of whose duties was keening – not the dead, but the dying:

> 'Well', she said, 'when we're called in, the first thing to do is to eat a good meal. Weepers work hard and you can't do that on an empty stomach. Then we draw up our chairs alongside the bed. The main thing is to prolong the agony so that before you leave you've helped that poor soul recall everything important that happened to him all during his life. I might say, 'do you remember, Ernest, the day of your First Communion, how little Mimi stood behind you and pulled your hair?' I grew up with him, you see, and I remember those things. 'Yes, yes, I remember', he sobs, and all three of us weepers groan and wail with him. Then it's the next weeper's turn. 'Do you remember the day you left for your military service when you had to say good-bye to the family? If he says yes, then it's the third one's turn, but if he says no, we try it again and again and add more and more details until he remembers. Sometimes, it's a really sad memory, like 'Do you remember Julie, the time you lost your little girl from the croup at the age of three?' When Julie cries her heart out, we follow along like a chorus. If it's a happy memory, we all laugh. And it goes on like that through the whole life of the one who's dying.[8]

It seems then that the death ritual of open weeping and lamentation by women, allied to extempore verse or chant, was an Indo-European (perhaps even a world-wide) phenomenon. Part of its function was, it seems, to propitiate the dead; another part was to help the survivors to get on with the business of living.

In Ireland, the keen was typically a series of incantatory extempore verses lamenting the dead person, chanted to a recitative type air, and punctuated at regular intervals by wailing cries. It was mostly sung/recited over the corpse at the wake; but keening might also be heard, for instance, on route to the burial or at the graveyard. On occasion the keening was carried out by the mother/nurse/wife/relatives of the dead man as each one of them arrived at the wake; more often – in the eighteenth and nineteenth centuries at least – it was the task of professionals, women hired to perform (just as one hires an undertaker today). A nineteenth century description of a professional keener refers to her as rocking rhythmically to and fro, closing her eyes, now raising, now lowering her voice as she recites her extempore verses, changing her tone dramatically as she proceeded.

As I say such a keener's lament would be extempore – but only to a point, for the keening woman would draw from the vast storehouse of themes and formulas used traditionally on such occasions and, of course, improvise on them as she proceeded with her composition. She would praise the bounty and heroism of a man (the lamented person was nearly always a man), she would recite his lineage; speak of his good looks and attractiveness to women; tell, perhaps, of a vision she had which foretold his death; declare that the very rivers and mountains bewailed his death. There is also found quite often in such keens a reflection of the concern – as in the wake itself – for ongoing life, for fruitfulness, for renewal in spite of death.

Fragments of various keens in this mould have been collected from oral transmissions, but very few extended keens on the scale of the *Lament for Art O'Leary* have survived. And of those which have survived none make in any way the same impact as Eileen Dubh O'Connell's composition.

Eileen Dubh herself – and indeed her husband Art – were probably quite unusual in their lifestyle in late eighteenth-century Ireland. After the fall of the old aristocratic Gaelic order (from c.1600 onwards), conditions of living for the conquered Irish became quite oppressive. Many descriptions of eighteenth-century Ireland speak of it as a land where the native population was submerged and downtrodden, a land of peasants living in hovels. Yet both Eileen and Art were of the stock of minor nobility – much reduced by the English conquest, to be sure – but still enjoying a very good living. Eileen was one of the O'Connell family of Derrynane, County Kerry, and aunt of the great Daniel O'Connell, known chiefly as the architect of Catholic Liberation in Ireland. Her mother (a poet herself and a relation of some of the learned poetic families), ruled a very large mansion, one of the few big Gaelic houses to survive under English rule. She, in fact, supervised with some style a large-scale smuggling operation between south Kerry and the European mainland, exporting goods such as hides and skins and importing other goods such as tea and wine. She also saw to it that her family – the boys at any rate – were formally tutored in Latin, French, English and possibly mathematics. Life in her house was self-contained, independent. Everything needed was grown there – or smuggled in. Servants and tradesmen abounded, silks were worn, wine was drunk, the furniture was mahogony. The O'Connells in fact were living or endeavouring to live as if the old Irish aristocratic order had not collapsed nearly two centuries previously.

If a death occurred in this type of house, not alone would the popular funeral and wake rituals (including a 'keen') be carried out lavishly, but one would expect more formal lamentations as well. For instance, it would have been usual that a bard or poet attached to the family would compose a learned elegy. A piece of music might also be composed in commemoration of the dead person (several such survive).

To understand the scope and tone of Eileen's keen it is necessary to understand some of this background; to understand that Eileen grew up in one of the last big houses in Gaelic Ireland where the full Irish cultural tradition, *aristocratic as well as popular,* could be inherited as a part of the normal daily routine. While the framework then for Eileen's lament is the popular extempore keen, it also clearly bears the marks of a literary and aristocratic environment. Throughout her lament one feels the clamour, the spaciousness, the haughtiness of the Gaelic big house in a way that is surprising to find in such a popular-type composition. She says to her dead husband, for instance, in a tone which reveals clearly her own upbringing:

> My friend and my dear!
> Oh bright-sworded rider,
> Rise up this moment,
> Put on your fine suit
> Of clean, noble cloth,
> Put on your black beaver,
> Pull on your gauntlets.
> Up with your whip;
> Outside your mare is waiting.
> Take the narrow road east,
> Where the trees thin before you,
> Where streams narrow before you,
> Where men and women will bow before you,
> If they keep their old manners –
> But I fear they have lost them.

This woman, after the death of her husband, had her two sons educated in Paris, and one of her grandsons ended up as a professor in the medical faculty in University College, Cork.

As for her husband, Art O'Leary, we heard of him in school as the pure heroic Irishman, unblemished and unbowed, murdered cruelly by English soldiery. The probable facts – as we deduce them from folklore and some documentary evidence – are somewhat at variance with this. Like many of the sons of the conquered nobility in eighteenth-century Ireland, Art was forced to go abroad to find a career, and served as a young captain in the Hungarian Hussars, under the Empress Marie Thérèse of Austria. (It is probable indeed that the empress herself acted as godmother to a child of Art's sister who was married to another officer serving under Marie Thérèse.) When Eileen first saw Art he was a young captain home on leave, living near Macroom, in County Cork, the scourge of the English yeomanry who ruled the district. He wore his sword in public (an act which was contrary to the anti-Catholic Penal Laws), sported fashionable clothes, performed feats of horsemanship and daring in public – in fact, baited his English overlords as often as he could. He was in trouble pretty soon after his marriage and was arraigned before a court on some charge or other, and found, it appears, not guilty. The charge probably emanated from a feud between himself and the former High-Sheriff of the district, Abraham Morris, and may have concerned the favours of a lady courted by them both.[9] Whatever of that, it is evident from statements made by acquaintances of his at this and at other times, that Art had what his brother-in-law termed 'an ungovernable temper'. The more we hear in documents and in folklore of the character of Art O'Leary, the clearer it becomes to us why Eileen's people objected strongly – as is commonly believed – to her marriage to him. The O'Connells were trying to live their own lives as anonymously as possible under English law, and an ostentatious rebel like Art was the last thing they needed in the family. Consequently they broke off all communication with Eileen, and seemingly did not even attend Art's funeral.

The immediate cause of his death was (it is reported) an incident at the local races where Art's horse outran the horse of his old adversary, Abraham Morris. Morris in a fury invoked an old penal law (scarcely ever invoked?) which decreed that a Protestant, under certain circumstances, could buy the horse of any Catholic – no matter how valuable – for five pounds. Art refused to sell the horse, they came to blows, and Art had to 'go on the run'. How long he was an outlaw we do not know; but it is thought that he managed to visit home surreptitiously now and again. Tiring of his life as an outlaw he resolved to have finished with Morris once and for all. On the morning of 4 May, 1773, he was home again to bid goodbye to Eileen, and set out on his own to ambush and kill Morris, who, with some friends was visiting a neighbouring gentleman's house. Art's intention was relayed by a local man called Cooney (?) to Morris, who collected a detachment of soldiers, and set off in pursuit of Art. Art seems to have got away, but later – baiting his pursuers, perhaps? – he delayed in a field near the village of Carriginima, thinking himself out of gun-range. He did not reckon (ironically enough) with a one-eyed soldier who shot him clean off his beloved brown mare.

The brown mare made its way back, it is said, to the O'Leary manor house, seven miles away. Tradition has it that Eileen, in bed, heard the horse pawing in the cobbled yard outside, rushed out, jumped on its back and was carried to where her husband's body lay, 'like a horse or ox' (as one version of the poem has it), still bleeding. The men and women of the village – for whatever reason – had in no way rendered aid. Eileen – if we are to believe the lines in the poem – cupped her dead husband's blood in her hands, and drank it. (This blood-drinking ritual occurs as a theme in early Irish literature.) There is some reason to believe that she began her famous keen over the body somewhere in the village or in the vicinity of Carriginima, and added to it on various later occasions. The dead man's sister from Cork city also added to the keen, as perhaps did his father.

Art was to be buried in the family graveyard, but it seems that Abraham Morris must have invoked one of the anti-Catholic penal laws forbidding this. Instead the body may have been buried in a common field, and much later transferred to an old monastic Abbey (or 'School') called Kilcrea. At the second burial Eileen seems to have added further to her lamentation.

Some of these verses are still being recited in the Irish-speaking districts of Cork and Kerry. (Fifty years or so ago they would have had much wider transmission.) In the two hundred years since their composition various verses must, of course, have been added to or altered. A bewildering array of fragments of the keen are preserved, in particular in the archives of the Irish Folklore Commission in Dublin. (These include verses where Eileen is found defending her husband against charges of heartlessness and wife-beating.) And all this great oral amalgam of verse is called *The Lament for Art O'Leary*.

Fortunately for us, however, two extended versions of the lament were written down in manuscript in the nineteenth-century from the oral recitation of a professional keening woman called Norry Singleton. The first of her versions may have been written down c.1800 (about thirty years after the lament was first composed), the second shortly before her death at a great age c.1870. These versions – though flawed on various counts – formed the basis of my own edition of *The Lament for Art O'Leary*, which consists of some 390 lines.[10] A previous edition consisted of 377 lines, and was mostly based on an 'amended' version of Norry Singleton's first recorded recitation, with some additions from her second recitation.[11] It did not always seem to follow, however, the sequence of events connected with the death.

Searching for the various fragments of orally-transmitted verse and collating them with the nineteenth-century manuscripts was one of the principal tasks I had to engage in. Searching out any folklore connected with the events, and checking it against available documentary evidence was another major task; this, in order to determine the probable order of events connected with Art O'Leary's death. Only when the order of events was determined to some degree, did it become apparent that the two nineteenth-century manuscripts I have mentioned reflected more or less this same order, and probably represented fairly accurately the main traditional version of Eileen Dubh's keen. Another heartening feature was that there was no really substantive differences between the oral version written down *c.*1800 (?) and the oral version written down about 1870. It meant at least that Norry Singleton, the professional keening woman, was not constantly adding her own creative lines to the first version she had given thirty years after the death of Art O'Leary. Adding to this what we know in general of the extraordinary retentive role of memory in the transmission of literature in Ireland, I am fairy confident that Norry Singleton's first version, in particular, is a close approximation to Eileen Dubh's original lament, and to the verses composed by Art's sister and father.

I should say, however, that my primary concern was *not* with the task of providing the earliest or closest approximation to Eileen Dubh's lament; such an objective may be possible where basic written texts are in question but in the case of an edition of a folk poem, is doomed to failure. (It may still be possible, for instance, that a minor fragment in the archives of the Folklore Commission is Eileen's original lament, and that what we know today as her lament is mainly a composition by Norry Singleton.) What I really was concerned with was providing the best version of *The Lament for Art O'Leary* as a poem, as an utterance; and in trying to provide that, I was quite unwilling to omit a few specially good lines, for instance, which Norry Singleton provided in her second version. This kind of literature above all is a collaborative event; while I am personally confident that Norry Singleton has transmitted most of Eileen Dubh's lines to us (if she herself has added a little creatively to them, that, for me, is not a critical issue). The only critical issue, I would submit for anybody who values literature in itself, is that the best version of the poem as a poem (within its own tradition) be provided; and a large part of the definition of what the 'best version' is, in this instance, would be its capacity to reflect both the events associated with Art O'Leary's death, and Eileen's grief.

So while I based my edition of the poem, for the greater part, on Norry Singleton's two versions, and primarily on her first version, I presented it in five distinctive movements which, I thought, reflected different moods and different events. *The Lament for Art O'Leary* emerges finally not alone as a powerful dramatic lyric, but also as an absorbing documentary of a tragic happening. One can experience, to some extent, its dramatic and lyric force without any knowledge of the events in the background. But familiarity with the storyline does not alone intensify one's appreciation of the verse; it also helps one see the whole poem fall into place as a structured utterance. That is why I have gone into some detail about the probable sequence of events associated with Art O'Leary's death.

The first section of Eileen's lament – which may have been composed
at Carriginima where Art was killed – mostly consists of memories;
memories of their life together, immediate memories of the murder. This
section ends with a lovely recapitulation where she urges the dead man
to arise and come home with her, where he would enjoy the very same
comforts and happiness she remembers enjoying from him (and of which
she speaks in the first paragraphs).

Eileen speaks:

I
My love forever!
The day I first saw you
At the end of the market-house,
My eye observed you,
My heart approved you,
I fled from my father with you,
Far from my home with you.

II
I never repented it:
You whitened a parlour for me,
Painted rooms for me,
Reddened ovens for me,
Baked fine bread for me,
Basted meat for me,
Slaughtered beasts for me;
I slept in ducks' feathers
Till midday milking-time,
Or more if it pleased me.

III
My friend forever!
My mind remembers
That fine spring day
How well your hat suited you,
Bright gold banded,
Sword silver-hilted –
Right hand steady –
Threatening aspect –
Trembling terror
On treacherous enemy –
You poised for a canter
On your slender bay horse.
The Saxons bowed to you,
Down to the ground to you,

Not for love of you
But for deadly fear of you,
Though you lost your life to them,
Oh my soul's darling.

IV
O white-handed rider!
How fine your brooch was
Fastened in cambric,
And your hat with laces.
When you crossed the sea to us,
They would clear the street for you,
And not for love of you
But for deadly hatred.

V
My friend you were forever!
When they will come home to me,
Gentle little Conor
And Farr O'Leary, the baby,
They will question me so quickly,
Where did I leave their father.
I'll answer in my anguish
That I left him in Killnamartyr.
They will call out to their father;
And he won't be there to answer.

VI
My friend and my love!
Of the blood of Lord Antrim,
And of Barry of Allchoill,
How well your sword suited you,
Hat gold-banded,
Boots of fine leather,
Coat of broadcloth,
Spun overseas for you.

VII
My friend you were forever!
I knew nothing of your murder
Till your horse came to the stable
With the reins beneath her trailing,
And your heart's blood on her shoulders
Staining the tooled saddle
Where you used to sit and stand.
My first leap reached the threshold,

My second reached the gateway,
My third leap reached the saddle.

VIII
I struck my hands together
And I made the bay horse gallop
As fast as I was able,
Till I found you dead before me
Beside a little furze-bush.
Without Pope or bishop,
Without priest or cleric
To read the death-psalms for you,
But a spent old woman only
Who spread her cloak to shroud you –
Your heart's blood was still flowing:
I did not stay to wipe it
But filled my hands and drank it.

IX
My love you'll be forever!
Rise up from where you're lying
And we'll be going homewards.
We'll have a bullock slaughtered,
We'll call our friends together,
We'll get the music going.
I'll make a fine bed ready
With sheets of snow-white linen,
And fine embroidered covers
That will bring the sweat out through you
Instead of the cold that's on you!

This is followed by a very strange contrasting section, where a caustic verbal battle occurs (in her own house, probably) between herself and Art's sister who had travelled from Cork city to the wake. This kind of battle between wives and sisters-in-law occurs in funeral laments as far back as ancient Greek times. It seems, however, to be more than a formal literary theme here: it most likely happened. It is said that when one of her children became hysterical with grief, Eileen lay down with him and his brother, and was found asleep when Art's sister arrived from Cork. The sister comments that many women, women with dowries, could have married Art – and none of them would have been found asleep the night of his wake. The reference to 'dowries' is a clear indication that Eileen on her marriage was cut off, without dowry, by her own family:

Art O'Leary's sister
speaks:

X

My friend and my treasure!
There's many a handsome woman
From Cork of the sails
To the bridge of Toames
With a great herd of cattle
And gold for her dowry,
That would not have slept soundly
On the night we were waking you.

Eileen speaks:

XI

My friend and my lamb;
You must never believe it,
Nor the whisper that reached you,
Nor the venomous stories
That said I was sleeping.
It was not sleep was on me,
But your children were weeping,
And they needed me with them
To bring their sleep to them.

XII

Now judge, my people,
What woman in Ireland
That at every nightfall
Lay down beside him,
That bore his three children,
Would not lose her reason
After Art O'Leary
That's here with me vanquished
Since yesterday morning?

Art O'Leary's father
speaks:

XIII

Bad luck to you, Morris! –
May your heart's blood poison you!
With your squint eyes gaping!
And your knock-knees breaking! –
That murdered my darling,
And no man in Ireland
To fill you with bullets.

XIV

My friend and my heart!
Rise up again now, Art,
Leap up on your horse,

Make straight for Macroom town,
Then to Inchigeela back,
A bottle of wine in your fist,
The same as you drank with your dad.

Eileen speaks:

XV
My bitter, long torment
That I was not with you
When the bullet came towards you,
My right side would have taken it
Or a fold of my tunic,
And I would have saved you
Oh smooth-handed rider.

Art O'Leary's sister
speaks:

XVI
My sore sharp sorrow
That I was not behind you
When the gun-powder blazed at you,
My right side would have taken it,
Or a fold of my gown,
And you would have gone free then
Oh grey-eyed rider,
Since you were a match for them.

The next section seems to be that part of Eileen's keen made over the corpse as it was being prepared for burial. Here she makes her statements with her traditional audience very much in view. She takes public pride in her husband as a hero of noble lineage. She trumpets his genealogy (as well as her own), secure in the knowledge that this had a profound resonance in the minds of those listening. Her reference to the possibility of the fertile districts associated with his aristocratic family blazing up in grief at his death, would be appreciated by anybody familiar with the traditional Irish and, indeed, Indo-European feeling that the rightful king was united in a mystic marriage-union with his own kingdom. And the fact that her own fertile marriage-union with her husband was now also at an end for ever, causes her to place a bitter curse on the head of Abraham Morris:

Eileen speaks:

XVII
My friend and my treasure!
It's bad treatment for a hero
To lie hooded in a coffin,
The warm-hearted rider
That fished in bright rivers,

That drank in great houses
With white-breasted women.
My thousand sorrows
That I've lost my companion.

XVIII
Bad luck and misfortune
Come down on you, Morris!
That snatched my protector,
My unborn child's father:
Two of them walking
And the third still within me,
And not likely I'll bear it.

XIX
My friend and my pleasure!
When you went out through the gateway
You turned and came back quickly,
You kissed your two children,
You kissed me on the forehead,
You said: 'Eileen, rise up quickly,
Put your affairs in order
With speed and with decision.
I am leaving home now
And there's no telling if I'll return.'
I mocked this way of talking,
He had said it to me so often.

XX
My friend and my dear!
Oh bright-sworded rider,
Rise up this moment,
Put on your fine suit
Of clean, noble cloth,
Put on your black beaver,
Pull on your gauntlets.
Up with your whip;
Outside your mare is waiting.
Take the narrow road east,
Where the trees thin before you,
Where men and women will bow before you,
If they keep their old manners –
But I fear they have lost them.

XXI
My love and my treasure!
Not my dead ancestors,
Nor the deaths of my three children,
Nor Domhnall Mór O'Connell,
Nor Conall that drowned at sea,
Nor the twenty-six years woman
Who went across the water
And held kings in conversation –
It's not on all of them I'm calling
But on Art who was slain last night
At the Inch of Carriganima –
That brown mare's rider
That's here with me only –
With no living soul near him
But the dark little women of the mill,
And my thousand sorrows worsened
That their eyes were dry of tears.

XXII
My friend and my lamb!
Arthur O'Leary,
Of Connor, of Keady,
Of Louis O'Leary,
From west in Geeragh
And from east in Caolchnoc,
Where berries grow freely
And gold nuts on branches
And great floods of apples
All in their seasons.
Would it be a wonder
If Ive Leary were blazing
Besides Ballingeary
And Gougán of the saint
For the firm-handed rider
that hunted the stag down,
All out from Grenagh
When slim hounds fell behind?
And oh clear-sighted rider,
What happened last night?
For I thought to myself
That nothing could kill you
Though I bought your habit.

The main substance of the fourth section is the keen made by Art's sister, where she speaks of their youth together and their old home, of a vision she had which portended evil, and of a plague in Cork city which caused the death of her friends and reduced her retinue at the funeral. Finally she seems to make a reference to Art's attraction to other women, prompting Eileen to defend him vigorously as a father, and to declare, in words which still dance with rage, that she will pursue his murderer to the very end. (Soon after this, indeed, an attempt was made on Morris's life and within two years a notice appeared in a Cork paper offering his house for sale, as the owner was going away 'for the good of his health'. He was dead a few months later.)

Art O'Leary's sister
speaks:

XXIII

My friend and my love!
Of the country's best blood,
That kept eighteen wet-nurses at work,
And each received her pay –
A heifer and a mare,
A sow and her litter,
A mill at the ford,
Yellow gold and white silver,
Silks and fine velvets,
A holding of land –
To give her milk freely
To the flower of fair manhood.

XXIV

My love and my treasure
And my love, my white dove!
Though I did not come to you,
Nor bring my troops with me,
That was no shame to me
For they were all enclosed
In shut-up rooms,
In narrow coffins,
In sleep without waking.

XXV

Were it not for the small-pox
And the black death
And the spotted fever,
That powerful army
Would be shaking their harness
And making a clatter
On their way to your funeral,
Oh white-breasted Art.

XXVI

My love you were and my joy!
Of the blood of those rough horsemen
That hunted in the valley,
Till you turned them homewards
And brought them to your hall,
Where knives were being sharpened,
Pork laid out for carving
And countless ribs of mutton,
The red-brown oats were flowing
To make the horse gallop –
Slender, powerful horses
And stable-boys to care them
Who would not think of sleeping
Nor of deserting their horses
If their owners stayed a week,
Oh brother of many friends.

XXVII

My love and my treasure!
And well they suited you,
Five-ply stockings,
Boots to your knees,
A three-cornered Caroline,
A lively whip,
On a frisky horse –
Many a modest, mannerly maiden
Would turn to gaze after you.[12]

Eileen speaks: XXIX

My love forever!
And when you went in cities,
Strong and powerful,
The wives of the merchants
All bowed down to you
For they knew in their hearts
What a fine man in bed you were,
And what a fine horseman
And father for children.

XXX

Jesus Christ knows
I'll have no cap on my head,
Nor a shift on my back,
Nor shoes on my feet,

Nor goods in my house,
Nor the brown mare's harness
That I won't spend on lawyers:
That I'll cross the seas
And talk to the king,
And if no one listens
That I'll come back
To the black-blooded clown
That took my treasure from me.

The fifth section of the poem is not as homogeneous as the others appear to be. It is rather a compendium of utterances made after Art's first burial. In a verse (which may have been fabricated and attributed to her at a much later stage), Eileen suggests that her own people, the O'Connells of Derrynane, would have come to Art's (second?) burial if news of his death had reached them. She now praises the women of Carriginima for keening the dead man (thus amending her previous view); she reviles the spy Cooney and fiercely curses her sister's husband, Baldwin (who, seemingly, yielded up Art's brown mare to Morris). Despite her great bitterness there is a sense now of everything really having happened in the past. This is nowhere more apparent than in the last two paragraphs. She speaks of life on her farm still going on – and of grief 'closed up' in her heart. And as her husband's body enters the old Abbey School grounds for reburial ('not to study poetry or song but to prop up earth and stones') we know her demonic grief is over. To quote a line from Samson Agonistes, she seems to end 'in calm of mind, all passion spent':

XXXI
My love and my darling!
If my cry were heard westwards
To great Derrynane
And to gold-appled Capling,
Many swift, hearty riders
And white-kerchiefed women
Would be coming here quickly
To weep at your waking,
Beloved Art O'Leary.

XXXII
My heart is warming
To the fine women of the mill
For their goodness in lamenting
The brown mare's rider.

XXXIII

May your black heart fail you,
Oh false John Cooney!
If you wanted a bribe,
You should have asked me,
I'd have given you plenty:
A powerful horse
That would carry you safely
Through the mob
When the hunt is out for you.
Or a fine herd of cattle.
Or the suit of a gentleman
With spurs and top-boots –
Though it's sorry I'd be
To see you done up in them,
For I've always heard
You're a piddling lout.

XXIV

Oh white-handed rider,
Since you are struck down,
Rise and go after Baldwin,
The ugly wretch
With the spindle shanks,
And take your revenge
For the loss of your mare –
May he never enjoy her.
May his six children wither!
But no bad wish to Máire
Though I have no love for her,
But that my own mother
Gave space in her womb to her
For three long seasons.

XXXV

My love and my dear!
Your stooks are standing,
Your yellow cows milking;
On my heart is such sorrow
That all Munster could not cure it,
Nor the wisdom of the sages.
Till Art O'Leary returns
There will be no end to the grief

That presses down on my heart
Closed up tight and firm
Like a trunk that is locked
And the key is mislaid.

XXXVI
All you women out there weeping,
Wait a little longer;
We'll drink to Art son of Connor
And the souls of all the dead,
Befor he enters the school –
Not learning wisdom or music
But weighed down by earth and stones.

In all cultures people have found need for various games or rituals to deal with life in general – and to deal, in particular, with the aspects of life associated with the *rites de passage*. It seems (as T.S. Eliot has said) that human beings cannot bear too much reality; to survive we all need to dramatize, eternalize our emotions, especially in times of great distress. There are people, however – and these quite often seem to be people of unusually refined or artistic temperament – for whom the ordinary rituals are not sufficient. To achieve satisfying emotional purgation, many such people need to express themselves through the form of one of the special games or rituals which we, in general, call art. So it was, I feel, for Eileen Dubh O'Connell. For her the traditional phrases, the traditional themes, the traditional framework of the keen were not enough. She used them,[13] and was guided by them, but by the intensity of her personal utterance she transformed them into another dimension, the dimension of poetry. (And it is the quality of the poetry which makes it impossible for me to conceive that the vast bulk of the work was composed by anyone other than by the woman whose husband was killed.)

While the keen of Art O'Leary is a most moving poetic utterance, it has few of the imaginative or exotic effects we usually associate with lyricism. Its imaginative quality is basically dramatic; in paragraph after paragraph, a situation is recalled or imagined, heightened, and utterly transmuted. Very few images or metaphors occur. Eileen rarely leaves the level of the 'earth and stones' of ordinary conversation, but still passes through a whole range of emotions – from bitterness to tenderness – with startling intensity. The human tenderness (in the original Irish poem, at any rate) is beyond praise and often beyond tears as in this passage, where her own name – the last time it was spoken by him – becomes the key-word for us:

XIX

My friend and my pleasure!
When you went out through the gateway
You turned and came back quickly,
You kissed your two children,
You kissed me on the forehead,
You said: 'Eileen, rise up quickly,
Put your affairs in order
With speed and with decision.
I am leaving home now
And there's no telling if I'll return.'
I mocked this way of talking,
He had said it to me so often.

The keen of Art O'Leary is finally not just a defence against death, against distress, but one of the greatest affirmations in literature of a woman's love for a man. What makes it most poignant is that there is not anywhere in it, or indeed in Irish keens in general (as Synge noted in Aran), any sense of fulfilment of that love in an afterlife. There is no sense of a spiritual life, no sense of spiritual comfort, no hope at all.

[1987]

7

The World of
Aogán Ó Rathaille

VERY FEW DETAILS of the life and career of Aogán Ó Rathaille have been established with any certainty. On the meagre evidence available, I think it probable - as was suggested by a nineteenth-century scholar - that his father was a County Cavan man who travelled to the Killarney area to study for the priesthood. Killarney seems to have been noteworthy at this period (c.1650-1690) for its schools and seminaries where *inter alia* Greek and Latin were taught. That seminaries flourished there at the time is due mostly, one thinks, to the fact that the principal English colonists (the Brownes), who had supplanted the native aristocrats (mainly McCarthys and O'Donoghues), were themselves staunch Catholics committed to supporting the activities of their Church.

It is likely that Ó Rathaille's father met and married in the vicinity of Killarney the daughter of one of the hereditary *ollaves* ('poets and learned men') attached to the principal McCarthy family in the district, the McCarthymores of Palice. Her family name was probably Egan, in Irish Mac Aogáin. Some special arrangements would have to be made, of course, so that the landless spoiled priest from northern Ireland and his wife would have a comfortable holding. That holding was secured, I would guess, by the McCarthymores from the Brownes in a barren and remote part of Sliabh Luachra, called *Screathan a' Mhíl* (Scrahanaveel), about ten miles east of Killarney where one of the minor McCarthy nobles was a close neighbour.

Ó Rathaille's mother and father married probably about the years 1670-75, and had a son called Aogán (Egan) - a name absolutely untraditional in the Ó Rathaille family annals in Kerry.

101

The two influential families, the Brownes and the McCarthymores, with whom the poet's parents probably had strong links,[1] played a dominant role in the highly complex social scene in Kerry at the time. The McCarthymore family, like Irish aristocratic families in general, had gradually lost most of its power and territory, during the seventeenth (and late sixteenth) century. By various legal and other subterfuges, however, they had retained a substantial estate (10,000 acres perhaps) at Palice, five miles east of Killarney. They also held, by traditional right, small parcels of land in other districts, one of them in the Sliabh Luachra district close to that granted *c.*1670 to the Ó Rathaille family.

The McCarthymores, in older times the chief family amongst the widespread McCarthy clan, were beginning at this period to accumulate vast debts, and in addition, were being rapidly Anglicized. The particular McCarthymore Aogán Ó Rathaille would have known in his youth was married to the daughter of an English lord, Lord Brittas, who fought on the side of the Catholic King James in 1690, but quite soon afterwards declared for the Protestant winner, King William. (His grandson, known as the last McCarthymore, was to become an officer in the British army.) Even though the McCarthymore in Aogán Ó Rathaille's time still maintained poets and learned men such as the Egans, their estate documents were now being written in English to comply with English legal requirements.

The Browne family on the other hand had prospered during the seventeenth century. They had come to Ireland as colonists in early Elizabethan times (*c.*1584), and during the following century had gradually acquired the confiscated estates of the McCarthys and other Irish families in Kerry, Cork and Limerick, so that in Ó Rathaille's time their vast holdings were in the region of 140,000 acres. The Brownes, like some early Elizabethan planters, were Catholic and in time intermarried with Irish aristocratic families. In fact the mother of the poet's landlord, Sir Nicholas Browne, was a McCarthy, sister of the chief McCarthy figure in County Cork.

It is in no way surprising that the Brownes were highly sympathetic to the Irish Catholic cause, and quite generous in their dealings with families such as the McCarthys – whose acquiescence in the new order of things was, of course, doubly assured by their acceptance of Browne generosity. Several minor McCarthy nobles, for instance, held large tracts of land from the Brownes at a nominal rent. Aogán Ó Rathaille's neighbour and friend, Captain Eoghan McCarthy, was one of these. He held an estate of *c.*3,600 acres on Sliabh Luachra for a mere two shillings a year. This arrangement ensured that Captain McCarthy, gentleman-tenant, having collected quite substantial rents from his undertenants, and having paid his own meagre rent to the Brownes, was able to live lavishly and maintain an open house in traditional Irish fashion for poets, scholars, musicians and wandering people.

We have no record of what rent Ó Rathaille's father paid but it is quite likely that it was also a nominal sum, enabling him to live comfortably as gentleman-tenant on the rents collected from whatever undertenants resided on his 300–450 (?) acre farm. So while the family holding may have been bleak, rough and remote, Aogán Ó Rathaille grew up, to some extent, in the privileged position enjoyed by poets from earliest times in Irish society.

We know nothing of his boyhood upbringing. We can only surmise that he herded cows like other children of his age, played games, listened to music and storytelling. He certainly received, somehow or other, a comprehensive education. It would appear from his poetry that he read some Latin; Ovid and Virgil, in particular. He read Old and Medieval Irish prose and verse from manuscripts, and wrote manuscripts himself. He probably knew English and perhaps a little Greek; there is some evidence (for instance his mention of Sancho Panza in a prose satire written in 1713) that he was not unaware of post-Renaissance literature in other countries.

Both his parents could have played an active part in his education. His father, the ex-seminarian, may have given him at home the rudiments of Latin and Greek; his mother may have helped him with his general reading and have sent him from time to time to study with his learned Egan grandfather on the McCarthymore estate, some twenty miles away. The likelihood, however, is that the greater part of his education occurred locally in Gaelic Big Houses and castles, several of which still existed within a radius of a few miles of the Ó Rathaille home. It is certain, for instance, that he visited the O'Donoghue castle in Glenflesk (eight or nine miles away), the home of a renowned aristocratic and poetic family. But it is altogether more likely that the home of his patron and friend, Captain Eoghan McCarthy, at Headford (four or five miles away) was his particular open university. In a poem (*c*.1700) lamenting Captain Eoghan's dispossession,[2] he tells us how one frequently encountered at Headford gatherings of poets, bards, priests and learned men. There cannot be much doubt that Ó Rathaille was accepted from an early age amongst this privileged band.

Ó Rathaille was possibly fifteen years of age, or thereabouts, when King James and the Jacobite cause was dealt a severe blow at the Battle of the Boyne (1690). In the next few decades the fairly stable world he had grown up in collapsed slowly but inexorably around him. In 1693 the 140,000-acre Browne estate – of which Scrahanaveel was a minute parcel – was confiscated because of Sir Nicholas Browne's allegiance to the defeated Catholic King. The confiscation, however, was to last only for the lifetime of Sir Nicholas (who fled for a time to England, and later to Belgium). Different sons-in-law – one of them an English MP – managed by stealth to keep legal or nominal possession of the estate for a lengthy period, but this did not prevent wholesale destruction and desecration of the property by the new Williamite colonists and by some local entrepreneurs. Trees from the great woods were hacked down and sold at sixpence each; various mining and smelting operations were set up in the Killarney area. Deploying a kind of image familiar to people in a nuclear age, Ó Rathaille declares that the sun had been blotted out by the smoke of these new 'smithies': *'sa ghréin níl taitneamh os fearannaibh, féachaidh,/is ceo na ceártan tá ar a sléibhtibh'.* He likens the young men who had fled abroad after the Boyne to 'young sapling trees, hacked down, dispersed': *'a slata fáis go scáinte réabtha/i gcríochaibh eachtrann scaipthe ó chéile'.* It is clear that he was being shocked into poetry by the stark details of the horror which was now engulfing his boyhood world.

Ironically enough, while the Anglo-Irish Brownes were dispossessed, the old Irish McCarthy family of Palice managed to retain possession of their heavily-burdened estate; this was probably due to their late switch of allegiance to King William. Other McCarthys, however, were not so fortunate. The poet's friend, Captain Eoghan McCarthy who had sided with King James, was singled out for dispossession. So also in time it seems were the O'Rahillys and a number of other important families in the Sliabh Luachra district. It would appear indeed that Sliabh Luachra, compared with other Browne territories, was given very rough treatment indeed. The reason for this calls for some comment.

It seems – and this is a further complicating factor in the social picture of the time – that a great part of Sliabh Luachra *c.* 1700 was a particularly lawless no man's land, a centre of continuing resistance not alone to the new Williamite colonists but also to the old Anglo-Irish colonists such as the Brownes. Chief amongst the resistance leaders were the O'Donoghues of Glenflesk, admired by Aogán Ó Rathaille and feared by gentlemen-tenants of the Brownes such as the Herberts, who were settled on former O'Donoghue lands. The O'Donoghues, who roamed the mountainy Sliabh Luachra district at will, struck terror into the hearts of all colonists. As late as 1729, the probable year of Ó Rathaille's death (at a time he had given up all hope for the restoration of the old order), a report on O'Donoghue activity against a new planter, who had got possession of a farm on Sliabh Luachra, shows clearly that the O'Donoghues, at any rate, had not given up. 'They burnt his crops,' the report states, 'and lifted his cattle . . . his steward was attacked . . . they cut off his ears and tongue, gouged his eyes, and finished their hellish work by stabbing his wife who was *enceinte*, and cutting out her tongue.'[3] That the forces of the new Williamite order would wish to root out such kinds of traditional resistance on Sliabh Luachra is quite understandable. Aogán Ó Rathaille was one of those who suffered grievously as a consequence.

It was most likely about the year 1703 Aogán Ó Rathaille, a married man with two daughters, was dispossessed of his family home. He may have lived for some years afterwards as an undertenant at Stagmount, a few miles from Schrahanaveel but finally (c.1707?) had to leave the Sliabh Luachra district completely. He most likely found himself a hovel by the sea – a gift, perhaps, from one of the widespread McCarthy clan – near Castlemaine, County Kerry.[4] In his poem *Is fada liom oíche fhir fhliuch* (*The drenching night drags on*), written on the occasion of a storm at sea, one senses that for the first time he was tasting grinding poverty. His inner desolation is palpable throughout the poem. The mood develops from being a sharp dramatic visualization of his own deprivation to a feeling of savage frustration at the humiliation suffered by his whole community:

> The drenching night drags on: no sleep or snore,
> no stock, no wealth of sheep, no horned cows.
> This storm on the waves nearby has harrowed my head
> – I who ate no winkles or dogfish in my youth!
>
> If that guardian King from the bank of the Leamhan lived on,
> with all who shared his fate (and would pity my plight)
> to rule that soft, snug region, bayed and harboured,
> my people would not stay poor in Duibhne country.
>
> Great Carthy, fierce and fine, who loathed deceit;
> with Carthy of the Laoi, in yoke unyielding, faint;
> and Carthy King of Ceann Toirc with his children,
>   buried;
> it is bitterness through my heart they have left no trace.
>
> My heart has dried in my ribs, my humours soured,
> that those never-niggardly lords, whose holdings ranged
> from Caiseal to Clíona's Wave and out to Thomond,
> are savaged by alien hordes in land and townland.
>
> You wave down there, lifting your loudest roar,
> the wits in my head are worsted by your wails.
> If help ever came to lovely Ireland again
> I'd wedge your ugly howling down your throat!

> (*D*, p. 141)

The poem has a typical Ó Rathaille structure, the last verse referring back to the first and revealing a great deepening of the initial mood. In the opening lines his poverty and hurt pride are captured passionately and exactly. There follows three traditional elegiac verses; the first of them lamenting the loss, most probably, of his immediate 'guardian king', Sir Nicholas Browne; the second of them bewailing the downfall of three great McCarthy figures of the mid-seventeenth century (the McCarthymore, the Earl of Cloncarty from Cork, the McCarthy of Kanturk); and the third verse, moving back further in time, bitterly recording the widespread plunder wrought by 'foreign hordes' on all the princes of Munster. The elegiac mood gives way here to raw anger, coinciding most tellingly in the last verse with the climax of the storm at sea. The inner personal storm and the outer physical storm converge in his final howl of desolation where, Lear-like (as Daniel Corkery sees it), he challenges the might of the sea.

It must have been soon after Ó Rathaille wrote this poem that the Stuart movement in Ireland got off the ground. In these years (c.1708–1709) the houses of Kerry nobles and gentlemen began to buzz with rumours from King James's residence in St Germain that the return of his son, the Old Pretender, was imminent and that the landing spot of the invading Stuart forces was quite likely to be on the Kerry coast. A Colonel Hedges, who was now the Williamite governor of the county and living in the former Browne residence at Ross, Killarney, was entrusted with the task of persuading the gentlemen of the county to take an oath of abjuration against the Stuart prince. Many refused and were jailed in Tralee; the jailed included Sir Nicholas Browne (who may have come back from London for his brother's funeral), and Randall McCarthymore (eccentric son of the deceased McCarthymore who had declared for King William). From this time on Ó Rathaille's poetry identifies increasingly with the Stuart cause, and begins to rail at the anti-Catholic laws passed by the British Parliament.

During these Stuart years, Ó Rathaille commented sharply on the absence of any McCarthy leadership. There is indeed no evidence that any of the McCarthys played a major role in the Stuart movement in Kerry. The leaders were in fact the old landed colonial families, surprisingly enough Protestant as well as Catholic, with very un-Irish names: Browne, Blennerhassett, Herbert, Crosbie, Rice, White, Lavallin. Colonel Hedges, the military governor, writing to Dublin Castle in 1714 says: 'I do not find the Papists so very confident of the Pretender's invading us with an army as another set of people are.'[5] That set of people consisted undoubtedly of the formerly privileged Anglo-Irish colonists.

It is not clear where Ó Rathaille lived at this period, but he seems to have spent a great deal of time visiting the houses of Anglo-Irish and Irish aristocratic families, writing praise poems and elegies for them. Indeed, about half of Ó Rathaille's opus consists of this kind of work where he is performing the traditional social functions of the hereditary Irish poet;

and, in these poems, while he often writes verses or lines of great distinction, the over-all effect can be tiresome, as the effect of poet-laureate work invariably is. Whether Anglo-Irish colonial families such as the Blennerhassetts understood the formal literary Irish of the poems written for them is an intriguing question which may now be impossible to resolve.

Another traditional poetic function which Ó Rathaille may have performed in his visitations to Big Houses was that of bearer of military intelligence. Indeed there is a slight indication that he may have engaged in some semi-military exploits himself. Whatever of that, his political poems, in particular his vision-poems (*Aislingí*), give us invaluable insights into the rapidly-changing political moods of the country at the time.

As far back as the eighth century, the sovereignty of Ireland was envisaged, in prose and verse, as a woman-queen whose beauty would bloom when she married the rightful king. This theme, Indo-European (if not universal) in its origins, was never shaped in lyric form in Ireland to reflect a poet's personal mood and situation, until Ó Rathaille's time. Such vision-lyrics were, however, written in other countries: in France in particular during the fifteenth and sixteenth centuries where they were quite clearly based on the *Pastourelle* and *Reverdie*-type love formula which by then had gained widespread European popularity.

Scores of French poets, including the famous Ronsard (1524-1585) wrote of walking out one fine morning and encountering in a vision the woman *La France*,[6] for instance, who complains of being in dire bondage to the English while her rightful king has abandoned her. There is some reason to believe that Irish literary men studying abroad in the seventeenth and late sixteenth century may have introduced this particular type of formula into Irish literature, and that Ó Rathaille was the first to successfuly merge the formula with traditional Irish thematic material. One doubts, however, if any other poet, at home or abroad, managed to shape this archaic mythic material into such intense contemporary lyric forms.

The earliest of his vision-poems is perhaps *Gile na Gile* (Brightness of Brightness), where the vision-woman, Ireland, is seen waiting patiently and somewhat hopelessly for the return of the Stuart Pretender. The poem, in story form, is a miracle of baroque workmanship, but despite its highly ornamented texture – or indeed, because of it – the story being recounted verse by verse is told most rapidly and dramatically, revealing some deep anxieties lurking beneath the surface. Decoded, it most likely reflects the mood of the years 1707-1709 when many of the poet's Jacobite friends (if not himself as well) were held in Tralee jail having refused to take the oath of abjuration. The feeling of incarceration is clearly present, and little hope is held out for any immediate action on the part of those advocating a Stuart invasion.

The desolate Sliabh Luachra country is the background to Ó Rathaille's crystal-clear vision:

Brightness most bright I beheld on the way, forlorn.
Crystal of crystal her eye, blue touched with green.
Sweetness most sweet her voice, not stern with age.
Colour and pallor appeared in her flushed cheeks.

Curling and curling, each strand of her yellow hair
as it took the dew from the grass in its ample sweep;
a jewel more glittering than glass on her high bosom
– created, when she was created, in a higher world.

True tidings she revealed me, most forlorn,
tidings of one returning by royal right,
tidings of the crew ruined who drove him out,
and tidings I keep from my poem for sheer fear.

Foolish past folly, I came to her very presence
bound tightly, her prisoner (she likewise a prisoner . . .).
I invoked Mary's Son for succour: she started from me
and vanished like light to the fairy dwelling of Luachair.

Heart pounding, I ran, with a frantic haste in my race,
by the margins of marshes, through swamps, over bare moors.
To a powerful palace I came, by paths most strange,
to that place of all places, erected by druid magic.

All in derision they tittered – a gang of goblins
and a bevy of slender maidens with twining tresses.
They bound me in bonds, denying the slightest comfort,
and a lumbering brute took hold of my girl by the breasts.

I said to her then, in words that were full of truth,
how improper it was to join with that drawn gaunt creature
when a man the most fine, thrice over, of Scottish blood
was waiting to take her for his tender bride.

On hearing my voice she wept in high misery
and flowing tears fell down from her flushed cheeks.
She sent me a guard to guide me out of the palace
– that brightness most bright I beheld on the way, forlorn.

The Knot

Pain, disaster, downfall, sorrow and loss!
Our mild, bright, delicate, loving, fresh-lipped girl
with one of that black, horned, foreign, hate-crested crew
and no remedy near till our lions come over the sea.

(*D*, pp. 151-53)

Intense anxiety and perplexity underlie the baroque surface of *Gile na Gile*. On the other hand *An Aisling* (*One morning ere Titan had thought to stir his feet*) is bouyant with hope and optimism, and with all the dreamy fruitfulness traditionally associated with the coming of the rightful king. It was most likely composed about the year 1714-15 when hopes were high again of the Pretender's landing on the west coast of Ireland to resume kingship over the recently proposed three kingdoms of England, Scotland and Ireland. In the last two lines, however, Ó Rathaille with his care to capture the precise feelings of his time cannot help puncturing the vision-woman's mood of optimism to record the ever-recurring doubts which must have accompanied the high hopes of these years:

> One morning ere Titan had thought to stir his feet,
> on the top of a fine high hill I had laboured up,
> I chanced on a pleasant flock of joyous girls,
> a troop from Sídh Seanadh's bright mansions to the North.
>
> A film of enchantment spread, of aspect bright,
> from the shining boulders of Galway to Cork of the
>   harbours:
> clusters of fruit appearing in every treetop,
> acorns in woods, pure honey upon the stones.
>
> Three candles they lit, of indescribable light,
> on Cnoc Fírinne's lofty summit in Conallach Rua.
> Then I followed the flock of cloaked women as far as
>   Thomond
> and questioned them on their diligent round of tasks.
>
> Then answered the lady Aoibhill, of aspect bright,
> they had cause to light three candles above the harbours:
> in the name of the faithful king who is soon to come
> to rule and defend the triple realm for ever.
>
> I started up - soft, sudden - out of my dream
> believing the good news Aoibhill told me was true,
> but found that I was nerve-shaken, downcast and morose
> that morning ere Titan had thought to stir his feet.

(D, pp. 153-55)

It is clear from his *aislingí* and from some other poems of his that the political freedom of Ireland, the notion of a nation-state, was not a matter of great concern to Ó Rathaille (as indeed it was not to Irish poets in general). That the Scottish Pretender should rule Ireland was as acceptable to Ó Rathaille, *under certain conditions,* as that the Brownes should rule in Kerry. The conditions were, of course, that the Irish way of life, Irish culture, be maintained, and specifically the poet's own privileged position within that culture. An understanding of this viewpoint is necessary if one is to come to terms with a good deal of medieval Irish bardic literature, and also with the literature of the eighteenth century. There is, for instance, a light good-humoured occasional poem by Ó Rathaille, *Do shiúlaigh mise an Mhumhain mhín* (*I walked all over Munster mild*), where the poet extols the virtues of a new colonial planter who lavished hospitality, and maintained Irish customs in a castle formerly owned by a famous member of the McCarthy family. Neither the poet nor his audience would, I think, have found his final declaration in any way time-serving or disloyal to the McCarthy chief who had died:

> God, Who created the world aright
> gave a generous man for the one who died
> to serve his household, scribes and poets
> – a true, great-hearted hero.

> (*D,* p. 145)

Aogán Ó Rathaille would have been alienated by any Irish society where the poet was not maintained and revered, given even the power of 'sanction by satire' which Irish poets enjoyed traditionally (and which, curiously, is recognized in an English legal document of the sixteenth century). Another of Ó Rathaille's rare poems in a light or humorous vein reflects a little ironically, one feels, on this view of the poet's function. It is a warrant, a 'Whereas', issued for the apprehension of an insignificant thief called Síobharán who stole a cock from a priest at the fair of Dingle. The first half of the poem reads like an elegant anecdote from happier – and more miraculous – medieval times, while the second half (with its plebeian bailiffs and its coarse verbiage) takes on all the detailed ugliness of an eighteenth-century criminal pursuit. One cannot help feeling that the contrast between the two halves of the poem accurately reflects Ó Rathailles view on how the cultural climate had changed. And in the final verse one senses strongly that Ó Rathaille is being as much ironic about his own inability to influence the course of justice, as he is satirizing the nonentity who stole the priest's cock:

> *Whereas* the learned Aengus
> a pious Christian priest
> came today before me
> to make a sworn complaint

that having bought a high-born cock
for his street – and household-hens,
of finest squawk, and blooming,
neck shaded every sheen,

and fifty lovely shillings paid
for this bird of beauteous comb,
some druid phantom snatched it
at the district's foremost fair.

Certain such a one requires
a squawking alarum cock
to guard him from soft slumber
at time of prayerful vespers.

For which cause I direct,
State-bailiffs of my court,
examine every highway,
and that with earnest care.

Omit no *lios* or fairy hill
where you hear cluck or cackle
but press pursuit of Síobharán
who did this plunderous deed.

WHERESOEVER hiding-hole
you find the little fatgut
bring him here on a piece of string
till I hang him like a wretch.

FOR YOUR SO DOING, as is required,
herewith my authority
by my written hand, done with a quill,
this day of the President's reign.

(*D*, pp. 147–49)

Despite his occasional foray into lighthearted verse, Ó Rathaille in the greater part of his work remains a gloom-filled figure, a Jeremiah. Hope recedes rapidly in most of his poems, including his vision-poems, as the years pass by. Paradoxically, the event which he most looked forward to – apart from the Pretender's invasion of Ireland – must have been the death of his former friend and patron, Sir Nicholas Browne. For in that event the 140,000 acre Browne estate would in law revert back to his eldest son, Sir Valentine, whereupon Ó Rathaille himself could hope to be restored to his own small family holding in Scrahanaveel. Sir Nicholas, however, took an unconscionable time in dying. He had left London for Ghent where it was reported: 'His Lordship was never so healthy, moderate or devout as at present. . . . He never drinks between meals, except with company worthwhile, and that seldom above two bottles at a time'. Finally, in 1720, Sir Nicholas died and for a short time joy unconfined flows through Ó Rathaille's verse. He immediately greets Sir Valentine as 'King', as a redeemer sent by God, and writes the happiest of epithalamia on the occasion of his marriage six months later. In his poem *The drenching night drags on* Ó Rathaille declares at the height of the storm at sea:

> If help ever came to lovely Ireland again
> I'd wedge your ugly howling down your throat.

In his epithalamium for Sir Valentine Browne, not alone does he conjure up an extravagantly fertile country on the accession of the rightful king, but he tells us that the storms have now ceased their ugly howlings in the harbours. The sea ceases to be a symbol of poverty and oppression; the hoped for saviour has crossed it, conquered it.

From what we know of Sir Valentine Browne[7] it would be difficult to imagine him as a patron/chieftain in Kerry at the beginning of the eighteenth century. He had been educated mostly in England, paying only a few visits to Ireland during his youth. He most likely had no knowledge of the Irish language. He read French and Greek, was a patron of the opera in London, played a gold flute – and complained inordinately of constipation. He seems to have been a kindly, though over-solemn, sort of man. On his accession he restored old leases to their proper owners, treated tenants well, subsidized priests and poets; all this despite the fact that his estate was heavily in debt, and in a disastrous legal mess, due to the machinations of numerous enterprising middle-men in the years 1693–1720.

It is clear, however, that Browne did not restore Aogán Ó Rathaille's lease on Scrahanaveel. It is quite possible indeed that he was unable to do so due to legal difficulties with that particular parcel of land; on the other hand, it may also be that he did not understand the necessity of treating an Irish poet as a privileged figure. He seems to have refused all of Ó Rathaille's pleas, whereupon the poet wrote him a poem of outraged bitterness and sadness. The McCarthys are now back in favour again; despite being under a 'cloud' (illness?) the McCarthymore becomes 'our Western Sun, Munster's right ruler', and all natural things are blighted because the wrong king rules:

> A mist of pain has covered my dour old heart
> since the alien devils entered the land of Conn;
> our Western Sun, Munster's right ruler, clouded
> – there's the reason I'd ever to call on you,
> Valentine Browne.

First, Cashel's company gone, its guest-houses and youth;
the gabled palace of Brian flooded dark with otters;
Ealla left leaderless, lacking royal Munster sons
- there's the reason I'd ever to call on you,
Valentine Browne.

The deer has altered her erstwhile noble shape
since the alien raven roosted in Ros's fastness;
fish fled the sunlit stream and the quiet current
- there's the reason I'd ever to call on you,
Valentine Browne.

(*D*, pp. 161-63)

After his bitter bout with Sir Valentine, Ó Rathaille seems to have resumed his Big House visitations. He also engaged in manuscript work. A copy of Keating's monumental history of Ireland, done at Drumcollogher, County Limerick in the year 1722 bears his signature. It is possibly about this time also he wrote his last vision-poem *Mac an Cheannaí* (*The Redeemer's Son*) - one of his few poems in popular metrical form where he gives us to understand that Spanish aid for the Pretender's cause was not now expected.

Sir Valentine Browne's aunt had been writing to her nephew in Killarney and to others in Ireland in the years 1719-1720 about the matter of Spanish aid. 'As for the King of Spain,' she writes, 'he never was so ill as was reported, and he is now better. The Pretender's friends are a little down at the mouth, but they are not out of heart and hope by the Duke of Ormond's being in Spain that some turn or other will happen to their advantage.'[8] Again she writes: 'I hear the Government and City of Dublin was extremely alarmed upon the report of the Spanish invasion, and I hear several ladies lay out of their houses . . .'.[9] It is certain that Ó Rathaille would have been *au courant* with this kind of news because of his Big House connections. But again, within a short time, the hopes of Spanish aid for the Stuart cause were finally dashed.[10] Given Ó Rathaille's perception now of the national position, and of his own personal position vis-à-vis the Brownes, it is not at all surprising that the mood of *Mac an Cheannaí* is of unredeemed despair. The woman-queen, Ireland, drops dead before his eyes:

A bitter vision I beheld
in bed as I lay weary:
a maiden mild whose name was Éire
coming toward me riding

with eyes of green, hair curled and thick
   fair her waist and brows,
declaring he was on his way
   - her loved one *Mac an Cheannaí.*

Her mouth so sweet, her voice so mild,
   I love the maiden dearly,
wife to Brian, acclaimed of heroes
   - her troubles are my ruin!
Crushed cruelly under alien flails
   my fair-haired slim kinswoman:
she's a dried branch, that pleasant queen,
   till he come, her *Mac an Cheannaí. . . .*

Her eye looks South day after day
   to the shore for ships arriving,
to sea Southeast she gazes long
   (her troubles are my grief!)
and a Westward eye, with hope in God,
   o'er wild and sandy billows
   - defeated, lifeless, powerless,
   till he come, her *Mac an Cheannaí.*

Her dappled Friars are overseas,
   those droves that she held dear;
no welcome, no regard or love,
   for her friends in any quarter.
Their cheeks are wet; no ease or sleep;
   dressed in black, for sorrow
   - dried branch she'll stay, with no man lie,
till he come, her *Mac an Cheannaí.*

I told her, when I heard her tale,
   in a whisper, he was dead,
that he had found death up in Spain,
   that no one heard her plaint.
She heard my voice beside her;
   her body shook; she shrieked;
her soul departed in a leap.
   Alas, that woman lifeless.

(D, pp. 157–61)

Ó Rathaille seems to have spent his last days back somewhere in Sliabh
Luachra country, half-reconciled with Sir Valentine Browne. The Browne

estate manuscripts for 1727 contains this report: 'Allowed Egan O'Rahilly, when his only cow was appraized last winter . . . for composing songs for Master Thomas Browne and the rest of his Lordship's children . . . £1.10.0.' The aristocratic families in the district, the Brownes, the McCarthys, even the ferocious O'Donoghues, had all been restored to their pre-Battle of the Boyne status, but the poet Ó Rathaille died an impoverished undertenant, owner of one cow. The £1.10.0 he received for his poems was no mean payment by today's standards: his fee might have enabled him to buy another cow (or at least a pig). Not alone that but he had no reason to fear he would want for comfort or food; his numerous relations, or the many McCarthy's or O'Donoghues in the district, would doubtless house or feed him. What must have been utterly dismaying for him, however, was the certainty that he, or his kind, would never again receive the special honour due to a poet in Irish society. Even if the Stuart Pretender, or some other Catholic prince, came to 'free' the country it would make no whit of difference to him now; it would, in effect, only strengthen the rule of the Brownes who had failed him. He was now the recipient of arbitrary small doles, instead of being a respected and prosperous functionary in society. And in his 'last' poem, *Cabhair Ní Ghairfead* (*No help I'll call*), he cries out:

> No help I'll call till I'm put in the narrow coffin.
> By the Book, it would bring it no nearer if I did!

By 'help' he meant, of course, some act or movement which would bring about the re-establishment of traditional Irish society as he knew it, and his own position within it. This now was unimaginable.

Of the two great aristocratic families he had special links with, the Anglo-Irish Brownes and the Gaelic McCarthymores only the McCarthymores – untrustworthy and Anglicized as they were – had any inkling now of the honour due to a poet in Ireland. And on the death of the last effective McCarthymore in 1729 (?), Ó Rathaille on his own death-bed makes a new kind of elegy, *Cabhair Ní Ghairfead*, not only for the last of the great McCarthy patrons, but for the Irish nation and, most poignantly, for himself.

The McCarthymore lamented in 1729 (?) by Aogán Ó Rathaille may have been a violent or eccentric type of character. We know at any rate that a spy reports in that same year 'that he has been struck and inhumanly pursued by a Milesian prince of a drunken and extravagant character called Mac Carthy Mór . . . as being a person who lives *extra legem* and matters not indictments nor any other prosecution.'[11] That the poet's last hope was such an anarchic person would have only served to deepen his despair.

Ó Rathaille begins his poem by starkly dramatizing his own personal situation now that the McCarthymore has died. His opening utterance, 'No help I'll call', is probably best understood in the context both of the poem and of his life, as more a statement of resignation than of defiance. As is clear from the second line 'By the Book, it would bring it no nearer if I did', he is willing to face the absolute reality of things as they stood without recourse to any self-deception.

There follows two verses lamenting, in traditional manner, the rape of the land of Ireland, especially since the time the 'Knave [William] skinned the crowned King [James]', at the Battle of the Boyne. Then there is a stanza predicting his own forthcoming death – his metaphor for death being that of the mythological indestructible pig or boar that 'no arrows wound'. In the fifth verse he bids farewell to the Brownes, referring kindly to Sir Nicholas ('lord of the Rinn and Cill'), but rather bitterly to his son, Sir Valentine. In his sixth verse he bids farewell to the royal McCarthys, and in the last verse he bids farewell to himself:

> No help I'll call till I'm put in the narrow coffin.
> By the Book, it would bring it no nearer if I did!
> Our prime strong-handed prop, of the seed of Eoghan
> – his sinews are pierced and his vigour is withered up.

> Wave-shaken is my brain, my chief hope gone.
> There's a hole in my gut, there are foul spikes through my bowels.
> Our land, our shelter, our woods and our level ways
> are pawned for a penny by a crew from the land of Dover.

> The Sionainn, the Life, the musical Laoi, are muffled
> and the Biorra Dubh river, the Bruice, the Bríd, the Bóinn.
> Reddened are Loch Dearg's narrows and the Wave of Tóim
> since the Knave has skinned the crowned King in the game

> Incessant my cry; I spill continual tears;
> heavy my ruin; I am one in disarray.
> No music is nigh as I wail about the roads
> except for the noise of the Pig no arrows wound.

> That lord of the Rinn and Cill, and the Eoghanacht country
> – want and injustice have wasted away his strength.
> A hawk now holds those places, and takes their rent,
> who favours none, though near to him in blood.

> Our proud royal line is wrecked; on that account
> the water ploughs in grief down from my temples,
> sources sending their streams out angrily
> to the river that flows from Truipeall to pleasant Eochaill.

I will stop now - my death is hurrying near
now the dragons of the Leamhan, Loch Léin and the Laoi are
    destroyed.
In the grave with this cherished chief I'll join those kings
my people served before the death of Christ.

(D, pp. 165-67)

In that superbly arrogant last verse, one knows clearly for the first time that Ó Rathaille has finally made a choice between the Brownes and the McCarthys. The Brownes, the Stuart movement - all things Jacobite, all things alien - are rejected. The land of Ireland has been lost; and only underground, with the McCarthys, is there now any hope of comfort. There is no mention of the glory or happiness of a Christian eternity. The happiness that awaits him is an eternity with the McCarthy dead: 'kings my people served before the death of Christ'.

One would need to know much more than any of us yet knows about Ó Rathaille's world - his values, the structure of his thought and feelings - before being able to make anything like a complete assessment of his writings. But it is clear that it was his Herculean efforts to come to terms with the destruction of the old Gaelic aristocratic order, to bring emotional order out of chaos, that made him the fine poet he was. He has little to say to us of the ordinary people or the ordinary daily life around him. Neither has he much to say of the beauty of the world, of trout leaping in the lakes of Killarney, or of the beauty of a sunset. His poetry is not that kind of poetry. This does not mean, of course, that he may not personally have been moved by such things. What it does mean is that the conventions of poetry he inherited did not allow for this kind of thematic material.

One can hardly say that one set of literary conventions is better or worse than another. The test of any artist surely is how creatively he can handle whatever conventions are available to him. A close analysis of the poems of his which I have discussed - as well as some others which I have not discussed e.g. *Aisling Mheabhail* (An Illusive Vision), *Tionól na bhFear Muimhneach* (The Assembly of Munstermen), *Epithalamium do Thiarna Chinn Mara* (Epithalamium for Lord Kenmare), *Do Dhonncha Ó hIcí* (For Denis Hickey) - suggests that Ó Rathaille, when deeply moved, transformed traditional themes and conventions into new and contemporary statements.

His best poetry is not very diverse or wideranging; it is narrow in scope, intense, turbulent, full of agony. The texture of the verse itself, however, is quite formal, elaborate, musical. The English poet I would think of comparing him with, stylistically and psychologically, is Gerard Manley

Hopkins: Hopkins focusing obsessively on God – and on himself; Ó Rathaille focussing obsessively on the Irish nation – and on himself.

It is difficult for us today to imagine such a poetry emanating from a bleak and desolate mountainside amongst the hills of Kerry. But, as is clear from earlier remarks in this essay, a place like Sliabh Luachra need not have been in any way culturally disadvantaged within the traditional Irish decentralized system of patronage. Because of this system Ó Rathaille was able, on the one hand, to be acquainted with the works of Ovid, Cervantes, or Gofraidh Fionn Ó Dálaigh; and on the other hand be acquainted with political and topical event in Paris, London or Spain. But he probably was the last of our poets to enjoy in any appreciable measure the old poetic privileges.

He remained in some way privileged to the end, for his last obsessive wish was granted: he is buried in Muckross Abbey, Killarney, with the McCarthymores, the kings his mother's poetic family, the Egans, served 'before the death of Christ'.

[1978]

8

Gaelic Culture in Crisis:
The Literary Reponse (1600–1850)

T HOSE IN THE sixteenth century who engaged in the planning of the
Tudor subjugation of Ireland may well have been unique in the at-
tention they paid to cultural as well as to territorial conquest. The cultural
philosophy espoused by English administrators was, in fact, the mirror
image of that promoted by Irish nationalists at the beginning of the twen-
tieth century. While nationalists in Ireland believed that re-establishing
an Irish cultural identity was a prerequisite in any effort to undo the con-
quest, the English empire-builders in the sixteenth century believed that
a prerequisite in any effort to carry out a successful conquest in Ireland
was to undermine the native culture. Consequently as early as 1537 an
Act was passed in the Dublin parliament to effect linguistic change in
Ireland.[1]

Young Irish noblemen and noblewomen were quite often at this time
sent to England for schooling or to be brought up as wards of court –
with the intention that they would learn to speak English and declare for
the new Protestant religion. Irish professional poets as well as priests were
jailed or hanged. A vast amount of Irish literature in manuscript was
destroyed. Edmund Spenser, Fynes Moryson, and Sir John Davies were
amongst those who philosophized at some length about measures such
as these.[2]

Spenser wrote in 1596: ' . . . it hath ever been the use of the conquerors
to despise the langue of the conquered and to force him by all means
to learn his . . . the speech being Irish, the heart must needs be Irish . . . '.
Moryson concurred: 'In general all Nations have thought nothing more

powerful than the Community of language.' The cultural destabilization of Ireland had progressed so satisfactorily by 1612 that the English attorney-general, Sir John Davies, declared: 'We may conceive and hope that the next generation will in tongue, and heart, and every way else, become English; so as there will be no difference or distinction but the Irish sea betwixt us.'

It is likely that the link being consciously forged between military and cultural conquest was not sufficiently appreciated in the early stages by the Irish themselves. In particular they did not seem to be sufficiently aware of the new English determination to bring about language change. That position is quite understandable. There had been an acceptance of English as a spoken language in many areas of Ireland for several centuries previous to this. Entering into alliances with English-speaking lords, who gave their loyalty to English monarchs, posed no problems for Irish chieftains or their bards. The classic weapon with which medieval Irish aristocrats intuitively countered cultural domination – in a situation where they outnumber the colonists – was intermarriage. The Norman will to conquer had been sapped in that manner. Some forty years after the initial Norman invasion, for instance, an Irish poet was writing learned dedicatory verses in Irish for the Norman de Burgos, who having found themselves Irish wives, could now be fêted as people 'who are become Gaelic, yet foreign'. The cultural success of the medieval Irish approach was such that no substantial English-speaking (or French-speaking) enclave survived in Ireland at the time Sir John Davies was speaking enthusiastically of the future of the English language in Ireland.[3] In such circumstances, it is not strange that extreme hostility to the English language as a symbol of conquest was slow to develop.

Sir John Davies, of course, was wildly optimistic in his projection as to the time the process of Anglicization would take, but he had every reason to believe that cultural change was now bound to occur in a much more extensive manner than previously. In face of the planned policies of a strong centralist state, the old Irish medieval approach would no longer be effective. The new procedures set in train had already ensured that many Irish aristocrats could now read and write English. Some key members of aristocratic families had embraced the Protestant religion. Above all, colonizers had been sent into Ireland and would continue to be sent in such numbers that the chance of a substantial number of them being Gaelicized, by intermarriage or otherwise, was very remote indeed. This was particularly so in view of the fact that only fifteen per cent or thereabouts of the native Irish population remained landowners a century or so after Tudor colonization began.

While Irish opposition to territorial conquest was not particularly effective, opposition to cultural conquest was surprisingly so. The cultural will to survive remained both flexible and obstinate for some three centuries after the initial programme for destabilization began. The extraordinary sense of nationality which existed traditionally in Ireland had much to do with the continuing durability of some of the main features of Irish culture. For while it may be true to say that medieval Irish aristocrats had a weak sense of *nationalism* in that (like the ancient Greeks) they saw no urgent need for political unity between their various small kingdoms in order to defend the whole land, its people and its cultural heritage, from foreign invaders, they had (again like the ancient Greeks), a strongly developed sense of *nationality* in that no matter how much fratricidal political strife they engaged in, they passionately identified with the one national culture which they wished to maintain and defend. Resistance to conquest had always stemmed more from cultural than from political ideals, and would remain so, for the most part, during the seventeenth and eighteenth centuries.

I

Because of the extremely decentralized nature of traditional Irish society – and because of the further fragmentation brought about by the various colonial settlements from early medieval times – the response of Irish literary people to the new efforts at cultural conquest in the seventeenth century was not always uniform. Irish literary figures in the first half of the seventeenth century did not, in general, seem to suffer acutely from the feeling that the language in which they were writing was threatened with extinction. This applies in particular, one feels, to poets such as Céitinn (Keating) and Haicéad (Hackett) who were ancestrally associated with 'Old English' families who, for many centuries, had flourished in a bilingual and bicultural milieu. Indeed Céitinn and Haicéad, as well as Feiritéar (Ferriter) who lived on the remote Dingle peninsula, were amongst those who themselves probably spoke, wrote or read English. The promotion of English did not put literary figures such as these under any new pressures.

Ill-feeling towards the English language in this period seems mostly to stem from the fact that the lowly labouring classes – formerly 'unfree' or unprivileged in the old aristocratic order – were now shamelessly identifying with the language of the colonists; identifying, in fact, with the conquest, and rapidly treating with disrespect the learned Irish poetic classes. The efforts of the lower classes to ape their new masters by speaking broken English and imitating English fashions of dress and behaviour were scathingly satirized. As the century progressed the indignation expressed by the poets at this turn of events became increasingly savage.[4] About the year 1650, the learned author of a Rabelaisian prose satire *Pairlement Chloinne Tomáis* (The Parliament of Clan Thomas) ridicules grotesquely the cultural pretentiousness of the formerly submissive lower classes.

General awareness that major linguistic change was an integral planned part of the colonization programme, and consequent hostility to the English language as a symbol of conquest, seems to have spread mostly from the second half of the seventeenth century onwards. Archdeacon John Lynch in his *Cambrensis Eversus* (1662) expresses what must have been a common bewilderment at the link that had been irretrievably made now between political loyalty and linguistic loyalty: 'For did the Welsh ever refuse to show obedience to the monarch of England by reason of the fact that they are steeped in the Welsh language? We don't see the Bretons in France or the Basques in Spain deny the authority of their kings because they happen to use a speech that differs from the language of their princes. Yet if the Irish have maintained their current and widespread ancestral speech, will they as an immediate result be said to hatch dangerous plots against their supreme prince? For I see no other reason why that language's abolition is insisted upon so vehemently.'[5]

The link between political loyalty and religious loyalty had been made much more rapidly. While there had been long experience in medieval times of dealing with language problems, the attempted Tudor imposition of the Protestant religion was a new and divisive issue which was avidly seized on as a rallying point by disaffected Irish or 'Old English' aristocrats. Ironically it is quite a debatable point whether the sixteenth-century Irish religious tradition can best be described as a Christian tradition with a strong pagan substratum, or a pagan tradition with a nominal Christian overlay.[6] However one describes their religion, it is probably true that while the value system of the Irish people in general does not appear to have been particularly influenced by essential elements in Christian teaching, reverence for authority figures of the Roman Catholic church, such as the Virgin Mary and the Pope, was probably quite intense. Consequently the Protestant demotion of these figures brought quickest reaction. 'Fúbún séanadh Mhic Mhuire' ('shameful the denial of Mary's son'), declares one mid-sixteenth century poet.[7]

The dissolution of the monasteries, and the resultant lack of training facilities for clerical students, brought religious issues sharply into focus. Large numbers of members of 'Old English' Gaelicized families, in particular – traditionally much more orthodox Catholics than the old Gaelic families – had been going abroad since the middle of the sixteenth century to study for the priesthood, or to complete their clerical education. As the ability of aristocratic Gaelic families to maintain poets and scholars declined, increasing numbers from such families also sought continental education. The reformed post-Tridentine Catholic church began in fact to supplement the Irish aristocrat as patron of learning and letters.[8] The immediate literary consequence of this was that a small but unique body of religious prose in Irish, advocating post-Tridentine reforms, was published abroad in the early seventeenth century. It is unlikely that this new material in printed form made any great impact on Irish society. Even elitist scholars and poets do not seem to have paid any great attention. To judge by the material which scribes preserved in the more acceptable manuscript form, the main interest continued to be the more traditional categories of literature, of poetry in particular. The prose works of the early seventeenth century which seem to have attracted most interest were not religious but historical. Céitinn's *Foras Feasa ar Éirinn*, for instance, an account of the mythology, legends and history of Ireland until the coming of the Normans, was immensely popular. And it was a work, it should be noted, which sought above all else to enhance the old Irish aristocratic order, and to bewail its passing.

Céitinn was one of the large number of Irish scholars who completed their clerical studies abroad. He took a doctorate in theology in Bordeaux, and probably lectured there. Yet one feels from his work that he is much more emotionally involved with the fate and reputation of the Irish aristocratic world than with the new Catholic Reformation. What really causes him horror and dismay is that the old noble families are being overthrown and their lands annexed. Indeed a little while after the flight of the Ulster earls to the continent, Céitinn had no hesitation in passionately putting forward the quite elitist viewpoint (a viewpoint that is echoed by other literary figures) that the way to proceed now was to winnow what was left of the noble wheat from the plebeian chaff - to gather the remaining Irish aristocrats and ferry them across the sea from Ireland.[9] The idea that an Irish culture - even a somewhat more Christianized version of Irish culture - was worth maintaining without its natural leaders was unthinkable.

The passing of the old order, the loss of hereditary property and patronage, remained the *leitmotif* of seventeenth-century literature. Of the major poets, Céitinn (1580-c.1644), Haicéad (c.1600-1654), Ó Bruadair (c.1625-1698), Mac Cuarta (c.1647-1733), Ó Rathaille (c.1675-1729), all shared this thematic material to one degree or another. Ó Bruadair and Ó Rathaille, in particular, worked out their reactions to the societal chaos in which they found themselves in most moving personal lyrics.[10]

Given that the land of Ireland had always been a central focus in the mythology and psychology of Irish people,[11] and that most Irish personal relationships depended in a special way on property arrangements, it is not at all strange that the rape of the land caused much more immediate cultural shock than the attempted imposition of the Protestant religion, or the promotion of the English language. The literary relationship which was possibly most affected was that of poet and noble patron. As ownership of property declined so did patronage. The decline of patronage was a long process, however, and did not happen at the same pace throughout the country. It is noteworthy that all of the five poets mentioned above, even those of them who lived well into the first half of the eighteenth century, seem to have had some measure of aristocratic patronage. A clearer understanding of the complex and varying cultural responses resulting from the decline of the poet–patron relationship may be got from a brief consideration of the manner in which two of these poets, Haicéad and Ó Rathaille, were affected by their own associations with supportive aristocrats or institutions.

II

Haicéad – himself of 'Old English' landed gentry – was born north of Cashel, County Tipperary, in Butler territory, and had close links through marriage with a cadet branch of the Butlers, the Earls of Dunboyne.

The main Butler family, the Earls of Ormond, was one of the four pivotal Anglo-Norman families in Ireland in medieval times. Unlike the Earls of Desmond, Kildare and Clanrickarde, the Earls of Ormond were quite slow to take to Gaelic ways. It is rather ironic that it was precisely at the time when they were in the process of being Gaelicized – to the extent of offering patronage to poetry in Irish – that the Tudor policy of cultural conquest began. One of the consequences of this policy was that the various Earls of Ormond were now brought up in England, and, in fact, became related through marriage to British monarchs. The eleventh Earl of Ormond, a contemporary of Haicéad's, had been educated in England and was a Protestant.

Other branches of the Butlers remained much more supportive of the Irish language and of Gaelic ways. In fact it appears that a major part of the new accentual poetry written at the end of the sixteenth and at the beginning of the seventeenth century emerged under the aegis of the Butlers. Haicéad's cousin, the third Earl of Dunboyne, was particularly revered by poets: for instance, three of them (including Haicéad himself) wrote him poems of deeply-felt commiseration when he suffered a severe leg injury. The third Earl seems to have consciously resisted Anglicization, yet one should remember that his father too had been educated in England and had actively aided the crown (and the Earl of Ormond) to quell the Catholic inspired Desmond rebellion.[12] While the Earls of Dunboyne remained Catholic and were in constant conflict with the Earls of Ormond about matters of family property, they were probably loyal in principle to the British crown. To judge from Haicéad's eulogies, even the third Earl did not think of offering opposition to British political hegemony in Ireland.

As an 'Old English' Catholic family the Dunboyne Butlers would have supported Haicéad in his clerical education at home, and abroad in Louvain. Haicéad returned to County Tipperary as a Dominican priest, intent on preserving the type of 'Catholic' culture he knew as a youth. In his later verse he becomes very much the truculent cleric, urging the people of Ireland to unite together in a holy war. The crunch came for him during the period of the Confederation of Kilkenny (1642–1649) when a national and international effort was being made to bind 'Old English' and 'Old Irish' families in an alliance to protect the interests of the Catholic religion. The Marquis of Ormond was amongst those who finally undermined the alliance and the 'Old English' left the Confederation. Haicéad was deeply embittered by these events, in particular as the fourth Earl of Dunboyne, son of his patron-cousin, was one of those who supported Ormond and was consequently excommunicated by the Pope. The poet's comments on all those who had jettisoned the Catholic cause are scathing:

> They are the evil progeny of their mother [Ireland]
> they are dishonourable sons in remote places,
> they are a heap of excrement from a leper-house,
> they are vipers in our breasts.

Haicéad never seems to have written a religious or didactic poem; indeed at no time does one feel that he wishes personally to urge the new Catholic reforms on Irish people. Nor does he seem to have had a basic aversion to a British political presence in Ireland, in that he would have been at one with his patron-friend, the third Earl of Dunboyne, who most likely valued cultural independence much higher than political independence. The difference which had now come about between himself and the fourth Earl of Dunboyne stems from the fact that for Haicéad the chief cultural mark of distinctiveness between Ireland and England had become that of religion, and special political arrangements had become necessary to protect that distinctiveness. These political arrangements having failed, Haicéad spent his last sad years back in Louvain meditating savagely on the heretics who had undermined the old Irish order, and seeking to have the Pope lift his excommunication on the fourth Earl, his former patron's son.

Literary patronage in the Butler areas receded rapidly after the collapse of the Confederation of Kilkenny and the subsequent Cromwellian wars and plantations. Many of the more Gaelicized Butlers suffered dispersal all over the European continent; a small number of them in Ireland managed ultimately to regain possession of some of their ancestral lands. But even in the case of those Butlers who somehow survived at home in the second half of the seventeenth century there is no record of any substantial patronage being offered by them to Irish poets or literary figures. It is interesting to note, however, that one of the most haunting of Irish folk poems, *Cill Chais* (*Kilcash*)[13] composed sometime in the eighteenth century, laments the fall of another Butler house where the Catholic brother of the eleventh Earl of Ormond lived in Haicéad's time. The author of 'Cill Chais', in a studied understatement, says of the house: 'Earls from abroad would visit there/and the sweet mass was celebrated'. The religious issue which divided the Butlers a century before were still very much alive in the popular mind.

If the events following the collapse of the Confederation of Kilkenny led to a major disruption of literary patronage in the Butler territories, the events following the Battle of the Boyne, half a century later, led to a disruption of similar magnitude in the 'Old Irish' McCarthy territories in the south-west of Ireland. This is specially traceable in the record of the relationship between Ó Rathaille and those patrons who supported him.

Ó Rathaille grew up on a holding near Killarney, County Kerry, which was leased by his parents from Sir Nicholas Browne. His primary loyalty, however, was to the McCarthys who formerly owned the territories now legally held by the Brownes.

The Brownes had been gradually acquiring confiscated McCarthy and other territories – some 140,000 acres – during the seventeenth century. They had come as colonizers to Ireland in the late sixteenth century, and were, somewhat exceptionally, Catholics. They intermarried with various Irish aristocratic families, amongst them the family they had supplanted – the McCarthys – and had become, at least minimally, Gaelicized. Their practice of allowing formerly privileged people (under the Gaelic order) to hold land at nominal rents allowed some of the remnants of the 'Old Irish' nobility (and possibly well-connected poets such as Ó Rathaille) to live in a certain luxury.

Historically, the main branch of the McCarthys, the McCarthymore family, had managed by devious means to hold on to a moderately large estate in the Killarney region, independently of the Brownes. With these McCarthys in particular Ó Rathaille appears to have had ancestral ties – probably through his mother's family who may have been hereditary poets and scholars to the main branch of the McCarthys. So it was that Ó Rathaille, for a time, was basically maintained on Browne territory, and was casually

patronized by various Catholic (and even Protestant) aristocrats in the en-
virons of Killarney, amongst them the Brownes and McCarthys. It is clear,
however, that at this stage any major literary patronage on the part of the
McCarthys was quite unlikely. Their estate was debt-ridden and they were
rapidly being Anglicized through intermarriage with Anglo-Irish gentry.

After the Battle of the Boyne (1690), the McCarthymore, by changing
his allegiance from the Catholic Stuart king to the Protestant King William,
succeeded in holding on to his estate. Not so Sir Nicholas Browne. He
had opted wholeheartedly for the Stuart king in the Jacobite war and, as
a consequence of the defeat at the Boyne, his vast estates were to be con-
fiscated for his lifetime. Ó Rathaille and some of the cadet McCarthy families
were accordingly dispossessed of their holdings on the Browne estate. One
of the most memorable poems in all Irish literature was composed by Ó
Rathaille on the occasion of his having to find shelter subsequently in
a hovel by the sea.[14]

Around the years 1707–1708 new efforts were made to re-launch the
Stuart cause from France. The Brownes, and their colonist friends, were
to the fore in preparing for a new invasion of the west of Ireland by the
Catholic king. In this movement Ó Rathaille – unlike many of the more
notable McCarthys – was quite emotionally involved, and some of his
vision-poems on the expected return of the Stuart king are amongst the
most vividly imagined and best-crafted of his works.[15] Hope of a Stuart
invasion finally petered out dismally about the years 1720–1723. Worse
was to follow when the heir to the Browne properties, an English educated
Catholic called Sir Valentine, came into possession of his father's former
estate (c.1720). Ó Rathaille, after initial elation, discovered to his horror
that Sir Valentine would not or could not (legally) restore him to his old
family lands.[16] Despairingly he proclaimed his loyalty in his deathbed
poem,[17] not to the Brownes but to the discredited McCarthymore fami-
ly, 'those kings, my people served before the death of Christ'. One of the
odd ironies of Irish history is that not many years after Ó Rathaille's death
the self-styled 'last McCarthymore' ended up in England, an officer in the
British army.

It is clear that the type of poetry written by Ó Rathaille in County Kerry
in the first half of the eighteenth century was dictated to a great extent
by the patronage that was available to him; so it was also with Haicéad
in County Tipperary in the first half of the seventeenth century. As a result
of this their cultural responses were different. In many ways Ó Rathaille's
reflect more centrally the medieval bardic traditon. Unlike Haicéad, who
was basically maintained by his religious order, Ó Rathaille (having lost
his property), had to depend on casual patrons for whom he sometimes
wrote formal eulogistic or elegiac verse, which from the point of view of

content, could well have been written in the sixteenth century. Despite the religious strife and persecutions, despite the efforts to disseminate post-Tridentine teachings, this kind of verse in particular shows very little evidence of any new religious awareness. Ó Rathaille does rail in a few of his more personal poems against anti-Catholic laws, but the ideals and virtues he attributes to his patrons, living and dead, are those of the heroic non-Christian type which we associate with the great bulk of traditional bardic work. In one poem only – an elegy on the death of a priest – does he imagine the ordinary Christian virtues to be part of a gentleman's character.

Ó Rathaille is not strongly motivated by religious issues in his wish to extirpate the forces of the Protestant king; nor does it give him any pleasure on his deathbed that the old familiar territories are once again under the rule of Catholic nobility. His emotional stand is based firmly on his desire to repossess his status as poet (and thereby his property) and to live in a society which would fully appreciate the traditions he represented. He could contemplate with equanimity an Ireland ruled by a foreign king,[18] or a former McCarthy stronghold inhabited by an English-speaking colonist,[19] provided that the cultural life he and his people enjoyed could still flourish. In all this he is very much at one with the medieval Irish mind.

III

For want of patronage during the eighteenth century, poets increasingly became wandering teachers, musicians or labourers, and fell more frequently into poverty. Yet one cannot account the poetry of the eighteenth century as in any way peasant poetry. All the major literary figures continued to compose with extraordinary virtuosity within the norms of the traditional aristocratic literary tradition. Mac Cruitín (c.1670–1755) berates the Irish uncultured classes for their boorishness and pretentiousness;[20] Mac Dónaill (1691–1754) savages a colonial landlord for not behaving as an Irish chieftain would;[21] Mac Cumhaigh (1738–1773) laments the disappearance of the aristocratic O'Neills;[22] and Ó Súilleabháin (1748–1784) hints at his own special status as poet and shows a certain reluctance to engage in lowly manual work.[23] Even a late poem such as the *Lament for Art O'Leary*,[24] composed in a popular keening tradition, bears all the marks of a mind nurtured in an aristocratic Gaelic milieu.

As one proceeds through the eighteenth century one feels that, while impositions such as unjust rents are resented[25] there is a reluctant acceptance of conquest and a more general awareness that the English language and the Protestant religion go hand in hand with brutish oppression. At the same time one cannot say that the teachings of the Protestant religion always caused revulsion. It is a matter of record, at any rate, that at least three of the better-known poets of the period (Mac Craith, Mac Gearailt, Mac Cumhaigh) flirted for a time with the alien religion, while some others did not show great interest in religious practices of any kind. Many of the eighteenth-century poets emerge as quite independent-minded figures. There is a sense of gaiety and recklessness about some of them (Ó Súilleabháin, Mac Craith, Mac Cumhaigh, Mac Giolla Ghunna) that one does not associate at any rate with the scholarly priest-poet figure such as Haicéad and Céitinn in the early seventeenth century. The jocular, and sometimes challenging, role they assumed in relation to priests (a number of whom were poets themselves) can be seen in a whole series of lighter poems such as the well-known *Barántaisí* (Warrants),[26] or in the more risqué verses addressed to some clerics by poets such as Mac Craith. It is undeniable that our poets did not always treat the sacerdotal figure with great reverence.

While it is true that the priest or priest-poet figure in the earlier period of the conquest carried great authority – and seemed for a time to be on the point of filling the hierarchical role in Irish society being vacated by the native aristocracy – from the second half of the seventeenth century on we see him lose dominance and status. As a result of penal measures against the Catholic religion, ministering clergy became quite thin on the ground – in the five years after Haicéad's death, for instance, only one bishop had residence in Ireland – and clerical training became rudimentary. Priests, when ordained, had to promise on oath to complete their education abroad. Yet of 1,089 registered priests in 1704, less than a quarter of them had gone abroad. A report on the clergy in Ireland in 1733 declared that the details 'would make a good Catholic's hair stand on end', and that many of the daily scandals were 'caused by an exorbitant number of priests roving about without any function but to say Mass and to marry young couples'.[27] The situation of semi-literate priests with little Latin and less learning caused great dismay to the declining number of scholarly ecclesiastics. Towards the end of the seventeenth century the Ulster author of the prose and verse satire *Comhairle Mhic Clamha* ridicules a newly ordained priest:

> Brother Arsaigh, may you live to enjoy the state of your new priesthood, and I pray you do not be depressed because of the poverty of your Latin, as the amount of Latin necessary for saying Mass for the common congregation is slight. . . . However, on beginning the *Introibo* bless yourself with a loud full voice and give your vigorous prominent body a firm sturdy aspect and let your two eyes be sloping and nunnish in your head while looking at the lord. . . . Then raise your voice to a sort of

melodious humming and wheezing and coughing. . . . O blessed loud-voice priest, as you are a fine fellow, a spendid bumpkin, a sweet-sounding rascal, a merry tippler and a big-heeled rattler of a priest.[28]

Given the situation of a semi-literate clergy, it is not at all surprising that the poets became the dominant community figures in the early eighteenth-century 'Hidden Ireland'. Of the many hundreds of poets whose work has been recorded, most were men of substantial traditional learning. They read or transcribed manuscripts which contained material going back to early Christian times, some knew Latin; some taught English, navigation, mathematics at hedge-schools. When they assembled in courts of poetry during the year,[29] they read their poems, exchanged views and manuscripts and engaged in extempore repartee in verse. On some occasions they fulfilled one of the most traditional roles of the poet in Irish society by imposing sanctions on wrongdoers and acting as arbiters of social issues. For instance, when four youg men from the district of Croom joined the British Army, a number of the poets associated with the court of poetry there condemned their action in various verses; similarly many of the same poets lampooned a Dominican priest who became a Protestant minister.

In no other sphere did the poets influence people so powerfully as in that of the issue of the country's future freedom. From earliest times in Ireland the notion of the whole country (in the guise of a queen figure) being united with a redeemer king had always been a vague aspiration, and the king's coming had been endlessly foretold. Now that the McCarthys, the Butlers and the various other 'Old Irish' and 'Old English' aristocrats – with their concentration on their own particular local territorial objectives – had departed the scene, the time became ripe for the popular development of the saviour-king theme which Ó Rathaille had handled so artistically in the *aisling* genre. Consequently scores of poets in the eighteenth century wrote vision-poems in which the exiled Stuart princes were imagined as the promised redeemers and rulers of the *whole Irish people*. Even though the return of a Stuart prince seemed most unlikely after the defeat at Culloden in 1745, no other redeemer-figure was at hand and the composition of the *aisling* genre continued unabated. It was after all 'a poetic dream, convenient for poetic purposes and for the unification of history'.[30]

If one is to judge by what has been preserved in oral tradition, of all the high literary work of the seventeenth and eighteenth centuries it would seem that it was the *aisling* which made most impact on the popular mind. Much of this, one suspects, is due to the fact that many eighteenth-century poets began to reach a much wider audience by writing their lyrics to well-known musical airs. The *aisling* therefore prepared a large section of the Irish people for a unique understanding of nineteenth-century nationalism, even though their sympathies seemed often to lie more with a monarchical nation-state than with a republican nation-state. Almost all the leaders of the late nineteenth-century revolutionary Fenian movement, for instance, 'at one time or another indicated that they were not wholly opposed in principle to monarchy.'[31]

In the absence of necessary dated or detailed evidence, it is exceedingly difficult to speculate fruitfully on how the conquest affected the development of the more popular types of literature, how the 'Irish mind' in general responded. Vast areas of this literature await analysis.

Two special branches of literature which were enjoyed and shared widely since medieval times by all classes were those of Ossianic lore and lovesong. As J.F. Nagy points out, the Ossianic tales and lays were afforded the type of reverential attention given to religious rituals in other cultures,[32] and are quite significant for the light they cast on the herofigure which Irish people most admired and identified with. In Nagy's fine structuralist study this figure emerges as one who is poet/sage and outsider;[33] who gives service to 'the kings of Ireland, who represent in medieval ideology the stability and prosperity of the entire island';[34] who at the same time could be a rebellious employee threatening 'the very authority of kingship';[35] who is 'righteous plunderer, avenger and agent of distraint';[36] 'reacquiring what one is legally entitled to within society';[37] and 'never attains full adulthood and the traditional sexual relationships that adulthood entails.'[38] One is tempted to ask whether it was such community expectation of a hero's attributes that threw up the rake-poet type such as Eoghan Rua Ó Súilleabháin who, in the late eighteenth century, was intent on making straight the way for the rightful king,[39] or, on a quite different plane, the majestic rogue/sage type of public hero such as Daniel O'Connell in the nineteenth century, and many others since. If so, the 'Irish mind' far from being eroded by the conquest continued to develop and adapt.

As with Ossianic literature the great Irish love-songs[40] were highly esteemed at different levels of society as very special works of art. The values which they reflect regarding love and marriage emanate from the mores of medieval Irish aristocratic society and are very much at variance with orthodox Christianity. The attitude to sex which they reveal contradicts in practically every detail that preached by early seventeenth-century reformist clerics such as Archbishop Aodh Mac Aingil in his *Scáthán Shacramuinte na hAithridhe*.[41] On the other hand, it seems clear that the mass of people had traditionally been quite stringent in their views as to how day-to-day matters regarding love and marriage should be conducted amongst themselves;[42] it was mostly, it appears, at the higher levels of society that 'unorthodox' behaviour was approved of and provided for by special economic arrangements.[43] Could it be, one is tempted to ask, that the extraordinary prevalence of love-songs in eighteenth-century society indicates a growing identification on the part of ordinary people with the 'unorthodox' non-Christian aristocratic values? If so, deteriorating economic circumstances in the nineteenth century and the English universal education system put an end for some time to any such tendency. There is little doubt, however, that ambivalent attitudes to sex and marriage continued and continue to be a feature of Irish society.

There is at least one major question to be asked if not to be answered finally: is not eighteenth-century Gaelic Ireland, in many respects, a period of extraordinary cultural growth rather than of decay? Under the new colonial landlord class the mass of people may have existed in fairly miserable living conditions and may have been denied their traditional rights or advancement; on the other hand – economic conditions apart – they were left more to their own devices. In the absence of native authority figures, attitudes to political, social and moral matters seem to have taken on new dimensions. There were considerable new literary developments in the genres of vision-poems, confessional poems,[44] comic warrants and occasional poems.[45] There is evidence for growing participation and interest in dancing, hurling, faction-fights and other entertainments. One feels that, as living conditions improved in the second half of the eighteenth century, both poets and people achieved a certain freedom to develop, denied to them in previous centuries. Allied to this freedom, one often experiences a great sense of gaiety, the sort of gaiety associated with the behaviour and *obiter dicta* of the poet Eoghan Rua Ó Súilleabháin, the sort of gaiety portrayed as late as 1827–1835 in the diary of Humphrey O'Sullivan.[46] The Hidden Ireland was in all probability a much merrier Ireland than we have been led to believe. This merriment, of course, may have been the sort that often emerges at a time of societal chaos.

The main feature of Gaelic culture which had visibly declined in the eighteenth century was the Irish language itself. Yet it is still likely that two out of every three people in the country habitually spoke Irish at the end of the eighteenth century, so that literature in Irish continued to be the predominant literature down to the middle of the nineteenth century. As one commentator points out, however,[47] the determining factor in favour of major language change at this stage was that all those people who wielded power in Ireland, who had formal education or professional careers, now spoke English as their preferred language. The training of priests – who now began to oust the poets as authority figures – came under the control of English-speaking authorities, and as a result the Church gradually helped to impose both Victorian religious values and the English language on Irish people. More significantly, perhaps, the universal educational system that had been established in 1831 with the objective of educating Irish children through English and in English, was an overwhelming success. While the numbers of English speakers increased rapidly, so too (due to unusual population growth) did the numbers of Irish speakers for some time. In fact, at the time of the Great Famine (1845–1847) there were probably more Irish speakers – as well as more English speakers – in Ireland than ever before in recorded history. When the Famine struck, vast numbers of the poorer Irish-speaking population, in particular, died or emigrated. From then on until the end of the century speaking and writing in the Irish language declined disastrously.

And so it happened that the wishes of Sir John Davies were finally fulfilled, to the extent that the majority of Irish people now adopted the English language. On the other hand Tudor policy regarding religion in Ireland failed completely. For in the same period that the Irish language came close to extinction the Catholic Church was able to re-organize itself in a highly efficient manner and become a power in the land.

[1988]

9

Love in
Irish Folksong

A FTER THE OVERTHROW of the Irish aristocratic order in the early
seventeenth century, the practice of love-poetry declined rapidly
amongst our learned poets. Ironically it was precisely at this period that
Irish popular love-poetry began to surface in abundance. The vast ma-
jority of Irish folksongs collected in the nineteenth and twentieth cen-
turies are, in fact, love-songs. Many of these must have been composed
in the period 1600–1850, but, for the most part, the models on which they
are based go back to medieval times.

W.P. Ker, one of the most eminent of medieval scholars, suggests that
it is in the twelfth century we must look for the main sources and models
of western European poetry and song: 'It is well to recognize,' he says, '. . .
that an old civilization with an elaborate literature of its own came to
an end in the eleventh century . . . and [that there is] great difficulty in
understanding the transition. Modern poetry, including the ballads, begins
about the year 1100.'[1]

The new European love-literature, shaped by the philosophy of *amour
courtois*, may have made an impact on Ireland, if not during the twelfth
century, at least quite early in the thirteenth century in the wake of the
Anglo-Norman invasion. Wherever in Ireland in the thirteenth century,
a Norman castle or enclave existed, it is likely that continental cultural
fashions prevailed. And as Norman chiefs, their poets and entertainers
became Irish speaking, they carried with them into Irish 'the matter of
France'. (This direct language change from French to Irish happened most
often, one surmises, in rural areas). English – and even Latin – sources

must also be reckoned with, particularly at a later stage. But the probability is that Norman-French influence, at this early period, was the major one. French was the second language – the prestige language – in Ireland for at least one hundred and fifty years after the Norman invasion (and indeed continued to be the British judicial language in Ireland down to the end of the fifteenth century). We know for instance of one poet, the Earl of Desmond, who composed verses in French in the early fourteenth century while his son, Gerald, composed much finer verse in Irish. This Gerald was the same man who, as Lord Chief Justice and upholder of the Anglo-Norman law in Ireland, was entrusted with the task of applying the Statutes of Kilkenny (1367), which themselves were enacted in French. The objective of the statutes was to enforce an apartheid between the two nations in Ireland – in fact to prevent the Normans being assimilated by Irish culture in general and, in particular, by that same language in which the Lord Chief Justice himself was most eloquently writing.

The Carole

One genre of the international literary love-movement for which there is early reliable documentary evidence in Ireland is that of the *carole*. The *carole* in France was primarily a light love-song with refrain to be danced to, in the form of a round. There is much reason to believe that the Normans were more taken with this form of love-song than with many of the more formal manifestations of *amour courtois*. Not having been long established in France themselves before they began their forays throughout Europe, their own literary traditions were thinly-rooted. Consequently wherever they went they seemed to have particularly cultivated the more popular levels of love-song and dance.

Of course, as many scholars have warned, distinctions between 'popular' and 'learned' as applied to medieval literature, can be quite misleading. It has been claimed, for instance, that 'popular' French refrains of the twelfth and thirteenth centuries express the basic philosophic notions of *amour courtois* as completely as the most elaborate learned lyrics of the period.[2] Such refrains, in association with the requisite *carole* dances, were engaged in by aristocrats and common-folk alike. *Carole* dancing and singing spread like a raging fever through all levels of western European society in these centuries. The great Norman Lord, Guillaume le Maréchal (d. 1219) who ruled the province of Leinster was known in France as being both an expert exponent and composer of the *carole*. According to the Norman-French poem, *Rithmus facture Ville de Rosse*, women and children helping to build the town of New Ross (*c*.1265) danced and sang their *caroles* on the way to work, after work, and during their lunch-breaks.[3] Priests – Franciscans in particular – were great disseminators of the fashion. Various clerics are known to have been singing *caroles* in English and French in the streets of Kilkenny in the middle of the fourteenth century. (It is noteworthy that their songs may have been mostly in English; English had begun to make a large impact on towns on the east coast of Ireland, just as English began to replace French as the literary language of England.) Sometime from the second half of the thirteenth century, comes a report of an Irish Franciscan who visited London and spent so much time a-carolling in the church precincts on Saturday night, that when he turned around on the altar on Sunday morning, instead of the necessary and liturgical 'dominus vobiscum', blurted out a dance-refrain sung on the previous night: 'swete leman þin ore' ('sweet lover have mercy on me').[4]

Such snippets of information do help us to imagine a little more deeply the medieval scene. They help us, for instance, to guess at the real life drama which may underly the lovely medieval *carole* adapted by Yeats:

> Ich am of Irlaunde
> ant of the holy londe
> of Irlaunde.
>
> Gode sire, pray ich þe
> for of saynte charite,
> come ant daunce wyt me
> in Irlaunde.

There is abundant internal evidence that these Anglo-Norman dance-song entertainments were assimilated into Irish-Gaelic culture. But the first clear documentary evidence we have that such activities were known in Gaelic Ireland comes from a description of carol dancing and singing in the O'Driscoll castle in Baltimore, County Cork, on Christmas Eve 1413. It was on the occasion of a visit by the Mayor of Waterford:

> . . . and so the Maior walked into the greate Hall, where O'h-Idriskill and his kinsmen and friends, sitting at boordes made ready to supp, commanded O'h-Idriskoll and his company, not to move or feare, for he would not, nor meant to, to draw no men's blood of the same house, more than to daunce and drinke, and so to departe. With that the said Maior toke up to daunce O'h-Idriskoll and his sonne, the Prior of the Friary, O'hIdriskoll's 3 brethren, his uncle and his wife and leaving them in their daunce, the Maior commanded every of his men to hold fast the said powers, and so after singing a carroll came away, bringing with them aboorde the said shipp the said O'h-Idriskoll and his company, saying unto them they should go with him to Waterford to syng their carroll, and make merry that Christmas.[5]

Not until the sixteenth and seventeenth centuries, do we come on a substantial range of references to round-dancing in Ireland from both Irish language and English language sources. Dancing in the seventeenth century was, we are told, 'the chief if not only relaxation of poorer classes'.[6] It is in these centuries also that English writers and travellers comment frequently on the 'Irish Hay/Hey' which from the descriptions we get must have been some type of round/*carole* dance. 'Hye' in French or 'Hay/Hey' in English were nonsense words which marked a stamping action in the burden of the *carole*. 'There can be hardly any doubt that the medieval Englishman,' says Richard Greene, 'often stamped his feet in a round dance in time wlth a "hey, hey" of this sort.'[7] English commentators in Ireland, including Spenser, described such round dances as 'country dances' or 'their old manner . . . of dancing'.

'Hey' or 'Hey Dery Daune' type of songs were anathema to most church authorities. Bishops throughout Europe consistently issued grave edicts from about 650 AD to c.1450 AD, condemning dancing as well as all types of love-songs. Bishop Ledrede had a more enlightened way of dealing with the problem in Kilkenny. The historian Edmond Curtis, writes: 'Richard Ledrede, who was bishop of Ossory, 1318–60, was an episcopal reformer. He was greatly scandalised at the frivolous ways of the clergy, who along with monks and priests were numerous in the gay little city. He found that they and their clerks were given to using on feastdays songs which were base, secular and only fit for mummers (cantilenae teatrales, turpes et seculares). Instead of these he wrote sixty hymns in Latin. He stole, however airs of the songs he meant to supersede.'[8] Bishop Ledrede, like Luther at a later date, obviously did not wish that the devil would have all the best tunes.

The songs sung to the *carole* dance seem generally to have been of the simplest, and were rarely of literary interest. One could say indeed that the *carole* was not a specific literary form at all: its theme could be any of the numerous love themes cultivated by poets internationally. A burden or refrain was a necessary element in all *caroles*, however, and due to the exigencies of the associated dance-steps, typical metrical forms were commonly associated with the *carole*. In England the Norman-English religious orders began gradually to adopt these metrical forms and the airs allied to them, for different types of devout songs. In fact five out of six carols written down in medieval England are religious songs to be sung at different feasts and festivals. By 1400 the 'carol' was going out of fashion and the word itself in English began mostly to mean 'song' (religious song) rather than 'love-song with dance'. By 1550 the carol was *passé*, an old fashioned entertainment – practised widely in Ireland, and in English rural areas.[9] Today the love-carol type of song is practically non-existent in collected English folksong. On the other hand Irish folksongs contains scores of carol-type verses on love themes – with only the rarest examples of carols on devout themes. All this seems to suggest that the models for most of our Irish songs today emanate most likely from the earlier Norman period (1200–1400), when the *carole* was inextricably linked with love, than from any later period.

The metrical forms[10] employed for the *carole* in France were chiefly A+C (one line with refrain) or 2A+C (two rhyming lines with refrain) or 3A+B+C (three rhyming lines with cauda and refrain). The refrain or burden often contained nonsense words such as *Haro, derin din, ding ding dong, avec la tourloura*, etc.; such nonsense words are found also in medieval English songs as well as in Irish folksongs, and in origin were sounds used by dancers, and possibly onlookers, to imitate the sound of pipes and other musical instruments (sometimes played as an accompaniment to the dance).

The A+C and 2A+C metrical forms seem to be linked with the most primitive type of *carole*, which has been traced back by French scholars to archaic women's dances at May-time. It is noteworthy that many of the examples of the A+C form extant today in Irish folksong are also linked with the coming of summer. 'Thugamar féin an Samhradh linn' is a widespread motif.

It was the form 3A+B+C, however, which mostly became identified with the *carole* in the high *amour courtois* period (*c.*1200–1400), when this type of entertainment became an elitist court activity for both men and women. Well-known troubadours and trouvères cast their *chansons à dancer* in this mould.

Irish folksong and traditional Irish poetry in general make abundant use of various versions of the form 3A+B+C. Amongst the simpler types of love-songs to do so are songs known in Ireland today to many school-children e.g. *Beidh aonach amáireach, Is trua gan peata an mhaoir agam, An Páistín Fionn*.

A breakdown of the metrical form might be outlined thus:

Song:	Beidh aonach amáireach i gCondae an Chláir,	(Ax3)
	Cén mhaith dhom é, ní bheidh mé ann.	(Bx1)
Refrain:	'S a mháithrín an ligfidh tú 'na aonaigh mé	(x3)
	A mhúirnín ó, ná héiligh é.	

This practice of casting the refrain in the same general metrical mould as the verse had become common already in medieval times, e.g.:

> My lady is a prety on,
> A prety, prety, prety on,

> *My lady is a prety on*
> *As ever I saw.*[11]

This particular form of the *carole* verse and refrain is widespread in Irish music and song today:

> Is trua gan peata an mhaoir agam,
> Is trua gan peata an mhaoir agam,
> Is trua gan peata an mhaoir agam,
>   's na caoire beaga bana.
>
> *Is ó goirim, goirim thú*
> *Is grá mo chroí gan cheilg thú*
> *Is ó goirim, goirim thú*
> *'S tú peata beag do mháthar.*

One suspects that it was the dance music, as W.P. Ker has observed, which was mainly instrumental in disseminating the *carole* form internationally.

Richard Greene refers to 'the principle that in Old French Lyrics derived from the dance riming lines were generally sung to the same musical phrase'.[12] This seems to be true of many light folksongs in Irish which are more or less in 3A+B+C *carole* form. The musical phrases often follow the structure of the verse. One finds, in particular, musical forms which can, I believe, be described as $A+A^1+A+B$ or $A+A^1+A^2+B$, corresponding generally to the elements of the verse forms. One finds also some examples of what seems to be a primitive form of *carole* music i.e. the exact 3A+B musical form, $A+A+A+B$ which seems quite unmusical to modern ears.[13] Folksong collectors in Ireland have reported their astonishment at hearing good singers sing their verses to such unpleasing and unsophisticated tunes. It may be indeed that Ireland is the only western European country in which this type of primitive *carole* music has survived into this century.

On the other hand, there are grounds for believing that elaborate developed forms of *carole* verse structures established themselves in Ireland as well. One popular form was that of the *rondel* or *rondeau de carole*, which is a common form used in may folk and literary songs in Irish. *Eibhlín a Rún*, for instance, is in a classic *rondel* form, a form which is frequently found in medieval French verse, as in the popular Robins and Mariete series. This stanza, for instance, could be sung without too much difficulty to the air of *Eibhlín a Rún*:

> En non Dieu! Robins en maine
> Bele Mariete!

> En non Dieu! Robins en maine
> Bele Mariete!
> C'est la jus desoz d'olive,
> Robins en maine sa mie,
> la fontaine i sort serie
> desouz l'olivete.
>
> (*Grá*, p. 235)

Among the Latin hymns composed by Bishop Ledrede in Kilkenny in the fourteenth century to popular *carole* airs, there are verse forms which seem to approximate closely to this type of *rondel* form.

The evidence that the Norman *carole* culture became deeply rooted in Ireland is very strong indeed. The extent to which it influenced the dance and dance music in Ireland may finally be gauged by the fact that the two extant words for dancing in Irish 'rince' and 'damhsa', derive from either English or Norman-French. The foreign rounds or ring-dances most likely became the models on which a great deal of 'traditional' Irish 'square' or 'round' dancing is ultimately based.

The Man's Love–Lyric

It is useful to have dwelt a little on the *carole* phenomenon as it gives some indication of one aspect of the deep Anglo-Norman penetration of Gaelic civilization. It should be remembered, of course, that not alone did the Anglo-Normans leave their own indelible mark on the tone and substance of our love-literature, but, more importantly, that they opened up the channels of literary communication on all levels between Ireland, England and France (including, one thinks, Provençe). Consequently some of the most solemn French of Provençal conventions in the man's love-lyric manifest themselves most astonishingly in our folksong literature as collected in the nineteenth and twentieth centuries. The Irish folk-memory is known to be particularly tenacious, so that the words of a well-known folklore scholar, Alexander Krappe, are especially relevant to Irish folksong studies. He says: 'It is equally clear that a considerable number of songs considered now old folk-songs have in all probability a literary origin. . . . In periods of intense literary activity, literary products will sink from the classes for which they were intended in the first place, to lower levels of the common people. When the songs of the medieval troubadours had charmed the knights and ladies, and even after they had ceased to charm them, they still appealed to the peasants.'[14]

J. M. Cohen in speaking of twelfth-century love-poetry adds to our understanding of the links between popular and learned:

> Twelfth-century poetry, nevertheless, is on the whole virtually anonymous. Just as we hardly know the names of the architects who in the same age were building the great Cathedrals, so we know very little about the troubadours or trouvères – as they were called in Provençe and Northern France respectively – who made the songs which the joglars or jongleurs sang. . . . The vernacular literature of the twelfth century was not designed for reading. The epic poems were composed to the simple music of the primitive fiddle, and the lyrics for singing to more complicated tunes, sometimes with refrains, or as a voice and fiddle accompaniment to a dance. There was, consequently, a very close relationship between the metres used and the traditional dance steps; and since most of the dances were popular in origin it was at this point that the cultivated lyric touched the folksong with the result that in some districts, in Northern France and Spain in particular, poems began to be devised on less sophisticated subjects by the jongleurs themselves, independently of the trouvères, to be sung at the festivities of the common people. It was the dance that bridged the gap between the art-forms proper to each caste.[15]

Detailed examination of the large corpus of popular Irish love-song as we have it today reveals that a preponderance of the material consists of the man's love-lyrics. Our folksong differs considerably in this from that of, say, England or France. While one finds an abundance of women's love-lyrics in English or French folksong, one finds only the rarest example of lyrics attributed to men. In Irish folksong there are literally hundreds of men's love-lyrics, most of them wedded to elaborately-structured music. The love-concepts expressed in them are uniformly of the idealized courtly kind; on the other hand the tone of the best of them can be quite intimate, informal, noncourtly. Here, for instance, is a fragment (probably of a *carole*) where the declaration of love evokes a mood of summer fruitfulness:

> She's the blackberry-flower,
> the fine raspberry-flower,
> she's the plant of best breeding
>   your eyes could behold:
> she's my darling and dear,
> my fresh apple-tree flower,
> she is Summer in the cold
>   between Christmas and Easter.

(D, p. 277)

This quality of lyricism is not maintained in our love-songs with any consistency, however; indeed the man's lyric tends to be effusive, eulogistic, lacking in poetic structure, owing a certain element of its tone to the rhetoric of praise-poetry as composed by professional bards and other poets, perhaps, in the medieval period (1200–1650). Lyric utterances tend to appear at random in a sudden astonishing verse (often reflecting a typical *amour courtois* motif):

> When my lady moves towards me on her path,
> The moon awakens and the sun shines forth,
> A honey mist spreads by night or day
> On each side of the road as she makes her way.
>
> (*Grá*, p. 280)

> When my loved one goes out
> The sun loses its heat,
> And the moon bows low in adoration.
>
> (*Grá*, p. 280)

> Honey grows in her wake,
> on her footprints on high ground,
> seven weeks after the feast of Samhain.
>
> (*Grá*, p. 280)

> My own dark head (my own, my own)
> your soft pale arm place here about me.
> Honeymouth that smells of thyme
> he would have no heart who denied you love.
>
> (*D*, p. 285)

The thematic material of these songs, when taken together, can be seen to correspond most accurately to that of French and Provençal *chansons d'amour*, both literary and semi-popular of the thirteenth and fourteenth centuries. The themes, of course, have sometimes suffered a sea-change; the Irish background to these songs, and the native literary traditions – praise poetry in particular – have left their marks. The images often stem from a non-courtly, non-philosophic rural environment, while such elements of traditional Irish prose and verse as the extravagant praising of the woman's hair take up an inordinate space in the typical continental description of the lady's beauties.

But taking these lyrics all in all they are as near *amour courtois* as one can expect folksong to be.[16] As in the typical *chanson d'amour*, there is everywhere in them absolute adoration of the lady; she, his secret love, is the most gifted of human beings, a saint from paradise radiating happiness, the mirror and flower of all perfection. Happy is the ground she walks on; she is, for beauty, the rose and lily commingled. She illumines the darkness – even the sun loses its brightness in her presence. Precious jewels (crystal, in particular) are likened to her beauty. Her eyes are green, hair blonde, breasts perfectly formed, neck slender as a swan's, eyebrows pencil-thin, waist slender, breath fragrant. The first time the poet sees her, he is stricken with the disease of love (or wounded by love's arrow), day for him becomes night, night day. He goes to church to see her, not to pray. He would (like the troubadour Bernard de Ventadour) brave snow and ice to visit her. Nature everywhere reflects the love-mood. One poet takes up a theme made famous by Bernard:

> It is well for small birds that can rise up on high
> and warble away on the one branch together.
> Not so with myself and my millionfold love
> that so far from each other must rise every day.
>
> She's more white that the lily and lovely past Beauty,
> more sweet that the violin, more bright than the sun,
> with a mind and réfinement surpassing all these . . .
> O God in Your Heaven give ease to my pain!

(D, p. 277)

The loved one is frequently, as in some medieval *chansons d'amour*, unmarried, but is more often than one would expect in folk poetry, a married lady (as is the case generally in the more formal *amour courtois* lyrics). The poet often addresses her by a secret fantasy name (akin to the early Provençal use of the *senhal*): she is the 'Little Dark Rose' or 'Pearl of the White Breast' who has afflicted him with the wasting disease of love, who has wounded him, has caused him to spend his time crying and sighing. Only she can be his doctor, cure him from certain death (with 'one kiss'). The joy she gives is greater than the joy of paradise. To sleep with her would be no sin. He prefers her to the wealth of kings or to God himself.

Not all of these motifs, of course, occurred with great consistency throughout the whole corpus of our folksong; some themes which more than likely are 'non-courtly' also make their appearance (e.g. marriage is sometimes envisaged; the lovers lack of means may become an issue). Where these songs differ mostly, however, from much courtly medieval French song is in the matter of tone. Adoration and unsatisfied desire are there, but the distance is different. The lady is no *dame soveraigne*: she tends rather to be made the poets equal, though still generally unattainable (for some reason not always specifically mentioned). The whole attitude of solemn feudal subservience is missing, as is generally any philosophic or feudal terminology of love. One does come, however, on an odd stanza which certainly seems to mirror consciously the troubadour idea that love ennobles e.g.

> It is so for the person
> Who turns his back on love
> As a tree on a hillside
> Whose leaves had withered.

> (*Grá,* p. 154)

Or still more succinctly:

> A tree without foliage
> Is a person who loves not, nor hates.

> (*Grá,* p. 154)

Generally speaking, however, one can say (with some modification) of these folklyrics, what G.L. Brook has said of the thirteenth and fourteenth-century semi-popular Harley Lyrics: 'The ennobling influence of love is not explicitly mentioned, but this does not mean that the poets did not believe in it. Two centuries had elapsed since the rise of the convention of courtly love so that anyone who was familiar with the minor conventions, as the poets of the Harley lyrics were, would probably take it for granted.'[17]

One philosophic viewpoint, however, which directly emanates from what has been rather colourfully called the 'heresy' of *amour courtois* is strongly and explicitly present in the Irishman's love-song, i.e., that without woman's love God is unattainable and only through woman's love can God be fully experienced. A story in the *Arabian Nights* tales has its hero say: 'I should not delight in life without seeing you, even were I in Paradise or the Garden of Eternity'.[18] And indeed it is more than likely that it was through the influence of a variety of Arabian poets and philosophers that this feeling became established in medieval Provençal and French love poetry, and later on in Irish love-songs (though not in learned medieval Irish love-lyrics). One folk-poet declares:

> Gan tú i láthair Dé na nGrásta
> Ní sásta bheinn gan gó.

> (*Grá,* p. 120)

> Without you being in the presence of
> the King of Grace
> Truthfully I would not be happy.

Another poet declares dramatically:

B'fhearr liom-sa bheith ar leaba léi á síor-phógadh
Ná mo shuí i bhFlaitheas i gCathaoir na Tríonóide.[19]

I would prefer to be in bed with her ever kissing her
than to sit in Heaven in the throne of the Blessed Trinity.

It is ironic that J.M. Synge's discreet adaptation of these and other lines from Irish love-songs in his *Playboy of the Western World* found little favour with an Irish audience in the Abbey Theatre in the year 1907. Victorian attitudes had by then taken over in English-speaking Ireland.

The *Pastourelle*

Several other song-types found in Irish folk-literature were professionally cultivated by troubadours in Provençe or by trouvères in northern France. Amongst those the *pastourelle* made a deep impact.

The *pastourelle*, in its assumptions, reflects the direct antithesis of the ideal love proposed in the *chanson d'amour*. It has been conjectured that the basic theme derives from old romance folksong which told of a young man sallying forth one summer morning, of his encounter with a young country girl, and of her escape from his advances. Whatever of its more remote origins, the twelfth or thirteenth-century learned poets in France and Provençe tended to place their own indelible seal on the theme: the young man becomes the poet himself, a knightly figure of the aristocratic class, who tells his tale in the first person singular; the young girl generally – though not always – is a shepherdess (*pastourelle*); she – after a fairly conventional love-debate – quite frequently yields to the poet's importunities, or is raped violently. This denouement was seen as necessary for the noble poet's ego: he needed to boast of his success. This poetic boast had its own technical term applied to it – the *gab* or *vanto*.

The twelfth or thirteenth-century *pastourelle* has since become the aristocratic prototype of the vast majority of the 'As I roved out' type of song in French and in English. The formula has been used loosely in English in countless love-adventure type of songs; most of these are simplified disingenuous versions of the classic *pastourelle* model where marriage rather than rape seems to be the desired outcome. There are, however, a few rare examples extant in English from medieval times which are quite close to the original formula.

There are in Irish, as in English, scores of folksongs of the love-adventure type which are loosely based on the *pastourelle* concept. It is possible that many of the models for these were introduced to Ireland at various stages of our post-Norman cultural history – especially, perhaps, from the Elizabethan period onwards when there seems to have been a great deal of cultural exchange of music and song between England, Scotland and Ireland. There is a significant core, however, of our Irish *pastourelle*-type songs which seem to reflect closely the twelfth/thirteenth-century French examples, and for which no prototype seem to be extant in the English language. It is conceivable that the models for these, at least, surfaced in Ireland in the early centuries after the Norman invasion. The classic *pastourelle*-type compositions in Irish include well known traditional songs, often of elaborate musical structure, such as *Seoladh na nGamhan, An Binsín Luachra, Eochaill, Risteard Ó Bruineann*.

There are, of course, some noticeable minor differences (due to cultural factors) between the classic Irish and the classic French *pastourelle*, e.g., in French the country girl is usually a shepherdess; in Irish she is more likely to be plucking rushes or herding calves. But the general structural and verbal similarities between some modern Irish examples and the medieval French texts – especially in the debate and denouement sections of the poems – seem quite uncanny. A few examples will confirm this (original text in italics):[20]

(a) The poet names the location where the adventure takes place:

Antre Aras et Douai/Between Arras and Douai.
Sor la rive de Seine/On the bank of the Seine.

Idir Caiseal agus Dúrlas/Between Cashel and Thurles
Ar maidin inné cois Féile bhíos/Yesterday morning by the
River Feale I walked

(b) The poet makes physical advances to the girl he encounters, but she demurs:

N'atouchies pas a mon chainse/Do not touch my chemise
Is é dúirt sí 'stad is ná strac mo chlóca'/She said 'stop, don't
tear my cloak'

Alleiz vostre chamin/Go on your way.
Is é dúirt sí liomsa, 'imthigh uaim'/She said to me 'be on your
way'

(c) The poet invites her to sleep with him – giving the lambs/calves the freedom of the meadows in the meantime:

Que nous dormons lez a lez/So we will sleep side by side
si lessiez voz aigneaux pestre aval les prez/and let your lambs
graze down on the meadow

. . . *cead síneadh síos led' bháinchnis*/leave to stretch out by
your white body

Agus gheobhaimid na gamhna amáireach/and we will find the
calves tomorrow

(d) She says she is too young; she fears her parents:

Trop per je sui jonete/Because I am too young.
Mar is maighdean mé ná táinig mh'aois/Because I am a virgin,
too young yet

Je n'os por mo pere/I dare not for my father
Och mo dhaidí féin go dúch insa mbaile/Och my own daddy,
disconsolate at home

ní fhéadaimse teacht ina láthair/I cannot appear in his presence

(e) The poet promises her the life style of a chatelaine:

Dame seras d'un chastel/You shall be chatelaine of a castle
robes et biaux joiaus assez vos donrai/dresses and a lot of fine
jewels I shall give you

Tá caisleáin gheala im choimeád 's teacht iarlaí im chúirt/
I own bright castles and earls visit my court

Gheobhaidh tú athrú den fhaisiún sin a rún go fóill/You will
get a change of fashion yet, my love

Gúnaí geala, sciortaí breaca, síoda agus sróill/Bright gowns,
dappled skirts, silk and satin

(f) When refused finally, the poet forces her violently into the sexual act:

Couchai la a terre/I laid her on the grass
tout maintenant/immediately
levai li le chainse/lifted up her chemise

lou jeux d'amors sens atendre/The game of love, without delay
le fix per delit/I engaged in with delight
Lors me sembla que fusse en paradis/Then it seemed to me I
was in paradise

In éineacht chun tailimh a treascradh sinn/We both tumbled
to the ground
Rug mé greim gúna uirthi is leag mé ar an drúcht í/I seized
her dress and brought her to the dewy ground

> *D'imríos cluiche den chleas nach neosfad* . . ./I played a game
> of a business I'll not describe . . .

> *Do shaoil an ríoghain gurbh í tír na n-óg í*/The princess
> thought it was paradise

(g) She, exceptionally, wants him to repeat the sex act:

> '*Faites le moi encor amis*'/Do it to me again, my love
> *lors recomensai san demor*/at which I recommenced without
> delay
> *le jeu k'elle m'avoit requis*/the game she had asked of me

> *Shin agat cead saor, agus déin é arís*/You have my full
> permission, do it again
> *Arís gan mhoill nuair d'éirigh liom*
> *do rinneas an scéal d'athnuachan*/Again, quite soon when I
> found it possible, I renewed the whole business

(h) The poet, exceptionally, declares (despite her pleadings) that he will
never return to her again:

> '*Revenés arier, biaus sire*' . . ./'Come back fine sir' . . .
> *mais por tot l'or de l'empire*/but for all the gold of the empire
> *ne fuisse tornes vers lors*/I would not return to her

> *Is é dúirt mo stór liom filleadh arís*/My love declared I should
> return again
> *Agus siúd mar a thréigeas féin mo bhuíon*
> *Agus nár chastar im shlí go bráth í*/And that's how I abandoned
> my loved one, and may we not meet again

Given the tight cliché-ridden nature of the genre, it is not at all surprising that *pastourelles* in any language rarely attain a satisfactory literary quality. Perhaps *Risteard Ó Bruineann* (D, p. 325) is the best of the few Irish compositions in this mode which have an element of poetic magic or stylishness about them. When sung to their own appropriate airs, however, nearly all of them impress as art-songs of a very high order.

Chanson De La Malmariée

The typical *chanson de la malmariée* generally speaking is also of little literary value. It is largely a woman's monologue on the unsatisfactory state of her marriage, and her desire for some younger man. Common motifs include the following: (a) she, a young woman, speaks (in the first person) of her anguish; (b) she blames her parents for marrying her off to an unsuitable - often aged - husband. (The description of the husband - especially in late medieval burlesque examples - can sometimes be unbelievably grotesque and ribald: he is humped, crippled; he coughs, grunts, whines at night; most of all, he is cold as lead, impotent, and completely fails to satisfy her desires); (c) she discloses that she is going to leave him for a young man (with whom she may already have an alliance); (d) she puts a malediction on her husband and wishes him a speedy death.

Gaston Paris traces the origins of the *chanson de la malmariée* to popular May Day festivals when the Queen routed her own husband, 'the jealous one', and sought a single man for herself.[21] Whatever of its archaic roots, the *chanson de la malmariée* was cultivated widely in France as a formal literary genre (composed inevitably by male trouvères) by the twelfth century. Only a few compositions of the type - albeit the earliest in date - are extant in Provençal. Northern Italy, which at the time was politically and culturally allied closely with France, seems to be the only other continental region where it was extensively cultivated. There is no evidence for its cultivation in thirteenth, fourteenth or fifteenth-century English, but there are a few burlesque examples in fifteenth/sixteenth-century English broadsides, in sixteenth-century Scots, and in English and Scots folksong. There are numerous examples of the ribald models in Irish literary and folk compositions, the most notable being the third monologue in Brian Merriman's *Midnight Court*. These models could have surfaced in Ireland at any period between the thirteenth and eighteenth centuries.[22]

The early trouvères, however, did not predominantly write burlesque or ribald *chansons de la malmariée*. They, in fact, sometimes put a very human lament for a failed marriage into the mouth of the young woman. A nucleus of such lyrics, 'An Pósadh Brónach' type,[23] is also extant in Irish folksong, but these are not found (to my knowledge) in early medieval English literature or in English folksong.

Other variants of the *chanson de la malmariée* were also practised by the trouvères and found their way to Ireland. For example debates between old husband and young wife, where she starkly tells him what she thinks of his prowess, are extant as far as I know only in the twelfth and thirteenth century French and in Irish folk and literary compositions. Another variant found in early French tells of the poet who wanders out one fine morning and hears two or three women debating their husbands' deficiencies. In Scotland, Dunbar (c.1460) has a version of this model, as has Eoghan Rua Ó Súilleabháin (1748–1784) in Ireland.

We find it curious today, perhaps, that learned poets in France, and indeed in Ireland, should have written lyrically of ideal love and at the same time should also have cultivated the bawdy versions of the *chanson de la malmariée* and the *pastourelle*. The poets themselves probably found this quite normal. Both ideal love and ribald lust were two sides of an imaginary poetic game they were playing in their disatisfaction with bourgeois marriage.

The Young Woman's Love-Lament

The greatest achievement of Irish folksong – perhaps, of most European folksong – is the young woman's love-lament. Some French scholars believe that the young woman's song, in general, is the oldest type of love-song extant in the Romance languages; it was, in their opinion, the most cultivated love-genre before the advent of the *amour courtois* type of lyric in the twelfth century.[24] It was clearly at odds, of course, with the purposes of trouvère and troubadour who in their *chansons d'amour* centrally placed the man rather than the woman in the predicament of ever-increasing desire and torment. Consequently, the learned poets did not to any great extent cultivate the young woman's song as a serious literary form, though they did exploit its themes in light dance-songs or in other popular compositions. On the other hand, the young woman's lament and other sub-literary love-models seem to have flourished widely in the new literary love-climate, so that French manuscripts of the fifteenth and sixteenth centuries are full of such compositions. And so also is French folksong.

It appears highly probable that themes associated with the young woman's song spread out from France to England and Ireland during the dynamic courtly love period (and that this material was itself in turn, influenced by the new male-centered courtly love themes). The Normans used its themes for their *caroles*. We know indeed that versions of the young woman's song were sung in English and in French to dance-tunes in Kilkenny in the early fourteenth century. At the same time it must be remembered that there existed already in Ireland, long before the Normans, a highly conscious and artistic tradition of the young woman's lyric – the only type of love-lyric, as far as we can guess from the remnants, which seems to have been cultivated in Ireland in the older period (600-1200 AD). So while it is likely that the twelfth and thirteenth-century international love-movement brought in its wake to Ireland and to England the young woman's song in popular form, it may be that Irish poets were already quite familiar with an analogous literary genre, and that a certain fusion of style and themes took place. It would appear from a thematic analysis, however, that the French or Norman-French models must have had an overwhelming influence on this type of lyric as we have it in our Irish folksong collections today.

The main themes and conventions of the young woman's love-lament (the principal type of the young woman's love-song), have proved quite durable and quite recognizable in a variety of western European cultures from Portugal to Ireland. The young woman speaks, in the first person, of the man she desires or loves; she may name him, praise his handsome appearance and his noble disposition. Frequently, he is gone from her, or about to go ('across the sea' quite often), leaving her abandoned in her anguish. He has made promises but is now false to her: he has deprived her of her virginity and may have left her with child; there is a suggestion sometimes of another woman on whose head maledictions are heaped. She sends him a letter, asks a bird to bring news of him, may imagine at night that her lover has returned – but on waking in the morning finds it was only a dream. Love for her is a dark burden to bear.

This is the common stuff of the young woman's lament which J.B. Entwistle in his *European Balladry* traces predominantly (with other types of women's love-song) to French origins. 'This preponderance,' he says, 'descends throughout all French literature and has spread into the other literatures of Europe.'[25] It has been pointed out, however, that some common motifs which occur in various European languages are not, in fact, extant in French literature or folksong. One of these mentioned by Alfred Jeanroy as occurring in Portuguese and Italian but not in French is:

Je n'ai point de batelier, et je ne sais pas nager.

(trans. Jeanroy from Portuguese)

I have no boat and I cannot swim.

The motif 'the sea is wide and I can't swim over' is, of course, common in Irish folksong, both in Irish and English:

Níl bád ná coite agam a chuirfinn 'do dhiaidh don Spáinn,
's go bhfuil an fharraige 'na tonna dearga, 's ni heol dom snámh.

(*Grá*, p. 103)

That this motif occurs in Irish as well as in Portuguese and Italian only serves to support the suggestion that the common language of dissemination was French. This and other motifs most likely made their way into

Irish folksong via French or English folksong or both.

One of the distinguishing features of western European love-song, both literary and folk, is that it has a common language of love, an 'amatory lingua franca'. Speaking of English folksong, Margaret Dean-Smith remarks: 'Alongside the crudities and vulgarisms of slang and the adroitly concealed but scorching double-entendre of many commonplace or innocent seeming folk-song texts there are innumerable instances of the metaphors, akin to mystical, chivalrous, and courtly poetry, elsewhere passed out of use'.[26]

As distinct from the man's bawdy *chanson d'aventure* type song, this amatory lingua franca is delicately deployed as a rule in the young woman's love-lament. Images and metaphors referring to gardens, flowers, fruit-trees, dew, birds, music, musical instruments, nearly always have sexual connotations. There are innumerable examples of such in late medieval French and in English and Irish folksong,[27] e.g.:

(a)   *My garden is over-run*
        no flowers in it grew.
            (English folksong; *Grá* p. 89)

        Tá an gáirdín seo 'na fhásach
        A mhíle grá bán, agus mise liom féin.
                (*Grá*. p. 89)

        This garden is a waste-land / dear loved one and I am alone.

(b)   *A ce poyrier y a ung fruict,*
        de le cueiller il est temps.
                (*Grá*, p. 89)

        On this pear-tree there is a fruit/it is time to pick it.

        Tá crann amuigh sa gháirdín le a bhfásann air sú craobh
        Ma baintear barr an bhlátha de ní fhásfaidh sé go héag.
                (*Grá*, p. 89)

        There is a tree outside in the garden on which raspberries flourish/if its flower is picked it will never grow.

(c)   *A maid again I shall never be*
        till an apple grows on an orange tree.
            (English folksong; *Grá*, p. 87)

        I mo mhaighdean óg ní bheidh mé go deo
        nó go bhfásfaidh úlla ar adharca bó.
                (*Grá*, p. 87)

A young virgin I shall never be/until apples grow on the horns of cows.

(d) The music motif is common to both the man's and woman's song:

Jouns nous deux de cette cornemuse.

(Grá, p. 89)

Let us both play on this bagpipe.

Tiocfaidh mo ghrá-sa le bánú an lae,
is seinnfidh sé port a's is tig leis é.

(Grá, p. 89)

My loved one will come with the dawn of day/and he will strike up a tune, as well he is able.

Despite the fact that it seems quite likely that songs on the model of the young woman's love-lament were mostly composed (as in other countries) by male poets, the woman's voice is vividly represented in them. The best of them have a poetic quality of rare distinction. In these generally one finds a dramatic stance, and a tendency to develop the poem creatively from situation to situation (which is perfectly in accord with our oldest literary tradition of the dramatic monologue). These songs are frequently more intense, nearer to life as lived, more assured in style, more finely structured than our other folk-lyrics. They are also full of that feeling for nature, that 'natural magic' which Matthew Arnold found to be a central feature of ancient Celtic poetry. A young woman, for instance, says to her lover:

Ní raibh id ghrá-sa ach mar a bheadh mám den tsneachta geal,
nó gainimh i dtráigh i lár na farraige,
nó feothan gaoithe thar dhroim na ngarraithe,
nó tuile thréan do bheadh t'réis lae fearthainne.

(Grá, p. 279)

Your love was merely a handful of white snow/or sand
on a beach surrounded by sea/or a gust of wind above
cultivated fields/or a stream, surging, after a day of rain.

Another young woman declares:

A stór má thagann tú, teara go caoitheamhail,
teara chuig an doras nach ndéanann aon ghíoscán.
Nuair fhiafrós m'athair dhíom cér dhíobh tú,
déarfa mé leis gur siolla den ghaoith thú.

(Grá, p. 281)

Love, if you visit me come at an opportune time/come to
the door which never creaks/When my father asks me
who has arrived/I'll tell him it was just a puff of wind.

Douglas Hyde published some remarkable examples of the young
woman's song in his *Love-Songs of Connaught*, a collection which was to
have a profound influence on Yeats, Synge and other writers associated
with the Irish literary renaissance. One of these lyrics, *Mo Bhrón ar an
bhFarraige* (*My Grief on the Ocean*) I have commented on elsewhere[28]
because of its beautifully achieved structure. Another finely created poem
is *A Óganaigh an chúil cheangailte* (D, p. 302) where the distance between
the girl's paean of ideal love is movingly offset at the end against the harsh
everyday reality. I give some verses of it in Hyde's own translation:

Ringleted youth of my love
with thy locks bound loosely behind thee,
you passed by the road above,
but you never came in to find me;
where were the harm for you
if you came for a little to see me;
your kiss is a wakening dew
were I ever so ill or so dreamy. . . .

I thought, o my love you were so
as the moon is, or sun on a fountain.
and I thought after that you were snow,
the cold snow on top of the mountain;
and I thought after that you were more,
like God's lamp shining to find me,
or the bright star of knowledge before,
and the star of knowledge behind me.

You promised me high-heeled shoes,
and satin and silk, my storeen,
and to follow me, never to lose,
though the ocean were round us roaring;
like a bush in a gap in a wall
I am now left lonely without thee,
and this house, I grow dead of, is all
that I see around or about me.

A few verses from the majestic *Dónall Óg*, a song known all over Ireland,
and in Gaelic Scotland as well, persuade us further that the line between
folksong and learned lyric is often a very fine one indeed:

Dónall Óg, if you cross the ocean
take me with you, and don't forget,
and on market day you'll get your present:
a Greek King's daughter with you in bed!

Last night late the dog announced you
and the snipe announced you deep in the marsh.
You were ranging the woods, out there by your self.
May you lack a wife until you find me!

You promised me (but you told a lie)
you'd be at the sheepfold waiting for me.
I gave a whistle, and three hundred calls,
and there was nothing but a lamb bleating.

A thing you promised, and it was hard:
a golden fleet with masts of silver,
a dozen towns, all market towns,
and a lime-white mansion beside the ocean.

A thing you promised, and it impossible:
you would give me gloves of the skin of fishes,
You would give me shoes of the skin of birds,
and a suit of the dearest silk in Ireland. . . .

It was on a Sunday my love I gave you,
the Sunday just before Easter Sunday.
I was on my knees as I read the Passion
and my two eyes sent you all their love. . . .

This heart of mine is as black as sloe
or a black coal in any forge
or the print of a shoe upon white halls
and a black mood is above my laughter.

You took my East and you took my West,
you took before and after from me,
you took the moon and you took the sun,
and I greatly fear that you took my God.

(D, pp. 289–93)

The stylishness of the language and the superb crafting of each individual
verse in *Dónall Óg*, as well as in many others of the woman's love-song
type, indicate that they emanate from some well-established medieval
literary tradition (though not from the learned bardic tradition).

The sense of moral anxiety revealed in the last line of *Dónall Óg* is rather
unusual. In general there is no equation between love-making and sin in

our folk-lyrics. A male poet defiantly says:

> Ní chreidim go bráth ó shagart nó ó bhráthair
> go bhfuil peaca ins an pháirt a dhúbladh.
>
> (D, p. 282)

> No priest or friar will I believe
> that its sin to couple in love.
>
> (D, p. 283)

The real sin as perceived by the young woman in her lament is not that
her lover has slept with her, but that he has abandoned her:

> Tuig, a mhíle stór, nach bhfuil ní sa domhan mór
> ná peaca ar bith is mó le déanamh
> ná maighdean bheag óg a mhealladh le do phóg
> agus fealladh uirthi go deo 'na dhéidh sin.
>
> (Grá, p. 286)

> Understand, my dear love, that there is no [evil]
>   deed on earth,
> nor any bigger sin to be committed,
> than to seduce with a kiss a maiden so young
> and to cheat on her forever after.

Other Genres

There are, several other examples of common European love-song types
which have found their way into Irish folklore. The *reverdie* – a variant
of the man's love song – has left a strong mark. This genre has been called
a *pastourelle* without the shepherdess, in that the woman the poet en-
counters in his spring morning adventure turns out to be a vision-woman.
In mood and structure the *reverdie* resembles popular Irish songs such
as *Fáinne Geal an Lae* (The Dawning of the Day).

On the other hand, the international type *ballad* has made surprisingly
little impact in Ireland, and curiously enough, whatever fragments of in-
ternational ballads that survive in Irish are concerned predominantly with
love-themes.[29]

Other love-songs in which the woman's voice is given prominence[30] in-
clude the *complainte* of a young woman for lack of a husband, various
chansons dialoguèes (a love debate for instance between a young woman

and her lover, or between a young woman and her mother), fragments of the *aube* and the *serenade*. It is intriguing to discover that the opening dialogue verse of *Éamonn an Chnoic*, a well known patriotic song, displays all the characteristics of the beginning of a mediterranean *serenade*, and that the popular drinking song *Tá 'na lá* contains as chorus a verse common to the *aube* where (as in *Romeo and Juliet*) the lover protests to the loved one that it is not yet day. The medieval French chorus line 'Est-il jors? Nenil encores' corresponds strangely with 'Chan fhuil sé 'na lá, a mhíle grá?'

All one can conclude with certainty about the origins of Irish love-songs is that the models for most of them established themselves in Ireland sometime after the Anglo-Norman invasion (1200–1600). Satisfactory thematic evidence to support this conclusion is found primarily in French (and Provençal) literary texts, and to a much lesser degree in English texts, both literary and folk. (There is a possibility, of course, that a much wider range of relevant English texts did at one time exist.) While transmission of thematic material through the medium of the English language is a possibility at all stages, the likelihood is, however, that the basic strata of love-song types and themes were transmitted predominantly through the French language in the immediate post-Norman period (1200–1400?). There are, as we have seen, many indicators which point to this – not least of them being the fact that the third Earl of Desmond (1338–1398), whose father wrote verses in French, composed some light informal *amour courtois* type verses in Irish which have undoubted similarities in tone and theme with modern Irish folksong.[31]

Irish love-song as we have it today emanates ultimately from the aristocratic medieval period when the prevailing ethic in matters of love and marriage in Ireland was, in many respects, non-Christian. Indeed even after the downfall of the aristocratic order in the seventeenth century, the strictures associated with modern post-Tridentine Catholic teaching on love and marriage only very slowly took root. 'Country marriage', a marriage-pact privately engaged in without benefit of clergy, was quite valid and possible in parts of Ireland down to the end of the eighteenth century.

While the basic models for much of our folksong may ultimately date back to the thirteenth and fourteenth centuries, most of those sung, or in our archives today, were, more than likely, composed between the sixteenth and eighteenth centuries. The composers of the best of them, one feels, must have been professional poets; poet-harpists, perhaps, of slightly lesser rank than the learned bards. In the Irish-speaking communities today those who sing or listen to these love-songs reckon a large number of them to be 'the great songs' ('na hamhráin mhóra'), the high artistic point of their literary and musical culture. This designation seems to refer, in particular, to the man's love-song, with its typically elaborate musical structure.

It is not easy to relate our love-songs to the lives of those who sang them in poor rural communities, where a rigid system of arranged marriage was the norm (even though one should remark, in passing, that the system was probably never as rigid as it appears, especially in pre-Famine days before the wide acceptance of new procedures relating to land inheritance). Peig Sayers (1873–1958), a traditional storyteller and reciter of songs, who even in extreme old age looked a remarkably beautiful woman, recounts how love and marriage came to herself on the wild west coast of Kerry: 'One night three men came in. . . . I couldn't make out which of them was trying to make a match with me, because I didn't recognise any of them. . . . My father came over to me. . . . "Will you go to the island?" . . . "I'll go wherever you want me to go" [I said]. "Good girl," he said.' It appears from another version of this story that Peig Sayers did indeed recognize the young man she was to marry and had in fact been attracted to him for some time previously. Whatever of that, one must concede that her first version expresses the expected attitude of a young Irishwoman of her time. At the same time, one suspects that the concept of ideal love she and her young husband inherited in their songs (and indeed in their folktales) was, despite some ambivalence, quite acceptable to them but practically impossible to imagine as having a central part to play in their own lives. Love as sung about, a near-magic event, did exist – but mostly for people of the nobler classes.

Much of our best love-songs, may be described in terms use by Richard Greene as 'popular by destination' rather than 'popular by origin'. A certain fusion took place, no doubt, in many of the song-types discussed here, of French and native stylistic traditions – both traditions having been originally shaped by literary classes who, in turn, mirrored aristocratic values. It seems clear, however, that the French tradition, however it was transmitted, overwhelmingly won the day. So much so that Irish people, on all levels of society, have been sharing with western Europe down through the ages a range of feelings and literary conventions about love – from the feeling that love is somehow a spiritual or ennobling event, to the kind of lingua franca, both delicate and bawdy, which one uses to describe it; from the detailed image in our imagination of what a beautiful woman should look like, to the *carole* form whose rhythms keep on dancing in our music and in our minds.

[1960]

PART III

EARLY MODERN IRISH POETRY
(1200–1600)

10

Background

NO WORTHWHILE LITERARY analysis has yet been made of most of the voluminous material in prose and verse written in the Early Modern Irish period (c.1200–1650). What is available of this literature in published form has been studied with most profit by linguists and historians.

It seems to be tacitly accepted that the Early Modern period – compared in particular, with the Old and Middle Irish period (600–1200) – produced little of aesthetic value. That is far from being true in my opinion. While a vast quantity of routine professional type of verse was composed in that period, a large and distinguished body of poetry was also produced – though admittedly even the best of this poetry lacks the lyric magic and the vibrant humanity one finds in the literature of the preceding Old and Middle Irish era.

Old and Middle Irish literature is arguably one of the great literatures of the world. The prose material – the sagas in particular – shows evidence of having been fashioned originally in a heroic society, probably in Gaul. Before being written down in Ireland, much of the prose and some of the poetry had probably been transmitted orally for several hundreds of years by the druidic order – professional priests, poets, historians, lawyers who were the custodians of literature both creative and non-creative. Following the introduction of Christianity and consequently of writing to Ireland, much of this material was recorded in manuscripts by monks in their monasteries or hermitages. That a number of these monks were also creative artists of a high order is attested, in particular, by the quality of the devotional and nature poetry written by them at that time. A classic precision, a dramatic immediacy, and an impressionistic verve are the hallmarks of this early Irish poetry, perhaps the greatest achievement of Irish civilization.

Things changed quite rapidly after the Anglo-Norman military invasion of 1169. In startling contrast with the older literature, much of what survives of Early Modern Irish literature appears at first glance to be a product of a most formalistic and conservative society. For several centuries after 1169, Gaelic Ireland, in perpetual conflict with a superior material culture, fights desperately to preserve itself; and in the effort of preservation tends to become conservative. The great work on illuminated manuscripts, and on precious metals, comes to an end; second-class Norman-Gothic becomes the main feature of the visual culture.

The conservatism of Irish society in this period is well exemplified by the institution of the Bardic School. With the collapse of the monastic schools, artistic authority passed again (c.1200–1300) into the hands of the lay-poets, successors to the ancient druidic order. From the school-system organized by such poet-professors emanated most of the surviving syllabic verse composed between 1200 and 1650.* The poet's principal function under this system became eulogistic; and most of his seven years rigorous training – in syllabic metres, Irish history and literature, Latin poetry and so on – was directed towards that end. Part of the poet's professional training was to learn a majestic mandarin-type language which remained the standard literary medium throughout Ireland and Gaelic-speaking Scotland for some four hundred years. When a young poet, always of a privileged hereditary 'poetic' family, had finished his apprenticeship, he normally seems to have found a position with one of the several hundred local 'chieftain/kings' or aristocrats who traditionally had given patronage to his ancestors. It has been frequently remarked that the service the bardic poet gave to his patron was not unlike that provided by modern journalists or public relations experts, to public figures and political parties. He was chronicler of great deeds, political commentator who eulogized and (on occasion) satirized his patron; and finally he was compiler of the requisite obituary notices. For this he was as richly rewarded as a best-selling author in our time. Payments for a poem might be twenty cows or twenty ingots of gold.

Poet-laureate praise poetry (and related genres) no matter how well-wrought, no matter how elegant in style, rarely makes for good art. The fact that a bardic obituary is in verse form gives no more artistic status to it than to the prose-obituary of a modern journalist; both types of obituary are best judged, generally speaking, by how well they fulfil their social function rather than by their artistic content.

---

*The classic description of bardic poetry is that of Osborn Bergin in *Irish Bardic Poetry*, pp. 3-22.

It is true that in a few isolated instances, a bardic poet (and indeed a poet of a later tradition such as Ó Rathaille or Haicéad) manages to develop in a praise-poem a personal creative insight, thereby transforming and recasting the traditional eulogistic material. But the risk of losing patronage by not properly conforming to the role allotted to them in Irish society must have actively discouraged even bardic poets of real quality from pursuing the near-impossible quest of shaping high art out of formal eulogy.

It is more than likely, however, that the view of Early Modern Irish verse as gleaned from extant Bardic poetry is a highly distorted or at least a partial one. It has to be borne in mind that our knowledge of the verse composed in this era is seriously circumscribed by the selective manner in which it was preserved in manuscripts; a substantial part of the verse surviving from that period is found in the private poem-books of the chieftains under whose patronage the work was composed. Furthermore, as noted by Katherine Simms, the extant verse is mostly from the end of the Bardic period: 'A higher survival rate from the end of the bardic period has meant that only half of the total, let us say a thousand poems, can be dated to a period earlier than 1566'.[1]

Given the limitations to our knowledge, no one can yet speak with great assurance of the scope and variety of Bardic verse. But it is almost certain that professional bards did also engage widely in varieties of occasional verse, in love poetry, in devotional poetry, in personal elegies and so on.* Whether they were encouraged in their schools to do so is unclear; but it is clear that many classic bardic poets, for instance Laoiseach Mac an Bhaird (c.1600), Eochaidh Ó hEodhasa (c.1600), Giolla Bríde Mac Con Mí (c.1260), Muiríoch Albanach Ó Dálaigh (c.1220) all produced verse which does not conform with the general stringent notion of professional school verse. Osborn Bergin remarks of the bardic poet: 'He might be a poet, too, if in addition to his training he was gifted with the indefinable power, that true magic of poetry'.[2] In fact quite a number of the bardic poets show in their occasional poems that they were capable of transforming their material into a truly poetic statement; so also do a variety of learned 'gentlemen' poets and other non-professionals, all operating – to a lesser or greater extent – within the bardic syllabic tradition. Until a comprehensive anthology of the best poetry of this era is compiled, we will not discover the extent of Ireland's contribution to the poetry of the later middle-ages.

[1995]

*Verse translation of some of this poetry is availabe. See, for instance, *An Duanaire*, pp. 2-57; *Kings, Lords and Commons*, pp. 57-89; *The New Oxford Book of Irish Verse*, T. Kinsella, 1986, pp. 87-110, pp. 125-67.

11

Love in the Medieval Irish Literary Lyric*

A ROMANTIC CONCEPT OF love does not seem to have played a large part in pre-Norman Irish literature. To judge by extant old Irish prose and verse, the heroic male rather than the loved heroine was the centre of the Irish literary universe up to 1200–1300 AD. In the old Irish prose-tales and sagas, especially in the categories called *Tochmarca* (Wooings) and *Aitheda* (Elopements), one indeed finds attention being paid to love-encounters; but the authors do not seem to be much concerned with the feelings of people in love. It is significant, however, that it is usually the woman – often a mythological figure – who pursues the love-affair. She is the aggressor, the risk-taker, the initiator of the love-contest. This is the manner, for instance, in which Déirdre encountered and conquered Naoise:

> Once when Naoisi was outside alone Deirdre slipped out to him as if she were going past him and he did not recognise her.
> 'That's a nice heifer that's going by me,' he said.
> 'Heifers ought to be big,' she said, 'wherever there are no bulls.'
> 'You have the bull of the province,' he said, meaning the King of Ulster.
> 'I'd choose between you,' she said, 'and take a little young bull like you.'
> 'No,' he said. 'Not after Cathbad's prophecy!'
> 'Are you saying that because you don't want me?'
> 'I am surely,' said he.
> She made a rush at him and grabbed his two ears.

*c. 1350–1650.

'Then two ears of shame and mockery on you,' she said, 'unless you take me with you.'

'Go on, woman!' he said.

'You'll have it,' she said.[1]

One does have fragmentary evidence in Old and Middle-Irish of the existence of a literary love-lyric attributed to women, but none at all of a man's love lyric. The woman's love-lyric was, in the opinion of some scholars, the most ancient form of love-song in the Romance languages, and seems to have been closely allied to folksong. We know nothing of folksong from the early Irish period. A likely assumption, however, is that if love-songs were in any way popular in the early Irish period, the most widespread type must have been the woman's song. In the few women's literary love lyrics and fragments that have survived from the early Irish period, there is a rare sophistication and – what is more important to our purpose here – a conception of an idealized personal love, as in this ninth-century lyric attributed to Liadan, a nun. Liadan, according to the story, was the love-aggressor: 'Liadan and Cuirithir were lovers, but Liadan resolved to enter a convent and Cuirithir then became a monk. She visited him in his cloister, *and he had to sail away from Ireland to avoid her* . . .'. This is her lament:

> Gain without gladness
>> Is in the bargain I have struck;
> One that I loved I wrought to madness.
>
> Mad beyond measure
>> But for God's fear that numbed her heart
> She that would not do his pleasure.
>
> Was it so great
>> My treason? Was I not always kind?
> Why should it turn his love to hate?
>
> Liadain,
>> That is my name, and Curithir
> The man I loved; you know my sin.
>
> Alas too fleet!
>> Too brief my pleasure at his side;
> With him the passionate hours were sweet.
>
> Woods woke
>> About us for a lullaby,
> And the blue waves in music spoke.

And now too late
>   More than for all my sins I grieve
That I turned his love to hate.

Why should I hide
>   That he is still my heart's desire
More than all the world beside?

A furnace blast
>   Of love has melted down my heart,
Without his love it cannot last.[2]

One finds in poems such as these, as well as in various passages in our prose epics, themes which we have come to associate with later medieval love-poetry: love hinders sleep; love wounds the heart, love is a sickness (which can waste even the mighty Cuchulainn to the brink of death); love can come in a vision or in a dream; love can be experienced for some one not seen (*grádh écmaise*); gazing at the loved one can be a sign of love. Furthermore, the descriptions of women in our prose epics such as *The Wooing of Étaín* and *The Destruction of Da Derga's Hostel* imply norms of beauty which surely suggest a certain adoration of ideal womanhood. For instance the famous description of Étaín in *The Destruction of Da Derga's Hostel*:

There was a famous and noble king over Erin, named Eochaid Fedlech. Once upon a time he came over the fairgreen of Bri Leith, and saw at the edge of a well a woman with a bright comb of silver adorned with gold, washing in a silver basin wherein were four golden birds and little bright gems of purple carbuncle in the rims of the basin. A mantle she had, curly and purple, a beautiful cloak, and in the mantle silvery fringes arranged, and a brooch of fairest gold. A kirtle she wore, long, hooded, hard-smooth, of green silk, with red embroidery of gold. Marvellous clasps of gold and silver in the kirtle on her breasts and her shoulders and spaulds on every side. The sun kept shining upon her, so that the glistening of the gold against the sun from the green silk was manifest to the men. On her head were two golden-yellow tresses, in each of which was a plait of four strands, with a bead of gold at the point of each strand. The hue of that hair seemed to the king and his companions like the flower of the iris in summer, or like red gold after the burnishing thereof.

There she was, undoing her hair to wash it, with her arms out through the sleeve-holes of her smock. White as the snow of one night were the two hands, soft and even, and red as foxglove were the two clear-beautiful cheeks. Dark as the back of a stag-beetle the two eyebrows. Like a shower of pearls were the teeth in her head. Blue as a hyacinth were the eyes. Red as rowan-berries the lips. Very high, smooth and soft-shining the shoulders. Clear-white and long the fingers. Long were the hands. White as the foam of a wave was the flank, slender, long, tender, smooth, soft as wool. Polished and warm, sleek and white were the two thighs. Round and small, hard and white the two knees. Short and white and rule straight the two shins. Justly straight and beautiful the two heels. If a measure were put on the feet it would hardly have found them unequal. The bright radiance of the moon was in her noble face; the loftiness of pride in her smooth eyebrows; the light of wooing in each of her regal eyes. A dimple of delight in each of her cheeks, with a variegation in them at one time of purple spots with redness of a calf's blood, and at another with the bright lustre of snow. Soft womanly dignity in her voice; a step steady and slow she had; a queenly gait was hers. Verily, of the world's women 'twas she was the dearest and loveliest and justest that the eyes of men had ever beheld. It seemed to King Eochaid and his followers that she was from the fairy-mounds. Of her was said; 'Shapely are all till compared with Étaín; dear are all till compared with Étaín.'[3]

Some of the feeling and thematic material in passages such as these, and in the women's love-songs, could quite naturally, one feels, be transposed into the later medieval type of man's love lyric. This is all the more probable when one considers that one of the women rapturously described in Irish texts (as far back as the eight century) is the vision-woman who identifies herself as the Sovereignty of Ireland. The later medieval Irish poet who formally made obeisance to the beauty of a flesh and blood woman might indeed be seen as merely exchanging one female sovereign for another.

The Courtly Tradition

Despite all this, however, it is indubitably true that medieval Irish learned lyrics (1350-1650), as well as Irish popular song, bear overwhelming evidence not of Old Irish influence, but of medieval continental influence. Even where it can be established that certain love themes existed already in Old Irish literature, when one encounters them again in post-Norman times (in both literary song and folksong) they seem to be fitted out anew in French or Provençal dress. For instance when one now comes on the theme of 'love as disease' all the symptoms are of the typical medieval European kind as described in the *Leys d'Amor* (*Grá*, p. 115). The lover can neither sleep nor wake, eat nor drink, distinguish heat from cold, wine from water. He spends his time sighing or crying (two activities which would have been anathema to Cúchulainn or indeed to any heroic personage in his love-ardour); but if he could manage just 'one kiss' – again a puny desire for a hero of older times – his cure would be complete. In the same way many of the medieval clichés describing a woman's beauty – the 'lily and rose' motif, for instance – supplant in our love-lyrics the older very lovely native metaphors or images, as found in passages such as that from *The Destruction of Da Derga's Hostel.*

Not until the post-Norman period does the Irish male poet become a love-lyricist. We know for certain, at any rate, that one poet in the fourteenth century, Gerald Fitzgerald, the third Earl of Desmond, composed light literary verses of love which were much of a piece with the 'semipopular' type of love-lyrics composed in aristocratic circles in France and England about the same time.

Gerald was born in 1338. He was made an Earl and married Eleanor Butler, daughter of the Earl of Ormond, in the year 1359. He was Lord Chief Justice of Ireland from 1367 to 1369 and died in the year 1398. Gerald was deeply involved in different strata of Irish life, from politics and administration to cultural and poetic matters. He was completely captivated, it appears, by the Irish poetic tradition; not alone did he compose a substantial opus himself in Irish, but he (and his family before him) gave continuous patronage to the most admired professional bardic poet of the age, Gofraidh Fionn Ó Dálaigh.

Some thirty-nine poems have been attributed to Gerald, most of which reveal a vibrant and outgoing personality; a man of Norman stock whose empathy with traditional features of Irish culture is quite remarkable. Two of his poems are particulary striking: one on the death of his wife, and one to the old hag who acted as guard in a prison where he was being held by a rival faction. Amongst his other poems are a handful of lovelyrics, which are clearly of the *amour courtois* tradtion. Gerald, as far as we know, is the first Irishman to compose verses which declare the poet to be in anguish, emaciated by his own sighs ('dam sheangadh tar éis m'osnaidh'), because of the absence of his loved one. His desire to be with her on an island or in an isolated place prefigures a theme and a tone which was later to surface in our popular love-lyrics (and to a lesser extent in our learned medieval love-lyrics):

> Dá mbeinn is mo chaoimhleannán
> in oiléan ar lár mhara
> ní ghéabhainn mar shaoibhsheachrán
> bheith ann faria go fada.
>
> (G, xvii)

> (Were I and my comely lady/on an island
> in the sea centre I would not think of it
> as wayward/to share her company a very
> long time.)

In another of his poems he sends a trouvère-type *salut d'amour* to his loved one; and in still another he sends a messenger – a typical *amour courtois* theme – to speak to her on his behalf. Furthermore he has a very graceful example of a renunciation-of-love poem, a type which became very popular later on in Renaissance love-poetry:

> Deachram feasta d'ionnraiceas;
> mithid bheith cunnaill céillidh;
> ní fada go bhfionnfaidhear
> mar do bhámar uair éigin.

> (*G*, xvi)

> (Let us from now on part in good
> faith/it is time to be sensible and
> discreet/quite soon it shall be dis-
> covered/what we were to each other.)

Gerald's love-poetry is not at all as studied or as conventional as the usual run of troubadour or trouvère verse. Nor is it as formal as most of those Irish learned love-lyrics which have been collected in one volume, *Dánta Grádha*, by T.F. O'Rahilly. It can be described rather as one of the types of 'semi-learned'/'semi-popular' love-lyric which seemed to flourish wherever the Normans imposed their culture, and of which the Harley lyrics (thirteenth and fourteenth centuries), and the poetry of Dafydd Ap Gwilm (c.1320-1370) seem to be other examples.

Dánta Grádha contains 106 poems in syllabic verse – only a small fraction, one thinks, of the number of learned love-lyrics composed in late medieval Ireland (c.1350-1650). The great bulk of those extant may belong to the sixteenth and seventeenth centuries. The poets generally are anonymous, but it is clear from their mastery of metrical techniques that a number of them were trained bards. Some fourteen poems are ascribed to well-known bardic figures of the sixteenth and seventeenth centuries, and about the same number to gentleman-poets of roughly the same centuries. The earliest ascribed poem is to Gerald, the Earl of Desmond (1338-1398). Over half the poems in the anthology emanate from the central *amour courtois* traditon of adoration of the inaccessible lady. Gaston Paris, who first coined the term *amour courtois,* thought of it as an ideal type of illicit love or desire governed by a certain code of courtesy which magnified the status of the inaccessible (married) loved lady and ennobled accordingly the poet who was in thrall to her in a kind of feudal relationship (*U,* p. 70).

Since then some literary commentators have been concerned as to whether there was any serious connection between life as lived and the code of courtesy to which the poets subscribed. Roger Boase who has, perhaps, written the most helpful analysis of the courtly love concept, says: 'Courtly love is inherently ambiguous. . . . Poetry is fictitious; it belongs to a world of make believe. . . . Courtly love was an expression of the play element in culture.'[4] The historian George Duby concurs: 'Courtly love was gratuitous, ludic, something apart from the serious things of life.'[5] Duby, however, does point out that the courtly love code had a central part to play in the new arrangements coming to the fore in France regarding marriage within the aristocratic feudal system (*U*, pp. 12, 84–85).

The lady we encounter in the more courtly and formal of the compositions in *Dánta Grádha*, is quite frequently the same ideal conventional lady we read of in the main stream of the *amour courtois* lyric. Her bodily beauties are innumerable; she may have 'green' eyes, white teeth, lily-white complexion tinged with red, a slender waist, round breasts, golden hair, and 'a slender eyebrow about which we fashion a poem'. For beauty, she is the sun itself; and the beauty of her mind is equally splendid. Because she is distant and inaccessible – either through being married or being of higher social rank – the Irish poet, using the feudal terminology of another time and place, gives her 'homage' and 'service' and pleads for 'mercy' from her.

Quite frequently, however, the lady to whom the Irish poet is in thrall turns out to be hard-hearted, shrewish, cruel, death-threatening – a feature which does not figure largely in the early troubadour and trouvère compositions. In regard to this, the French scholar Jean Frappier reminds us that the term *amour courtois* has been used to describe different strands of European love poetry from about 1100 AD to 1500 AD; more notably: 'la *fine amor* des troubadours, la galanterie chevaleresque des romans d'aventure, l'adoration mystique de Dante pour Béatrice, ou de Pétrarque pour Laure, les souffrances stylisées de l'amant martyrisé pour la belle dame sans merci dans la poésie lyrique des xive et xve siècles.'[6] It was in the fifteenth century, in particular, with the publication of Alain Chartier's *La Belle Dame sans Merci*, that the beautiful but cruel lady and her martyr-lover became dominant figures in western European love-poetry.

'La belle dame sans merci' and 'l'amant martyrisé' are also the dominant figures in our learned Irish love-lyrics. Other fourteenth and fifteenth-century features commonly occur as well: a poem may be sent to a loved one in the form of a letter; the name of the loved one (rarely if ever mentioned in earlier centuries) is disclosed in the form of an anagram or an acrostic. There are poems which are parodies of the love-malady, and there are poems which renounce love. The link between love and the moods of nature, so strongly emphasized in the early troubadour poetry, is practically non-existent as it is also in later European love poetry. It appears that the bulk of the poetry in *Dánta Grádha* can be described as fourteenth or fifteenth-century type *amour courtois*.

The question has to be asked, however (in view of the fact that both English and French had virtually died out as spoken languages in Ireland by the end of the fifteenth century (*U*, p. 81)) how this fourteenth and fifteenth-century thematic material reached Ireland. Did it come by way of French or English sources, or by way of both?

The evidence available at the moment does not permit a confident answer, but it seems most likely to me that the material reached us at various stages by way of books, manuscripts and *chansonniers*; mostly, perhaps, by way of French sources in the fifteenth century, mostly by way of English sources after that. There is strong evidence to suggest that the learned classes were frequently in touch with both France and England. A large number of Irish students studied in Montpellier and in Oxford; there was constant traffic of priests, friars and soldiers between Ireland, England, and the continent. We have very little information about what books were held in monasteries and big houses in medieval Ireland, but in one great house, the castle of Gerald the Earl of Kildare (1451–1513), we know that there was a good library of Irish, Latin, French and English books. It is noteworthy that French books were the more numerous, and still more significantly, it appears that only in the French collection were there love-lyrics of a kind which could have been models for our own *dánta grá*. These collections included *Le Jardin de Plaisance*, a much sought after anthology of love-lyrics which included work by Alain Chartier, Deschamps and other poets of the fifteenth century. Other French books in the library were the love-Bible of the middle ages, *Le Roman de la Rose*, as well as *Le Tryumph de Damez*, *Le Brevier de Nobles*, *A French boke in parchement*, *A boke of Farsses in French*, etc. *Troilus* was the only book in English in which the material related to *amour courtois*. It is not unlikely then that French remained the prestige foreign language of love-poetry in fifteenth-century Ireland. Of course, French did remain the legal language of the English state in Ireland until the final quarter of that century.

Fifteenth-century western European *amour courtois* tends to be much more conventional than the classic *amour courtois* of the twelfth and thirteenth centuries. The cruel *dame* and her martyr-lover become boring cyphers. The conventional love-material – three hundred years a growing – proves too heavy a burden for the run-of-the-mill poet, whether he be French, English or Irish. It is not surprising then that many of the more formal lyrics in Irish are somewhat trite, a little leaden. But so is the bulk of professional *amour courtois* verse everywhere. 'Suirghe an cheard do chleachtamar', says one poet: 'wooing was the craft we practised'. And indeed one is persuaded that most Irish poets understood absolutely what their fellow-poets abroad took for granted: that the notion of ideal love was basically a game, an elaborate social code to be adhered to in verse – if not in life. There is in their work much more evidence of the feudal and philosophical vocabulary of love than in our folksong, but not at all as much as in, say, English courtly love-poems of the fifteenth century. The idea of the ennobling effect of love is understood rather than articulated. The major conceptual concern is possibly with the idea of love as death, or wasting sickness – a concept, one notes, which was not at all alien to the composers of old Irish sagas.

Even in the less interesting of our learned love-poems, however, one often perceives an epigrammatic or dramatic tone of voice, one of the new native Irish dimensions of *amour courtois*. Consider for instance, the poem *Uch, fa-ríor* (*DG*, no. 68) which echoes some of the ordinances of the medieval *Leys d'Amors*. These laws describe inter alia the contradictory sensations a person in love should feel: 'one feels sharp cold when it is warm, and an overwhelming heat when it is cold', etc. (*Grá*, p. 115). The Irish poem, in the main, is merely an epigrammatic gloss on this notion e.g.: 'Alas, alas!/I can't distinguish water from wine,/I can't distinguish day from night/woe to him whose disease is eternal love.' Before the end however, the anonymous poet reverts to archaic pre-troubadour notions about love: 'Alas again/that I have not a charter on her cool skin,/a woman of the accomplished fairy-host of Aodh Fionn/has deprived me of sleep.'

Uch, fa-ríor is an undistinguished poem; by and large, none of the clichéd matter has been transformed into a poetic insight. But the style itself (in the original poem) is quite brisk and workmanlike, moderately efficient: one line in particular (quoted above) has a John Donne 'metaphysical' type of imaginative daring about it: 'alas again/that I have not a charter on her cool skin'. It is instructive to note how the native literary tradition has tempted the poet into identifying his lady love, not as a beautiful flesh and blood chatelaine but as a vision-woman of the *sidhe*. So the continental and native stylistic and imaginative traditions intermingle. The influence of the native vision-literature is widespread; perceptible, also, is the influence of the native storytelling tradition, as well as that of bardic praise-poetry. And while our poets readily accept the international mythological love-figures of Venus, Narcissus or Absalom, they are quite happy to see Irish mythological love-figures, Déirdre, Gráinne, or Diarmaid, cheek by jowl with them. Robin Flower has this to say of the particular intermingling of traditions which took place in the *dánta grá*: 'It is thus without any surprise that we find them sharing this peculiar art of love-poetry with that other aristocracy of alien conquest or tribal right. . . . In this happy union the aristocrats of position contributed the subject, the aristocrats of art the style. By their intermediation the matter of European love poetry met the manner of Irish tradition. And in these poems we see how perfect was the fusion, how happy the result.[7]

As Robin Flower suggests, what does distinguish medieval Irish love-poets – even the dullest and most fatuous of them – from the main body of French or English love-poets of the same period, is their fine feeling for style. This stylistic flair had stemmed from one of the oldest and most refined literary traditions in western Europe, and had been cultivated meticulously in different genres by the bards throughout the entire medieval period. One rarely encounters the solemn aureate tone so familiar in English or continental love-poetry of the fifteenth century; one hears rather the finely-edged epigrammatic, dramatic or 'metaphysical' voice which in the midst of triteness may quite nonchalantly proclaim: 'alas that I have not a charter on her cool skin'. Syllabic verse, as developed by the Bards, was a stylistic instrument of great delicacy and potentiality.

There is in *Dánta Grádha* a substantial number of conventional lyrics which succeed by style alone. These rarely contain fresh insights into love, or new moods experienced by lovers; rather they depend on stylistic *brio* and intellectual agility to give fresh expression to threadbare themes. The following poem, for instance, provides a teasing lighthearted version of *la belle dame sans merci* which has to be admired for its professional adroitness:

> She's my love,
>   who only gives me trouble;
>   although she has made me ill,
>   no woman serves me as well.
>
> She's my dear,
>   who breaks me and doesn't care;
>   she yawns when I take my leave,
>   O she won't grieve on my grave.
>
> She's my precious,
>   with eyes as green as grass is,
>   who won't touch my bending head,
>   or take presents for caresses.
>
> She's my secret,
>   not a word from her I get;
>   she's deaf to me as the skies,
>   and never lets our eyes meet.
>
> She's my problem
>   (strange, how long death takes to come),
>   this woman won't come near me,
>   still I swear, she's my loved one.[8]

On the other hand, there is also a surprising number of formal 'courtly' poems where style merges magically with artistic insight. Some of these deserve recognition as being amongst the most elegant love-poems in medieval literature. It is worth glancing at a representative sample of them.

Dónal Mac Cárthaigh, first Earl of Clancarty, (fl. *c.*1540) is the author of *Och! och! A Mhuire bhúidh* (*DG*, no. 30), in which conventional *amour courtois* material is handled with aplomb. This translation by Frank O'Connor, although straying at times quite far from the original, captures much of its lyrical quality:

> My grief, my grief, maid without sin,
>> Mother of God's Son,
> Because of one I cannot win
>> My peace is gone.
>
> Mortal love, a raging flood.
>> O Mother Maid,
> Runs like a fever through my blood,
>> Ruins heart and head.
>
> How can I tell her of my fear,
>> My wild desire,
> When words I speak for my own ear
>> Turn me to fire?
>
> I dream of breasts so lilylike,
>> Without a fleck,
> And hair that, bundled up from her back,
>> Burdens her neck.
>
> And praise the cheeks where flames arise
>> That shame the rose,
> And the soft hands at whose touch flees
>> All my repose.

[Her perfectly shaped limewhite body/has robbed me of my senses. The sweetness of her voice and speech/has wasted me away.]*

> Since I have seen her I am lost,
>> A man possessed,
> Better to feel the world gone past,
>> Earth on my breast;

* This stanza is omitted by O'Connor.

> And from my tomb to hear the choir.
>   The hum of prayer;
> Without her while her place is here,
>   My peace is there.

[The song of her mouth/as sweet as incense/Has
maddened me to death/What better reason?]*

> I am a ghost upon your path,
>   A wasting death,
> But you must know one word of truth,
>   Gives a ghost breath –
>
> In language beyond learning's touch
>   Passion can teach –
> Speak in that speech beyond reproach
> The body's speech.[9]

The material being handled here by the Earl of Clancarty is the main fifteenth-century *amour courtois* theme of the lady who brings about the 'death' of her love. Seeking spiritual comfort he confides his trouble to the Blessed Virgin in the first two stanzas; in the last two stanzas he pleads directly with his own earthly 'virgin' to succour him with her 'body's speech'. In the main section of the poem he tells how his unspoken love brought about his destruction.

In describing his love the poet has recourse to the conventional catalogue of the lady's beauties. He adds to them, however, what seems to be a very personal observation that 'the sweetness of her voice and speech' was a major cause of his malady, and he further imagines in an extended piece of native imagery other voices, monks, singing at his own burial. All this finally prompts him to emphasize that what mostly is causing his love-death is the musical voice of the young woman – a voice as sweet as the incense wafting over a dead body.

This is the point where the original insight of the poet finally breaks through the hallowed conventional material. We now sense in the poem the very voice of the lady, whose formal beauties only had been mentioned previously. And, in compensation for his 'death', he pleads now for the healing speech of her body. The word in Irish 'comhrá' (i.e. conversation) which is translated above as 'speech', is common shorthand in folksong for sexual intercourse.

There is a personal passionate pulse in this poem which one does not usually expect in formal *amour courtois*, and the rhapsodic accentual flow of the original verse – which is not the norm in syllabic poetry – tends to intensify the underlying mood. It is not too fanciful to imagine it being

---

*This stanza is omitted by O'Connor.

recited, to the accompaniment of a bronze-stringed harp, in the great hall of the McCarthy Castle in Blarney, County Cork.

One hundred years or so later, another poet intimately acquainted with the refinements of castle-life, Piaras Feiritéar (*c.* 1600–1653) wrote a series of poems of friendship to men and a series of love-poems to women. He seems to have been influenced by the Elizabethan and/or Cavalier poets of the sixteenth and seventeenth centuries and may, in fact, have written in English as well as in Irish. In *Léig dhíot th'airm* (*Lay your weapons down*). Feiritéar is also concerned with the *la belle dame sans merci*, but in this case, as in some English poetry of the same era, she is imagined as wielding her bodily beauties as if they were dangerous weapons. Shakespeare (who wrote: 'Her pretty looks have been mine enemies . . ./. . . but since I am near slain/kill me with looks, and rid my pain')[10] would have been quite at home in Feiritéar's world of love weaponry:

> Lay your weapons down, young lady.
>   Do you want to ruin us all?
> Lay your weapons down, or else
>   I'll have you under royal restraint.
>
> These weapons put behind you:
>   hide henceforth your curling hair;
> do not bare that white breast
>   that spares no living man.
>
> Lady, do you believe
>   you've never killed, to North or South?
> Your mild eye-glance has killed at large
>   without the need of knife or axe.
>
> You may think your knee's not sharp
>   and think your palm is soft:
> to wound a man, believe me,
>   you need no knife or spear!
>
> Hide your lime-white bosom,
>   show not your tender flank,
> For love of Christ let no one see
>   your gleaming breast, a tuft in bloom.
>
> Conceal those eyes of grey
>   if you'd go free for all you've killed.
> Close your lips to save your soul;
>   let your bright teeth not be seen.

Not few you have done to death:
   do you think you're not mortal clay?
In justice, put your weapons down
   and let us have no further ruin.

If you've terrified all you want,
   lady who seek my downfall.
now – before I'm buried in earth –
   your weapons, lay them down.

What your surname is, young lady,
   I leave to puzzle the world.
But add an 'a' or an 'é'
   and it gives your Christian name away . . .

                (*D*, pp. 97-101)

The voice in this poem is not in any way similar to the glowing warm
lyric voice of the Earl of Clancarthy. The poet speaks coldly, abruptly, to
the lady as if she were a soldier in a hostile army, blocking his way. In
early *amour courtois* the lady's eyes were frequently seen as death-dealing
weapons, but here her breast, her flank, her rounded knee, her curled hair,
the palm of her hand, are all life-threatening. From head to toe she is,
in fact, dressed to kill, a cavalier in the hostile army of love.

The manner in which the poet extends a traditional image of *la belle
dame sans merci* is very impressive indeed; his strong links with some
of the military activities in the seventeenth century wars and uprisings
may, of course, have conditioned him to develop this feeling of love as
armed conflict. One misses in this poem, however – as well as in his other
love-poems to women – a certain intimacy of tone which one finds in
his poems of friendship to men. It has been suggested that Feiritéar was
a homosexual; if true, this may help to explain why his best poem, *Léig
dhíot th'airm*, owes its creative energy to what seems to be an underlying
coldness to the female sex.

Quite often our poets take just one element of the conventional *amour
courtois* material and completely transform it. Here, for instance, the typical
troubadour theme of love for a married woman – expressed by 'one kiss'
– is posed in a new and starkly simple way:

Keep your kiss to yourself,
   young miss with the white teeth.
I can get no taste from it.
   Keep your mouth away from me.

I got a kiss more sweet than honey
   from a man's wife, for love,
and I'll get no taste from any kiss
   till doomsday, after that.

Until I see that same woman
   (grant it, gracious Son of God)
I'll love no woman young or old
   because her kiss is - what it is!

(D, pp. 3-5)

The imagination at work here again, as in some of the best of our lyrics,
is a dramatic imagination. The young lady, who proffers a kiss, is spoken
to harshly and directly by the poet as if in the presence of an audience.
This imagined situation gives way to the memory of another kiss 'sweeter
than honey' given to him by a married woman. The whole focus finally
is on the durability of that kiss, and of his love for the married lady 'ós
í a póg atá mar atá'. This durability is emphasized not alone by the
authoritative hammer-beat of the last three words, but also by the poet's
confidence in invoking the help of the Son of God to aid him bring his
adulterous pursuit to fruition.

A theme which occurs in fifteenth and sixteenth-century semi-popular
verse (in France, at any rate) is that of the poet who cannot manage to
be alone in the company of his loved one. This theme appears in a few
of our *dánta grá*, imagined situationally. The best of these poems is one
by the seventeenth-century Scottish poet Niall Mór Mac Muireadhaigh,
where a new dramatic dimension is added to the traditional material: the
poet's discomfort is greatly magnified by the thought of the secret joys
of love-making experienced by him the previous night. He feels trapped,
isolated, surrounded by watchful people. Only his eyes can speak to her,
and when they do, they speak in the popular terms used by lovers in the
international aubade: 'Keep for me this night again . . ./oh go put out
the sun my love / let not daylight in so fast'. The contrast between the spon-
taneous singing quality of these lines, and the taut dramatic quality of
the preceding verses, creates an unusual passionate surge towards the end:

Farewell last night; 'tis bitter pain
to see it dimly thus receding:
if I were to hang for it -
I would it were again commencing.

There are two within this house to-night
whose looks of love betray their secret;
tho' lips may neither speak nor kiss,
eyes - pinpointed - are fiercely meeting.

Good sense demands restraint
on the roaming glances of the eyes;
what good the silence of the mouth
if the eyes reveals its love.

Alas, across this jealous throng
no phrase or word of mine can reach you:
but list to what my eyes are saying
to you, apart, in silence seated:

'Keep for me this night again
would that it might forever last,
oh go put out the sun, my love,
let not daylight in so fast.'

Mary, nurse and mother mild,
Queen of poets and minstrelsy,
hear me now and take my part –
farewell last night, most enviously.

The final courtesy stanza once again invokes supernatural help to aid the lovers in their carnal desires. This time, however, the poet looks to the Virgin Mary for miraculous intervention, mirroring on one hand the Irish bardic tradition of appending a final stanza in praise-poems in honour of the lady of the house (and in religous poems in honour of the mediatrix, the Virgin), and on the other hand the *chanson d'amour* tradition of the poet's appealing to Christ/God to bring his adulterous love to its proper fruition. It is doubtful if a better single example could be cited for the fusing in our lyrics of Irish and European features.

One of the most unexpectedly beautiful of all the poems in *Dánta Grádha* is *A bhean fuair an falacháin* (O lady duly veiled) (*DG*, no. 13). Because of its paean in praise of the loved one's hair, Robin Flower has said: 'This might well be the praise of Étaín out of fairy-land'. At first glance this poem is the kind of ornate praise-poem to which many modern readers will react negatively. It contains puns, learned references, high rhetoric, but, at the same time, one senses a true poetic sensibility behind its baroque framework. I give it here in a near-literal prose translation:

O lady duly veiled/I see about your threadfine tresses/
something which puts to shame/the hair of Absalom son of David.

On your radiant waved hair/lies a flock of curls (birds) in debility;/these birds (curls) do not give voice,/yet they have troubled every man.

Your long ringletted fair locks/reach down about your lovely eyes:/the round crystalline eyes/are like precious stones in a setting.

A new fashion you have embraced/wherever its place of origin,/your hands without the appointed ring,/and a hundred rings about your throat.

> Your soft yellow hair has looped / right around your erect neck; / that
> throat (prisoner) is encompassed by rings, / a prisoner (throat) it is quite
> truly.

'Praise of the lady's hair' is a common feature in Irish eulogistic literature,
both in old Irish and modern Irish. Eighteenth-century poets such as
Eoghan Rua Ó Súilleabháin cultivated it inordinately. There is no other
poem to my knowledge, however, where the poet manages with such com-
plete success to use his praise of the lady's hair as the true *objective cor-
relative* of his personal love for her.

In the first stanza a general courtly statement is made: the hair of Absalom
(a common image in *amour courtois* love-poetry) cannot match the beau-
ty of his loved one's hair. From this statement emanate four images which
gradually intensify our perception of what all this means to the poet: in
the first image (the most alien one perhaps to modern readers) her head
is imagined as being covered by a flock of *ringlets* = birds (a recurring
pun in Irish literature), which, though they do not sing, have caused anguish
amongst men; in the second image her hair is a transformational device
which, reaching down over her eyes, causes them to glow like jewels in
a *ring*, in the third image her hair is testimony to a new fashion – though
no *ring* (bracelet?) adorns her hand, there are a hundred *rings* (of hair)
about her neck and shoulders; in the fourth image the hair, with its
multiplicity of *rings*, has twined itself around her neck – she is entwined,
a prisoner, in the rings of her own hair.

It is the poet, of course, who is really imprisoned in the rings of the
lady's hair. And were it not for this feeling of a captive poet's adoration
of his lady (as well as the reference to Absalom) one would not think
of applying the term *amour courtois* to this poem. The raw material of the
poem has been dictated mostly by bardic praise-poetry; the love-philosophy
by the spirit of *amour courtois*; the artistic sensibility by an anonymous
poet of, perhaps, the sixteenth century.

Amongst the aristocratic composers of love-poems, Mánas Ó Dónaill,
chief of Tír Chonaill, deserves special mention. Five poems are attributed
to him in *Dánta Grádha* (nos. 49–53). Three of these are very much con-
ventional *amour courtois*, but the two other lyrics, which are infinitely better
poems, are quite difficult to place in context.

Mánas is thought to have been born around the year 1490 – some hun-
dred years after the death of Gearóid Iarla, some hundred years before
the birth of Piaras Feiritéar. When, in the year 1510, his father departed
for eighteen months on a pilgrimage to Rome, Mánas took responsibility
for the territory of Tír Chonaill. Later on, in 1526–1527, he had a splen-
did castle built for his use at Lifford, County Donegal; and in 1532 he

dictated a vast absorbing prose work *Betha Colaim Cille* (The Life of Colm-cille), which is mainly based on material collected for him, from oral transmission and from manuscripts, by a group of scholars. He spent much of his life in conflict with his father, and when he died in 1537, Mánas became chief of his clan and engaged continually in national and inter-national politics. From about 1548 he seems to have been in conflict with his own son, An Calbhach, who got the whip-hand when Mánas suffered ill-health in 1555. Mánas died in his castle in Lifford in 1563 and was buried in the Franciscan cemetery in Donegal.

Mánas was widely known in his time for his charm and extravagant per-sonality. A modern historian has dubbed him 'Manus the Magnificent', considering him to have had the stature and attributes of a Renaissance prince (*U*, pp. 37-40). He certainly cut a princely figure the day he came by river in a rowing boat to parley with Lord St Leger, wearing 'a coat of crimson velvet with aglets of gold, twenty or thirty pair; over that a great double cloak of right crimson satin, girded with black velvet; a bonnet with a feather, set full of aglets of gold'.

On the political front he was quite astute, managing by a combination of diplomacy and military action to maintain the independence of his ter-ritory. He took a major part in the Geraldine league – 'Gaelic Ireland's first organised resistance to the Tudor state' (*U*, p. 38). He cultivated trade and political links with France and England. It is reported that when on a visit to the King's palace in Scotland he was accompanied 'by a right sober and learned young man' who had been reared in France. He was much involv-ed with the French-speaking order of the Observantine Franciscans who settled in *Tír Chonaill c.*1480. He himself founded a new monastery; the Franciscans seemed to have considered him in every way a major patron.

Mánas was a patron of poets in particular, and was known for his own gifts as poet and witty versifier. His three mainstream *amour courtois* poems, (*DG*, nos. 49, 50, 51) are however, dull, relying over much on a conscious play on a theme which was common-place both in formal and semi-popular love-poems in France from about the fifteenth century on. This was the notion that the lover had lent his heart (soul) to his lady love. It appears that one, at least, of these poems refers to a central episode connected with the Geraldine league.

When the rebellion of Silken Thomas Fitzgerald (1534–1535) petered out and seven of the Geraldines were put to death on the Tower of London, Eleanor Fitzgerald (daughter of the Earl of Kildare, at Maynooth) took her son (the remaining Geraldine heir), firmly under her wing and joined with other Irish aristocrats in the Geraldine league in an effort to save him. Mánas Ó Dónaill at this stage was a widower (his wife Siobhán having died in 1535) and he persuaded Eleanor that the best protection for the young Geraldine would be that she should marry himself and live in Tír Chonaill. She agreed to the marriage in the same year (1537) that Mánas became Chief of his clan. By 1540, however, when the marriage did not suit the political purposes of Mánas (and perhaps of Eleanor), the young Geraldine was put on board ship to France, and Eleanor returned to Maynooth.

It is reasonably certain that it was during his courtship of Eleanor that Mánas composed *Cridhe so dá ghoid uainne* (*DG*, no. 49). He refers in one verse, to his difficulty in giving his heart to the Earl's daughter because his own heart is full of sorrow (since the death presumably of his wife Siobhán): 'A pity the Earl's daughter/has not a loan of my heart/so that she would realize the impossibility/of winning over a heart full of sorrow'. This personal pain, admittedly, gives a slightly new dimension to a well-worn theme, but it does not manage to bring substantial creative life to the rather cliché-ridden poem in its entirety. Two of his other poems (nos. 50 and 51) are still more conventional in their declarations of love.

On the other hand both *Cridhe lán do smuaintighthibh* (*DG*, no. 52) and *Goirt anocht dereadh mo sgéal* (*DG*, no. 53) are lyrics that reveal a highly individual poetic sensibility. Some heartrending separation is at the core of *Cridhe lán do smuaintighthibh*:

> A heart full of turmoil/is my fate at separation,/no man is so arrogant/that a woman does not deprive of intellect.

> Sorrow like the growth of a vine/has been my life for sometime past,/no shame on me my black despair/since I am encompassed now by ghosts.

> It is the parting of a bird from spring-water,/or the quenching of the bright sun,/my parting with wearing sorrow/after the friend of my heart.

While there is some difficulty in interpreting one or two lines of the original text, it is clear that this poem is full of the hurt of separation or departure. In stanza I the poet's heart and head have been separated by the woman's (?) departure; in stanza II the depression caused by separation has grown 'like the growth of a vine' (leaving the poet open, perhaps, to the eerie feeling of having departed the material world for ghostly territory?); a separation which cannot happen, i.e., his own separation from deep sorrow after the departure of his loved one, is the main mood of stanza III – this is as impossible to imagine as that a bird should forsake spring water, or that the sun might be quenched.

There are none of the clichés or attitudes associated with *amour courtois* in this poem; one notes, in particular, that the love-genre 'Renunciation of love/Separation of lovers' leaves no mark.[11] The poem, indeed, seems more an elegy on the death of a lover than any lyric declaration of love at separation. If so it is likely to be a poem on the death of his wife Siobhán, a poem which imaginatively and movingly builds up the mood of a separation which will never end.

Goirt anocht dereadh mo sgéal is also a poem which owes little, one thinks, to the *amour courtois* tradition:

> My story bitterly ends this night -/most strong men are ultimately laid low -/even if Dian Céacht were living still/the wounds of my flesh he could not cure.
>
> My sorrow truly knows no ebb -/a full sea over headland surging -/the damage wreaked on me by pain/was nothing at all until now.
>
> I have finally found out, alas/that wine rarely comes without the lees;/ sorrow is a bitter lotion/corrosive to the bitter end I think.

The bitter hurt the poet feels is developed in this poem through its imagery of wounds, sea, and the lees of wine. Only in the last stanza, in fact, do we realize that the bitterness emanates from some happy circumstance in the poet's life having now ended: 'wine rarely comes without the lees'. We do not know, however, what happy era in the poet's life has ended. What we do discern is that the wounds inflicted are so grievous, that, even if Dian Céacht (the mythical doctor) were alive, he would fail to cure them. The poem could well be, indeed, another elegy by Mánas on the death of Siobhán, his wife.

If these two poems by Mánas are indeed love-elegies, they are in no way exceptional within the Irish tradition.

The Anti-Courtly Tradition

About a half of the poems in *Dánta Grádha* stem from the mainstream courtly tradition. The rest may generally be labelled anti-courtly in that their authors, while conversant with courtly love ideals, either ignore or reject them. (A small number of the poems, in fact, could more properly be termed 'non-courtly' in that it is not clear if their authors were conscious in any way of the philosophy of *amour courtois*).

A large section of the anti-courtly verse tradition is comprised of poems of satire and ridicule. Irony is their major characteristic, about which Robin Flower, writing of Irish literature in general, made one of his most perceptive judgements: 'There has always been in the Irish nature a sharp and astringent irony, a tendency to react against sentiment and mysticism, an occasional bias to regard life under a clear and humourous light. This could easily be illustrated from the older epic tales . . . and from Mac

Conglinne to Merriman the light of this inexhaustible irony plays upon Irish life and letters. We miss the point of much in the literature if we forget this.'[12]

It would be rather rash, however, to attribute the large ironic or humourous vein in our *Dánta Grádha* to the Irish tradition alone. The truth is that irony, humour, ridicule – in the goliardic vein – are valid component parts of the international courtly love movement: 'the integral connection' according to one critic 'between satire on women and courtly love.'[13]

In his book *Burlesque et Obscénité chez Les Troubadours*, Pierre Bec remarks: 'La plus grande aventure lyrico-érotique du Moyen Age, celle des troubadours, commence par un contre-texte . . . gaillard et truculent, subversif et iconoclaste. . . . Nous avons sans doute des troubadours une image trop angélique.'[14] This 'contre-texte' reveals itself even in the earliest Provençal love literature. The first recognized troubadour, Guillaume IX (1071–1127) wrote not only some bawdy love-poems but also a series of compositions which could be said to be seriously at variance with court- ly philosophy. Only a small number of his poems can properly be regarded as being imbued with the spirit of *fin amor*, the most idealistic type of *amour courtois*. While most succeeding Provençal poets did cultivate *fin amor* to an inordinate degree, satiric love-poetry continued to flourish in their work as well as 'une sorte d'infra-littérature'. The 'contre-texte' was at its strongest in Provençe in the thirteenth century. From about the second half of the fourteenth century, well into Renaissance times, anti- courtly love poetry flourished in northern France and England.

One cannot claim then that Irish poets were in any way the pioneers of certain kinds of satiric love-poetry. They did however, accept and develop various strands of it in an unique and dynamic way. They are absolutely at ease with the connection between love and satire; they often feel a genuine need to puncture any feeling or idea they find over-solemn or romantic. The 'amant martyrisé', for instance, is a favourite whipping boy. One poet says 'Christ why should I die (of love)/when women are available to me alive' (*DG*, no. 9).

F.L. Utley in his book *The Crooked Rib* discusses the various types of satiric love-poems in English literature.[15] He lists nine examples of poems from the fifteenth and sixteenth centuries 'in which the disconsolate lover's malady allows him to sleep and grow fat' and thirteen examples of 'parody defence and the satirical panegyric of one's lady'. *Dánta Grádha* offers an abundance of this kind of thematic material. One poet declares (*DG*, no. 8) that love has kept him in perfect health and disposition:

> I have preserved my flesh and my blood. . . ./I eat my fill, I soundly sleep,/I constantly enjoy music of all kinds.

Similarly an English poet declares:

> I am sorry for her sake,
> ye may wel ete and drynke;
> Wann ye slepe ye may not wake
> so muche on here ye think.[16]

The satiric eulogy of the lady's beauty is found at least as far back as Hoccleve in English and Deschamps in French (*U*, pp. 42-43), who described their loved ones thus:

> Grosse de corps, ronde comme une pomme;
> (Deschamps, fourteenth century)

> Hir comly body shape as a foot-bal;
> and she syngith ful lyk a pape-jay. (Hoccleve, fourteenth century)

The sixteenth century (?) Irish poet, Riocard de Búrc, is not very demanding either (*DG*, no. 5) of the conventional marks of beauty: 'I find it no fault if she is dark and yellow/I love all women when they are swarthy'. De Búrc reckons, in fact, that the only defect any lady can have is advanced years, but then he finds them 'young at forty'! This kind of extravagant ridicule is grist to the Irish mill. It is not often accompanied, however, by an individual artistic insight.

The most interesting and most artistically developed of the Irish anti-courtly poems are those which Utley labels 'Renunciation of Love' (or loved one). This theme seems to have become popular internationally from about the fifteenth century onwards. 'Je me repens de vous avoir amée' a French poet says; 'I lothe that I did love' an English poet says; 'I exchanged my love for hate' an Irish poet says (*U*, p. 43). The feelings dominating such statements are sometimes ironic or humorous; on occasion, however, the viewpoint put forward seems to be, sincerely and unambiguously held.

Irony rules openly in one of the better known of our poems of renunciation, *Ní bhfuige mise bás duit* (*I will not die for you*) (*DG*, no. 99) where the courtly adoration of the loved one is turned topsy-turvy. The poet lists the conventional beauties of the lady, which might affect inane lovers but not the Irish poet who has been weaned away from romantic nonsense:

> I will not die for you,
>   lady with swanlike body.
> Meagre men you have killed so far,
>   and not the likes of me.

> For what would make me die?
>   Lips of red, or teeth like blooms?
> A gentle hand, a lime-white breast?
>   Should I die for these?

Your cheerful mood, your noble mind?
    O slender palm and flank like foam,
eye of blue and throat of white,
    I will not die for you.

Your rounded breasts, O skin refined,
    your flushed cheeks, your waving hair
- certainly I will not die
    on their account, unless God will.

Your narrow brows, your hair like gold,
    your chaste intent, your languid voice,
your smooth calf, your curved heel
    - only meagre men they kill.

(*D*, pp. 7-9)

Three of the poems of 'renunciation' are of unusual quality: *Meabhraigh mo laoidh chumainn-se* (*DG*, no. 95); *Cumann do cheangail an corr* (*DG*, no. 81); *A bhean lán do stuaim* (*DG*, no. 100).

There is no irony in *Meabhraigh mo laoidh chumainn-se*. The poet's hurt pride because of his lady's falseness, and his desire to separate from her, are presented in a measured graceful manner, reminiscent in tone and metre of the poem by Gearóid Iarla discussed above:

Take my song of love to heart,
    lady of the lying love:
you and I from this time on
    must endure each other's loss.

If you hear them talk of me
    in the cottages or the big house
don't discuss me like the rest.
    Don't blame me or defend me.

In the chapel, in the abbey,
    the churchyard or the open air,
if we two should chance to meet
    don't look, and I won't look at you.

You and I, we mustn't tell
    my family or Christian name.
Don't pretend, and I won't,
    I ever looked at you before.

(*D*, p. 5)

Concealed behind the facade of this simple lyric lies a well developed artistic statement in which one of the basic theories of *amour courtois* is employed in a novel manner. One of the fundamental tenets of ideal love states that it is by proper use of the senses that love is attained. One version has it thus: 'Looking, addressing, touching, kissing, then love. Unless you shun touching the act of love is bound to follow' (*U*, p. 46). The poet here deploys the antithesis of this. If the different senses in turn can be employed to bring love to fruition, these senses being gradually withdrawn can, on the other hand, spell the end of love. So in the first stanza the poet declares an end to bodily contact; in the other stanzas speaking (to each other, or of each other), looking (at each other), are not to be envisaged so that the poet can finally say:

> Don't pretend, and I won't
> I ever looked at you before.

Given that it is through the eyes that love is initiated in the philosophy of *amour courtois* the last two lines imply that the erstwhile lovers should act in future as if no love ever existed between them. With the withdrawal of the senses the separation is complete, love is dead.

Cumann do cheangail an corr also treats of false love, but in a throwaway ironic fashion. While it is not a very profound statement on the theme, it has a certain stylistic elegance about it and a lively teasing quality:

> They tied the loving knot: a crane
>   and the fox from Brí Ghobhann.
> The fox vowed to the crane
>   their knot would never break.
>
> Unwise, in a wilderness,
>   to cleave to such a mate. . . .
> When he's been fasting a while
>   put not your trust in William.
>
> The crane soon fell asleep.
>   he caught her by the throat;
> I won't go on. In short,
>   he parted her head from her body.
>
> Know it was she who did it –
>   and goodbye to my ladylove!
> She the fox and I the crane,
>   and our loving much the same.

> (*D*, p. 7)

Animal stories, *fabliaux*, were popular with medieval European writers and scholars. Generally speaking these stories were recounted and valued for the moral lessons which could be learned from them. I know of no other poet, however, who used the genre, as this poet does, to tell of his personal love-affair. The affair is narrated symbolically in three swift stanzas, ending up with the fox's decapitation of the crane. The ironic personal twist occurs where, unexpectedly and untraditionally, the lady is identified as the fox and the poet as the decapitated crane: 'She the fox and I the crane/and our loving much the same'. A bittersweet real life love-story may well lie half-concealed beneath these four stanzas (*U*, p. 47).

Some use of a sense-withdrawal technique may also be present in the magnificent *A bhean lán do stuaim*, but otherwise the poem is difficult to relate to any of the *amour courtois* models of the love-lyric. It has been ascribed to the priest Séathrún Céitinn (an ascription difficult to accept in light of the mediocrity of his other verse-compositions):

> O lady full of guile,
>   take away your hand.
> Though you sicken for my love,
>   I am not an active man.
>
> Consider my grey hairs.
>   Consider my slack body.
> Consider my tired blood.
>   What is it you want?
>
> Don't think I am perverse.
>   You need not tilt your head.
> Let's love without the deed
>   for ever, spirit slender.
>
> Take your mouth from mine:
>   grave is your condition.
> Touch not skin to skin
>   – the heat leads on to lust.
>
> Your branching curly hair,
>   your eye as grey as dew,
> your sweet pale rounded breast
>   excite the eye alone.
>
> All deeds but that of the flesh
>   – and lying in your quilt –
> I will do for love of you,
>   o lady full of guile.
>
>   (*D*, pp. 87-89)

Unlike the usual practice in courtly love poems, here it is the woman who seduces and the male who refuses. The man claims he is too old to love but still does not wish to risk sensual contact: 'Touch not skin to skin/–the heat leads on to lust'. He obviously accepts that lust is morally wrong (a concept at variance with the philosophy of *amour courtois*) as are 'all deeds' of the flesh. Consequently even though there is no mention of 'sin' or of 'the afterlife' in it, *A bhean lán do stuaim* seems to reflect to a limited degree the concerns of *memento mori* poems of the Catholic Counter-Reformation – didactic poems on love of which there are a few examples in *Dánta Grádha* (nos. 98, 102, 105, 106). Such poems can sometimes contain a catalogue of the lady's beauties in true *amour courtois* style only to emphasize at the end that everybody, including the lady, will end up as 'food for worms' (*DG*, no. 98).

It has been suggested[17] that the type of situation envisaged in certain sixteenth-century English poems dealing with the theme of 'The Aged Lover Renounceth Love' may have been the major influence on the author of *A bhean lán do stuaim*. This may well be; it is also possible that Céitinn's (?) poem echoes a traditional situation in Irish literature in which the priest or saint refuses a woman, as did Daniél, Abbot of Lismore, in the ninth century.

Whatever of the fragments of traditional or contemporary morality underlying its poetic mood, *A bhean lán do stuaim* is in the final analysis, a unique love-poem: a poem in which the poet, in stark anti-courtly fashion, refuses carnal love to a lady while proclaiming in courtly fashion his ideal love for her; a poem in which sensual pleasure is denounced, yet is awash with sensual feeling. It is true that some of the early troubadours and trouvères maintained that love without the sexual act was the ideal kind of love, but I know of no poet in the *amour courtois* tradition who refuses sex to his lady. It is difficult to imagine that there are many other poems in world literature so majestically poised between lust and love. The poet manages in stately measured lines stripped of rhetoric, to denounce and magnify human love, at the one time, in the one poem.

There are quite a few other anti-courtly compositions in *Dánta Grádha* which are difficult to discuss in the context of *amour courtois*. At least three of these (*DG*, nos. 92, 93, 94) are concerned with ridiculing jealous husbands. Ideal male love is not the issue here:

> O jealous one, go risk the shower,
> get out about like all mankind;
> and if you wish to be at ease –
> cease to probe your wife's mind.

> Whatever pain of it will come
> she needs must be a woman first;
> she is a hired hand of love's,
> she is not mistress of herself.

and again:

> You're jealous of your wife?
> a curious plight you're in:
> if you realised aright
> you'd leave your melancholy.
>
> A shapeless surly wife
> has rarely wrecked a home;
> strange as it may seem –
> your wife is still your own!
>
> There you stand on guard
> in secret misery
> shielding your wife's charms:
> a fence without a field.
>
> Not one in many thousands
> lives as safe a life
> from sharp and wagging tongues
> a-scandalling his wife.
>
> So if all the world should come
> to swear she's been untrue –
> no need to flee the land:
> she knows no bed but yours.

Romantic female love is satirized more pointedly still in a poem (*DG*, no. 11) by Laoiseach Mac an Bhaird (*c.*1600), a prolific professional poet who is mostly known as a scholarly composer of formal bardic verse. At first glance this poem, *Tuirseach sin, a mhacaoimh mná*, might appear to be another of his routine professional compositions. But the following Frank O'Connor translation of it – while not quite achieving the mock-scholarly tone of the original manages to highlight its underlying playful ridicule:

> Really, what a shocking scene!
>   A decent girl, a public place!
> What the devil do you mean,
>   Mooching round with such a face?

Things can't really be so bad,
    Surely someone would have said
If - of course the thing is mad,
    No, your mother isn't dead.

Sighing, sniffling, looking tense,
    Sitting mum the whole day through:
Speaking from experience
    I can guess what's wrong with you.

Roses withering in the cheek,
    Sunlight clouding in the hair,
Heaving breasts and looks so meek -
    You're in love, my girl, I swear.

If love really caused all this
    So that looks and grace are gone
Shouldn't you tell me who it is?
    Even if I should be the man.

If I really were the man
    You wouldn't find me too severe,
Don't think I'm a puritan,
    I've been through it too my dear.

And if you'd whispered in my ear:
    'Darling, I'm in love with you'
I wouldn't have scolded, never fear;
    I know just what girls go through.

How does it take you, could you say?
    Are you faint when I pass by?
Don't just blush and look away -
    Who should know love if not I?

You'll be twice the girl tonight
    Once you get it off your chest;
Why - who knows? - you even might
    Win me to your snowy breast.

Make love just the way that seems
    Fittest to you, 'twill be right.
Think of it! Your wildest dreams
    Might come true this very night.

That's enough for once, my dear
    Stop that snivelling and begin:
Come now, not another tear -
    Lord, look at the state you're in.[18]

The inventive dramatic flourishes employed here are reminiscent of the techniques used by certain comic dramatists, Oscar Wilde, for instance. A simple commonplace situation is imagined, and in a swift series of situational transformations becomes a matter of open laughter. It is doubtful indeed if many other poets in their love-lyrics have managed to say, so nonchalantly and so outrageously, to their female friends:

> Why – who knows – you even might
> win *me* to your snowy breast.

Outrageous in another sense, is the poem *A bhean na lurgan luime* (O bare-shinned woman) (*DG*, no. 97) by another professional bard Mac-con Ó Cléirigh. This is a highly vindictive piece on the poet's wife, or so it seems. The tenor of his ugly, highly effective (comic?) diatribe – which is wholly, one thinks, in the Irish satiric tradition – is maintained throughout the poem in lines such as these: 'Your aged physiognomy hard as iron/resembles nothing human'. Amongst our *Dánta Grádha*, it is difficult to find any other poem so remote from idealized love.

Amour Courtois: National/International

In one sense the concept of *amour courtois* is indefinable. We have seen a French scholar pointing to four different manifestations of it in European literature. The Irish *dánta grá* can probably be seen as adding still another dimension to the European models. The influence of Irish praise literature – which catalogued in minute detail the features of the lady's body from foot to hair – is omnipresent. Satiric and vision-type literary traditions also leave a heavy trace. It is, however, in its general imaginative stance and in its stylistic energy that an identifiable Irish voice reveals itself. One finds little in this voice of courtly obeisance or solemnity, such as one finds in the work of Chaucer or Charles d'Orleans. The voice is an intimate and homely one, which speaks to us suddenly and dramatically – often in a very sensual tone:

> Let me share your quilt, o gentle slender one/let us lay down our bodies side by side. (*DG*, no. 45)
>
> Do not sit beside me in that fashion/do you not see we are observed. (*DG*, no. 39)
>
> Keep your kiss to yourself. (*D*, pp. 3-4)
>
> I would much prefer to an earldom/to plunder your virginity. (*DG*, no. 32)

Dangerous to have revealed in my presence/your throat and rounded breasts. (*DG*, no. 32)

It is clear that the distance between poet and lady in the majority of our *dánta grá* is unique, Irish, different. That this is so is symptomatic, no doubt, of what happens when any international movement makes an impact on a strong individual national culture. The merging of literary traditions, in particular, is a reflection of the merging of two different sets of cultural values, attitudes, social structures.

Given what we know of society in Ireland in the middle ages, one cannot imagine the Provençal *fin amor* ideal of the adorable but unattainable lady being treated with unmodified solemnity. One has to remember, first of all, that the Irish professional poet himself was one of the very privileged people in that society. He was feared and respected: 'the poet was a sacred personage, almost a priest or magician'.[19] Legally he ranked as high as a 'petty' king – whose bed he might share. One cannot imagine him or, indeed, some of the lesser ranked poets, as suppliants in the sense their continental counterparts often were.

Then again sexual affairs in Gaelic Ireland were ordered in a way which must have particularly discouraged the cultivation of ideal romantic love. The Christian ideal of monogamous marriage – which, according to George Duby[20] was to a large extent accepted in principle, if not in practice, by French aristocrats from the beginning of the thirteenth century – had made very little impact on Gaelic aristocratic society right down to the seventeenth century. A modern historian has written:

> In no field of life was Ireland's apartness from the mainstream of Christian European society so marked as in that of marriage. Throughout the medieval period, and down to the end of the old order in 1603, what could be called Celtic secular marriage remained the norm in Ireland and Christian matrimony was no more than the rare exception grafted on to this system.[21]

The secular ('Celtic') system of law permitted – to the Gaelic privileged classes at any rate – polygamy, divorce and certain 'incestuous' relationships. Marriages were rarely celebrated in churches. Priests and bishops were frequently married (or were 'living with concubines' in the eyes of the Roman Catholic church). Children born out of wedlock were not thought to be illegitimate, or unfit to be priests or bishops. (Fr Canice Mooney informs us that at least eighteen bishops in the sixteenth century in Ireland were born out of wedlock.)[22] Travellers – some friendly, some hostile – from Raimon de Perelhos in 1398 to De Tocqueville in 1835, report Irish men as 'amorous', 'much given to whoredom'; and Irish women as not being especially conscious of the need for 'modesty' and reticence in matters of dress and behaviour.[23]

It is reasonable to assume then that up to 1634 (the year the British parliament passed an act forbidding polygamy amongst the Irish), Irish Gaelic society was structured in a way that was far removed from the western European norm. Love poems emanating from societies differently struc- tured will of necessity display different assumptions, different tonalities, different distances at which one plays (or denies) the game of love. It is more than probable at any rate that the Irish noble lady could not be thought of – from the poet's point of view – as having the same inaccessibili- ty as the wife of a feudal lord in France or Provençe. The daily pattern of Irish life, especially its sexual mores, must account to a great extent then for the homely intimate voice and the open sensual feelings we find in the *dánta grá*.

Allowing for peculiarly Irish variations – and sometimes even transfor- mations – of theme and tone it is very clear that the European medieval love-movement made a startling and profound impact on the learned Irish literary tradition (as well as on the folk tradition). No matter how sophisticated the older tradition of love in Pre-Norman Ireland had been, not alone do we now encounter in our poetry new thematic material, new tonalities, new images, but more significantly we experience a new revolutionary concept of love which (as J.M. Cohen says of the medieval love-lyric in general) 'reversed the habitual relations of the sexes'.[24] Ideally now man replaced woman as the adoring one, the tearful one, the sub- missive one, in Irish as well as in western European literature. Like most ideals, of course, including those of Christianity, the new concept made only spasmodic impact on real life, in Ireland as elsewhere.

It is probably true to say, of course, that at a rather simple general level *amour courtois* was no new concept in Ireland, or indeed in several other countries, even non-European countries. Peter Dronke has written: 'the feelings and conceptions of *amour courtois* are universally possible'; 'we find (in ancient Egypt) the characteristic thought and feeling of *amour courtois*'.[25] But so also one could argue that a variety of dynamic philosophies – from existentialism and romanticism to Christianity, na- tionalism or socialism – were not entirely new concepts in their time. 'Movements,' says Frank Kermode, referring to literary movements, in particular, 'are never as new as they look; it is one of the duller laws of literary history'.[26] One should add that defining the philosophy of such movements so as to take account of their varied manifestations is well- nigh impossible. It would not be feasible, for instance, to reconcile, in a definition of Christianity, Christ's teaching on loving one's enemy with the actions of the Roman Catholic inquisition in Spain.

The major factor, I would guess, in the creation of a new exciting love-dynamic in Provençe c.1100 was that an aristocratic feudal society (with certain problems about the codifying of the laws of marriage and property) came into intimate contact with Arabian love-poetry and philosophy, with its glorification of the inaccessible noble lady.[27] It was this particular ideal concept of love, especially that element in it of *amor purus* – identified by some of the early troubadours as unsatisfied sexual desire – which, in my opinion, energized the whole love-movement; a love movement which occurring at a crucial point in the evolution of Provençal and western European society in general fused together or gradually took under its wing a multitude of disparate love-themes and attitudes.

During the centuries in which the new philosophy of love was developing and changing a new Europe was coming into being. The Romance languages were emerging, universities were being founded, heresies were spreading, the Gothic arts began to flourish (as did also popular entertainments such as carol-dancing). A new western European sensibility was being created. A vital part of that complex western European sensibility was the Provençal feeling of an idealized love which, though 'ludic' in nature, envisaged a new possibility for living, to be approved of or reacted against.

The strength of this new feeling in western Europe may be gauged by many criteria, not least the extent to which it made an impact on Irish medieval literature which is often seen as a product of the values and life-style of an archaic and conservative aristocratic society. On one hand the Irish poet – at whatever level of professional expertise – functioned as composer of eulogy, satire and elegy precisely as he had done in heroic times; on the other hand he composed a most un-heroic type of sentimental poetry, the Irish version of *amour courtois*.

While the medieval Irish poet did not in any way enjoy the level of daily living enjoyed by many of his counterparts abroad, he did produce in his own society a literature of love which would be difficult to surpass for its elegance and refinement.

[1988]

PART IV

OCCASIONAL

12

Some Highlights of
Modern Fiction in Irish

WHEN ONE SPEAKS of the collapse of literature in Irish in the nineteenth century, one is mainly speaking of the collapse of the poetic tradition. The prose tradition had for long been of much less significance: one could even say with some truth that real creative prose-writing in Irish had died out after the twelfth century. Whatever of that, it is true at any rate that the novel – or the drama – had never made any worthwhile impact on the Gaelic literary tradition until just at the point where it seemed that the language itself was doomed to extinction. And so it was that in *The Gaelic Journal (Irisleabhar na Gaeilge)* in 1894 was published what one may call the first novel in Irish: *Séadna* by Father Peadar Ó Laoghaire. One may conveniently date the beginnings of all modern literature in Irish to the foundation of the *Gaelic Journal* in 1882; the first period lasting from 1882 to 1939, the second period from 1939 to the present day.

Séadna was highly thought of in its own day both as a work of literature and a textbook for learners of Irish. P.H. Pearse declared on its publication in book form in 1904: 'Here at last is literature.' Douglas Hyde in 1920 spoke of its uniqueness in the canon of European literature. Nowadays, however, it is suffering something of an eclipse. Some modern commentators are inclined to view it as a folktale, denying it the nomenclature and status of 'novel'. It can be very convincingly argued, however, that *Séadna* is no folktale but a very creditable folk-novel, far removed from the few pages of oral narration on which it is based.

The basic story is the international type folktale (on which *Faust* is based) of the man who sells his soul to the devil. Séadna, the principal character, is no magniloquent Doctor Faustus; rather he is an ordinary rural Irish shoemaker who finds himself trapped in Satan's clutches due to a minor indiscretion. With a little supernatural aid, and a great deal of native cunning, he finally releases himself from his evil pact. The three hundred page story ends with his departure from his native district into what seems to be some sort of purgatorial state.

The writing in *Séadna* is somewhat uneven: it contains some *longueurs* and a few awkward passages, as well as many beautiful stretches of lucid folktale type narrative. But what is most impressive is the manner in which the author, while observing the folktale conventions, manages to sustain a complete development of theme and character from beginning to end. The gullible easy-going shoemaker who appears in the initial pages gradually gives way to the wiser and more finely tempered character, who sharpened by his ordeal, departs the final scene. This is precisely the kind of development one does not get in a folktale, where all character is static.

Fr Ó Laoghaire in his voluminous writings never again achieved the creative level reached in *Séadna*. It is probable that the main reason for whatever success he had in *Séadna* was that the only mode of narration he felt comfortable with was the traditional folktale which he had inherited naturally by his own fireside. His efforts at more orthodox novel-writing or fiction were consequently a failure.

A much more conscious *littérateur* was Galway born Pádraig Ó Conaire, who appeared on the scene as short-story writer in the early decades of this century. Influenced by French and Russian masters, his ideas about the function and uses of literature would have been anathema to the author of *Séadna*, as indeed they would have been to the mass of Irish people until quite recently. In an essay written in 1908 he stated:

> The objective of the writer's art is to move the human heart. . . . They realise that horror and wonder still exist, as they have existed from the beginning of time . . . that their own hearts are as strange as any wonder that has existed . . . that man himself is the source of all wisdom and the soil of all wonder. . . . When (modern continental) writers emerged from the pit in which they were excavating they held something smeared and dirty in their hands which had the shape of a human being . . . and they cried out: this is man! this is the human being! this is the truth! But little attention was paid to them for some time. It was thought that the smeared and dirty shape they held was too ugly to be man.[1]

In his short stories Ó Conaire succeeded, to some extent, in giving form to the ideas expressed in his essay; and after him (and Pádraig Pearse) the short story became the prose form most expertly used by writers of Irish down to our own day: Liam O'Flaherty, Máirtín Ó Cadhain, Donncha Ó Céileachair, Tomás Bairéad, Séamas Mac Grianna, and so on. Where already there was a magnificent oral tradition of short tale-telling, and where publishing outlets were mostly in small magazines, this development of the short story was virtually bound to take place once a writer such as Ó Conaire had made such a promising start. Consequently, despite the praise lavished on *Séadna* in its own day, the novel took a back seat from the beginning in the revival of literature in Irish.

Ó Conaire himself, however, did produce one novel *Deoraíocht* (Exile), a fascinating attempt to tell a story situated on the fringes of circus life in London through the medium of Irish. There is undoubtedly in this short work the feeling of seedy living, minutely observed and experienced; but one doubts if the author manages to discover an appropriate style to give credibility to this rather grotesque tale of the love affair of the hero with the fat woman in a circus.

It can be said that a major difficulty – if not *the* major difficulty – encountered in their work by the authors of *Séadna* and *Deoraíocht* was the absence of a novel-writing tradition in Irish; an absence of stylistic models to guide, or to react against. This difficulty was to manifest itself again and again in later decades. The gradual introduction of Irish as an essential school subject in the twenties and thirties naturally required, as a corollary, the rapid production of suitable reading material. One of the aims of *An Gúm*, the government publications office established in 1926, was to encourage native speakers of Irish to produce modern novels for students as well as for general readers. Most of the novels emanating from this policy left – as one might expect – a great deal to be desired. The models, consciously or unconsciously followed, seem to have been in most cases those of the English love-novelette or adventure story. *Caisleáin Óir* (Golden Castles) by Séamas Mac Grianna, and *Ceol na nGiolcach* (Music of the Reeds) by Pádraig Óg Ó Conaire are two of the more genuine achievements of that period, both authors making special efforts to recapture the talk and life-style of the Donegal and Connemara Gaeltachts respectively. But here again, although these writers tried to keep their eyes on life as lived, the convention of the love-novelette finally defeats them: both novels contain a hero and heroine as pure and white (and static!) as alabaster, who have an abiding sentimental love for each other, who are more sinnned against than sinning, more acted against than acting – in short no relation to human kind!

There are a few other novels from the first period of our Gaelic literary renaissance which require special mention. Foremost amongst these is *Cúrsaí Thomáis* (The Story of Tomás). First published in 1927, it was written by Eamonn Mac Giolla Iasachta, the author of several other novels in Irish and English, and well known (under the English equivalent of his name, E. McLysaght) as a historian and genealogist. *Cúrsaí Thomáis* is, without doubt, one of the most authentic pieces of novel-writing, in Irish or in English, to come out of the Irish countryside during this period. Situated mainly in Irish-speaking west Clare, it tells in diary form of the adventures of the vagabond Tomás from the time of his return from Canada until he inherits the farm he works on from his friend and employer Stíofán Mac Conmara. The novel traces in easy conversational style the development of Tomás's relationship with various members of the community until he finds himself obliged to leave. He then makes for Dublin and the dissolute life (the least convincing part of the narrative), until finally he is enabled to return, with great relief, to his beloved farm in West Clare.

For us today *Cúrsaí Thomáis* is in some ways an awkwardly written old fashioned novel with no profound insights, yet one experiences in the main body of the work the feeling of a real world inhabited by recognizable characters. The small-farm background is clearly and lovingly observed, with situation and character naturally evolving from it. In short there is good organic interdevelopment of the basic storytelling elements which many more pretentious novels never attain.

Another novel worthy of critical note is *An Druma Mór* (The Big Drum), by Seosamh Mac Grianna, the more talented younger brother of the author of *Caisleáin Óir*. Written in the 1930s it has only recently been published (the long publication delay being apparently due to *An Gúm's* overcautious approach to a possible libel action.) The main theme of the book is a politico-cultural one, which even forty years later has a fascinating ring of truth about it. It concerns the machinations in a small Donegal community, before the founding of the Irish State, as to who would control 'The Big Drum' – the local name for the pipe and reed band – in the annual St Patrick's Day procession. 'The Big Drum' probably represents symbolically – though not quite successfully – the cultural soul of the community which is being fought over by different political interests, principally the Ancient Order of Hibernians, the Friendly Sons of St Patrick and Sinn Féin. Of these, Sinn Féin finally wins the day, thereby quenching the ambitions of the main character and anti-hero, Proinnsias Bheagaide, one of those mealy-mouthed gombeen-type politicians who have kept on emerging down to our day in Irish rural communities.

An Druma Mór – viewed as a product of Irish writing in the 1930s – reveals the emergence of a writer of astonishing potential and refinement. As the work stands, however, one doubts if it can be accounted as a satisfying novel: its conceptual basis is not realized artistically; a world in which the events happen and in which the reader can believe, is never established stylistically. A major factor here once more is the lack of a credible traditional narrative convention for this type of literary opus. The narrative style alternates disconcertingly between saga, burlesque and a more naturalistic type writing, leaving the reader hanging uncertainly between different levels of fantasy and realism. The undoubted impact which Mac Grianna could have made on any of these levels is accordingly lost.

The most lasting achievement of Irish literature in the 1920s and 1930s was not in the field of storytelling but in autobiography (veering sometimes, it must be said, towards the autobiographical novel). Such autobiographies were a natural result of the investigation of learners of Irish into Gaeltacht speech and traditions. Native speakers of the language were encouraged to write (or often to dictate) their life stories. From all parts of the Gaeltacht have since flowed scores of autobiographies or books of memoirs describing in rich colloquial style different aspects of life in those western rural communities which have inherited the magnificent Irish poetic tradition, and which are still, to a large extent, influenced by medieval concepts and practices. There is scarcely a single one of these books which has not got immense value as a social and as a linguistic document.

From the Blasket Islands, in particular, has come a handful of autobiographies which by common European standards are *sui generis*. Books have frequently been written about isolated communities – generally, however, by people on the outside, or by members of the community who became writers and were not bound by the daily routine of life in their communities. These Blasket Island books to which I am referring, however, have been written/dictated by serving members of this highly-cultured but nonliterate community. Everything in them is reported from the inside, with very little reference to outside standards of living, of belief, or of writing. (The only vaguely comparable series of books known to me is that by Indian chiefs describing their ancestral life before the white man's conquest.)[2]

Three of the Blasket books are rightly regarded in Ireland as classics: *An tOileánach (The Islandman)*,[3] *Peig*,[4] *Fiche Blian ag Fás (Twenty Years a-Growing)*.[5]

Fiche Blian ag Fás, the more immediately attractive of these three books, is by Muiris Ó Súilleabháin, who received more formal education than the others, and who left the island ultimately to become a civic guard. Despite this, the book is all of a piece with the general run of Blasket books. E.M. Forster, in his foreword to the translation – which by now has run to, at least, six editions in World Classics – has expressed his astonishment at the magic and authenticity of this book: 'here is the egg of a sea-bird – lovely, perfect, and laid this very morning'.

A few passages, in translation, may give some idea of the book's quality.
Ó Súilleabháin here tells of a dream he had about his friend Mickil:

> After a while it seemed Mickil fell asleep. I was looking at him, he snor-
> ing fine and easy. While I sat thinking what a strange thing was that
> same sleep, what would I see come out of his mouth but a pretty white
> butterfly. It began to walk down over his body. . . . Down went the but-
> terfly through the meadow, I after it, ever and ever, till it came to an iron
> gate. It began to climb the gate, from bar to bar, slowly and easily, I watch-
> ing. When it came to the top of the gate, down it went on the other side.
> . . . It came down into another meadow where there was an old skull
> of a horse which looked as if it had been there for years. In went the
> butterfly through the holes of the eyes, I watching intently.
> It must have been five minutes before I saw it coming out again through
> the mouth of the skull. Back it came to the gate, up each bar and down
> the other side, just as it had done before, then up through the meadow,
> I following it ever and ever till it went back into Mickil's mouth.[6]

And here is the last page of the book where the author tells of his return
to the island after two years' absence:

> When we came into the quay in the Blasket I thought I would never
> reach the house.
> 'Oh King of Angels', cried an old woman, 'isn't it a fine man you have
> become!'
> 'Musha how is every bit of you?' cried another.
> 'Musha, isn't it you have the great shell of flesh!' cried a third, till at
> last I was mad with them. As for the little children, though I was putting
> my two eyes through them, I was unable to recognise most of them. As
> I approached the house, I saw my grandfather standing in the doorway.
> When he saw me, he remained there standing, shedding tears of joy.
> 'Musha, how are you since, daddo?'
> He could not speak yet, but embraced me.
> 'Musha my heart', said he at last, laughing, 'its many a savage dog and
> bad housewife you have met since.'
> 'No doubt of it', said I, walking in.
> Rose was at the fireside before me, greatly changed, with no thought
> of fawning on me now. Soon my father came in. My grandfather poured
> out the tea.
> After tea I wandered out through the village. Everyone I met on the
> road stopped to welcome me.
> There was a great change in two years - green grass growing on the
> paths for lack of walking; five or six houses shut up and the people gone
> out to the mainland; fields which once had fine stone walls around them
> left to ruin; the big red patches on the sandhills made by the feet of

the boys and girls dancing – there was not a trace of them now.

When I returned home the lamps were being lit in the houses. I went in. My father and grandfather were sitting on either side of the fire, my grandfather smoking his old pipe.

A more authentic or more moving *cadenza* has rarely been achieved even by the most renowned of novelists.

Peig Sayers, who dictated her own book, was one of the great extempore speakers and storytellers of her time. A poet at heart, she tended to place even the simplest events of her life in a somewhat dramatic or imaginative setting. This facility of hers tends to detract somewhat from her book, if viewed as the factual life story of an islandwoman. Nothing, however, can detract from her talent as storyteller. She had most of the gifts of a natural writer: pace, descriptive ability, vivid dialogue, dramatic juxtaposition.

The author of *An tOileánach,* Tomás Ó Criomhthain, had very few of the natural literary gifts of Ó Súilleabháin or Peig Sayers. Imaginativeness, humour, inventiveness, natural storytelling ability – all these he seemed to lack to a degree. Yet, paradoxically, his book is reckoned – and rightly so – to be the masterpiece of Gaeltacht literature. It could be said of Ó Criomhthain that his very literary deficiencies saved him to a great extent from the major criticism that can be levelled at his co-authors from the Blaskets: that their works are not on the one hand completely factual autobiographies, nor on the other hand sufficiently composed to merit the title of autobiographical novels. Generally speaking one feels that Ó Criomhthain's narration remains as close to the events as one can hope from any author who has inherited the Irish storytelling tradition.

An tOileánach is more the biography of an island community than of a single islander. By the time one has read through it several times, one realizes that Ó Súilleabháin's and Peig Sayers's books, delightful as they are, are mere personal addenda to this majestic sociological document. Personal life, especially that of a woman, was somewhat at a discount in a neo-medieval community such as the Blasket Islands. Even births, marriages and deaths, were seen to a great extent in the light of their importance to the community. One senses this public masculine mind revealing itself everywhere in an *An tOileánach*. The language the author uses throughout – rich, immediate, incisive – has little of his own personal stamp: it is the colloquial community language. His stark reportage contrasts vividly with the somewhat overcomposed descriptions of Ó Súilleabháin and Peig Sayers. He tells here, for instance, of the wrecking of a grain ship off the island:

There were no sails whatever on this ship but one tatter only on the front mast. He (the captain) had to make for the White Strand. She hit far out, because she was loaded. The men on board threw out a chunk of wood on the end of a rope, but they failed to make land. The people said they never saw a day so stormy. The wind blew right out through the strand. In spite of everything a block of wood from the ship finally reached somewhere on the strand. The people inside, and the men outside, pulled on the rope, it broke and the men were swept out through the storm. The island people were never again in the better of that sight. The ship split shortly after. . . .

The island people saved thousands of bags of wheat which was enough to feed them, and all who belonged to them, for a long time. No one would be living in this island only for it. . . .[7]

What one senses in this book is the pulse, the true dimensions, of a unique island: this island of highly cultured non-literates where the physical limitations are such that a trip to Dingle (the nearest mainland fishing town) is something akin to a trip to Paris or San Francisco for the ordinary mortal; where the killing of a seal can take on the proportions of an epic act of Achilles; where the wrecking of a grain ship off the island ranks in importance with a *coup d'état* in a Latin American state; where the singing of the 'big songs' (the more structurally complex of folksongs) marks the high point of aesthetic pleasure. And there is still something beyond all that. For Ó Criomhthain is emotionally involved in his island life in a way a professional sociologist could never be. His feeling, concealed or restrained, is present at all times, lending a grave intensity to many passages. Here he is, for instance, describing in spare heartrending phrases the fate of his wife and children:

Ten children were born to us, but ill-luck dogged them, God help us. The first child of mine christened was seven or eight years of age when he fell down the cliff and was killed. From that time on as quickly as a child came, another went. Two of them died of the measles, and every disease that came swept some one from me. Donal was drowned trying to rescue the lady on the White Strand. I had another fine boy, growing up and helping. Shortly he was taken from me too. The sorrow of all these things affected their poor mother, and she was taken from me. I was never blinded until then. . . . One boy only is with me now at home. Another boy in America. That is the end my children came to. God be with them - all of them who are dead - and with the poor woman whose spirit broke because of them.[8]

The events recounted in this short paragraph might well have been the material for another man's book. That it is not so in Ó Criomhthain's work clearly proclaims that he is a voice from another epoch.

Due primarily to the success of the Blasket classics, the autobiography or memoir became for some time one of the fashionable literary forms in modern Irish, both for native speaker and learner alike. The publication of *An Béal Bocht* (The Poor Mouth) by Myles na Gopaleen in 1941 is sure evidence of this. Here the mystique of the 'unique' native speaker, and some of the more misguided efforts of the Irish revival movement, are joyously and successfully satirized. Reread today, *An Béal Bocht* still retains a good deal of its bite and relevance. Indeed its author is to be ranked highly with others such as Liam O'Flaherty, Mícheál Mac Liammóir, Risteard de Paor (Richard Power), Eoghan Ó Tuairisc (E.R. Waters), and Brendan Behan as writers who, since the war, have produced creditable fiction in both Irish and English. Myles na Gopaleen's satire, however, did not stop the flow of autobiographical works. They still appear regularly, year in, year out - the more noteworthy now being written by non-native speakers of Irish. *Dialann Deoraí*[9] by Domhnall Mac Amhlaigh, for instance, is as authentic a book in its own right as is *An tOileánach*. It is an account of life amongst the Connemara navvies in London by a Kilkenny man who has lived and worked amongst them. The author's writing skills are such that scenes and dialogue on English building sites come marvellously alive.

Perhaps, however, the autobiographical work by an established writer of Irish which would mostly attract attention because of its purely literary qualities is *Mo Bhealach Féin* (My Own Way) by Seosamh Mac Grianna (author of *An Druma Mór*). This book, published in 1940, might more accurately be described as an autobiographical novel, because what it does primarily - in the manner of Joyce's *Portrait of the Artist* or Jean Genet's *Notre Dame des Fleurs* - is to create the resonance and taste of an unusual personality. Mac Grianna, who later was to experience severe mental illness (which effectively finished his writing career), depicts himself in this turbulent and volatile book in a most scrupulously honest and poetic fashion. A man who seems to have spent much of his adult life in dingy lodging houses dreaming up heroic deeds, he in turn joins the Salvation Army and the IRA (or so he says); raises money to go to Algiers and instead finds himself in London looking at pictures by Turner; plans to have himself set up as the leader of the coloured races in Britain; and finally ends up - for no apparent reason - trudging wearily through Welsh mining valleys until the poetry atrophies, in himself and his work. The telescoped staccato style of writing, and the surrealistic quality of the author's imagination, makes this, for the most part, a fascinating book.

From about 1939 onwards opportunities for creative writers in Irish increased considerably. Literary prizes were offered by different agencies, small magazines were founded, adventurous publishing houses like that of Sáirséal agus Dill were established. And in 1947 a book club was organized which guaranteed a readership of, say, 1,500-3,000 people for an acceptable book in Irish. From this point on poetry and short-story writing in Irish made dramatic advances – but novel-writing still languished (as indeed did novel-writing in English down to the 1960s).

Séamas Ó Néill's novel *Tonn Tuile* (Floodtide), published in 1947, can be looked on as the first skilful attempt to depict urban living realistically in modern Irish. It concerns the life and strife of a young couple in Dublin during the war years. Here the general (i.e. urban) reader of Irish is brought into a world which is more immediately recognizable to him than the world of *Séadna* or *Cúrsaí Thomáis* or *An tOileánach*. The novel, however, though well crafted, lacks power and conviction. A major difficulty – completely outside the author's control – is that of creating the life and mood of a city in a language which is not an urban community language. The style, especially the dialogue, is denotative rather than connotative, so that the different events and the principal characters remain inert, uncreated.

The better of our recent novels have generally eschewed the realistic representation of the urban scene. Eoghan Ó Tuairisc, for instance, turned his fertile mind to the lyric-historical mode. In *L'Attaque* (1962) he deals with the effect of the French landing in the west of Ireland, in the year 1798, on the life of a typical countryman of the time. In *Dé Luain* (Monday), written in 1966, he attempts an imaginative documentary of some of the events of the 1916 rising. In both works there is great inventiveness and lyrical verve, but again, in the final analysis, there is, one thinks, a failure to match style with content.

Diarmuid Ó Súilleabháin (d. 1985) was the most dedicated writer of novels in recent times. His untraditional use of Irish and his experimental modes of narration make him also, one suspects, our most unread novelist of recent times. This is unfortunate for he was a writer of undeniable talent. The most noteworthy of his novels is possibly *Uain Bheo* (Live Moment). Written in 1968, it deals with the dissolute fringes of contemporary urban life in a style which is nervous, impressionistic, and a little bewildering for anyone brought up on Gaeltacht Irish. It is still difficult to assess Ó Súilleabháin's achievement; but one wonders whether in this, or in his other novels, he managed to develop any deep personal insights about human beings or human living. Yet there was plenty of passion in his work, and great scope for development.

The one post-war novel which continues to make a large impact on contemporary readers of Irish, was written as far back as 1949. It is *Cré na Cille* (The Graveyard Earth), by Máirtín Ó Cadhain, the major figure in twentieth century Irish prose.[10]

Máirtín Ó Cadhain (d. 1970) was the most remarkable example in modern Ireland of the writer *engagé*. His commitment was such as one rarely encounters amongst writers of the major European literatures: the main purpose of his life and work was that of rescuing the very language he was writing in - and therefore the nation it belonged to - from oblivion.

The part of the Galway Gaeltacht where Ó Cadhain was reared - unlike some other Gaeltacht areas - had not a strong literary tradition. His natural heritage was rather the magificent Irish oral literature. So much was this a part of his nature right up to his later years that on a trip to the USSR, as he tells it to us in a famous autobiographical essay,[11] he found himself instinctively identifying the Soviet Republic of Kirghizia with 'the well at the end of the world,' and the horses of Genghis Khan with 'the slender brown steeds' from the stories related by his father and grandfather. One can better gauge how inextricably rooted in his own culture Ó Cadhain was when one considers that this same man, whose imagination was lit up to the end of his life by oral literature, spoke and read some half dozen European languages, and that the works of Shakespeare, Dante, Stendhal, Dostoyevsky, Mauriac, Chekhov, Joyce, Valéry, Gogol, Tolstoy, Balzac, De Chardin, Saunders Lewis, Swift, Eliot, Aristotle, Croce, Roman Jakobson, René Wellek, formed only a small part of his voracious and meticulous reading.

Ó Cadhain wrote the most consciously-patterned and richly-textured prose that any Irishman has written in this century, except Beckett and Joyce. For all that, what seemed to give him greatest pleasure was not that he was widely regarded by Irish critics as a writer of stature but that parts of his writing, such as his novel *Cré na Cille*, were being avidly read by the ordinary people of his own district, Cois Fharraige. In his view, however, - as against the view promulgated by Father Peadar Ó Laoghaire and others at the beginning of the Irish revival - current idiomatic usage, even that of his own district, was no sacred cow. Colloquial speech was of course necessary in any dialogue purporting to represent native Irish speakers, but Ó Cadhain insists, quite rightly, that generally speaking it can only act as the necessary and fragile base of sophisticated writing. So it happened that it was he, above all other writers of modern Irish, who most sought and succeeded in making the language a flexible and compelling instrument of modern thought and feeling. Nobody in Ireland, of course, had a more complete and scholarly knowledge of his own dialect. He had, as well, an overall knowledge of other Gaelic dialects, Scottish and Irish, and obviously had read practically everything worthwhile in Old, Middle, and Modern Irish. With help from all these sources he built up – sometimes skilfully, sometimes clumsily, always passionately – a prose style which, whatever its faults, has an undeniable sweep and grandeur.

The quality of his writing can only be properly experienced in the original, but a few passages in translation, from his autobiographical essay, may help to give some indication of its pungency and lucidity, as well as alerting us to some of the problems the fiction writer in Irish has to face in modern Ireland:

> It frightens me when I hear a person declare that he wrote something to prove that one can deal with modern life in Irish. One can. But I know that it causes me the greatest distress to deal with even the most random thought that occurs to me, and I feel the case is similar for other writers, or I hope it is. Words should be handled as carefully as eggs through which the unborn chicks are breaking.[12]

> The kind of style I am endeavouring to cultivate is, perhaps, a little clumsy, but not as clumsy as it was. The new stories I am writing now are not at all concerned with my own district, or with Galway. . . . I am a longer period in Dublin now than I ever had been in my native place. I had to garner a very accurate knowledge of the city, a knowledge more accurate than many true Dubliners have, when I was an active member of the IRA. There are more of my near relations in Dublin than at home. Very many of my neighbours and people from my native district are living quite close to me. We are a kind of ghetto, perhaps. Kafka and Heine, to mention only two whose work I know, both came from ghettoes. As far as I can see Dublin consists entirely of ghettoes. One could not say that it has been a community since Joyce's day, when the town was very much smaller, more integrated, more dynamic. It was Joyce who wrote the first of Dublin's novels, and perhaps the last. Neither of them is a novel of conflict or action. *Ulysses* is of the picaresque type, a type which is not at all dissimilar to *Diarmaid and Gráinne*. . . . I feel that a large labyrinth like Dublin lends itself easily to picaresque storytelling.[13]

> Irish is a new, though narrow medium, and it is to me a challenge. It is my own, and this I cannot say about any other medium. In the desolation of my heart I heard – I still hear:
>
>> the cry of the blackbird of Leiter Laoigh
>> and the music made by the Dord Fiann.
>
> I am as old as the Hag of Beara, as old as Brú na Bóinne, as old as the great deer. There are two thousand years of that stinking sow which is Ireland, revolving in my ears, my mouth, my eyes, my head, my dreams.[14]

Ó Cadhain's creative work, however, mostly took short-story form. He published five volumes of short stories, in two of which he endeavours to come to grips (not entirely successfully) with life in Dublin. His novel *Cré na Cille*, however, emanates from the heart of Ó Cadhain country, the Connemara Gaeltacht (as seemingly does another novel of his - *Athnuachan* (Renewal) - a prize-winning work, still unpublished).*

Cré na Cille is a dynamic Rabelaisian piece of work, written virtually entirely in dialogue form, each character identifying himself by his own verbal 'signature tune'. The main action takes place in a Connemara graveyard, amongst the dead, who themselves engage in various human activities - from running elections to organizing cultural circles. The heroine, Caitríona Pháidín, is an eloquent virago, and as each new body descends into the earth (at the beginning of each chapter) the story of her alienation from her sister is unfolded - as is the reason for herself being buried in the less respectable part of the graveyard. The plot itself is of no great consequence. What is highly impressive is the revelation of the way Gaeltacht people think and talk, and the bitingly satiric jibes at certain aspects of life in modern Ireland. The style throughout - except for the rhetorical introductions to each chapter - is superb: the reader is swept along in a non-stop flow of scarifying verbal exchanges and repartee. The characters in *Cré na Cille*, however, remain static, typed, under-developed, so that however valid a picture *in general* the novel is of a Connemara Gaeltacht, it is not in any way a deeply felt depiction of *personal* human life, in its complexity, as lived within that community.

Máirtín Ó Cadhain will continue to be the main model for writers of fiction in Irish, in particular for short-story writers, for the foreseeable future. It may also be that, with the success of *Cré na Cille*, the fantasy or non-realistic novel will continue to be seen for a long time as the most viable novel-genre for the writer of Irish in modern Ireland.**

[1975]

*Publication of *Athnuachan* is due in 1995.

**Much notable work has been done since this essay was written. The novels of S. Mac Annaidh and the short fictions of Alan Titley and Seán Mac Mathúna deserve particular mention.

13

A Writer's Testament

MÁIRTÍN Ó CADHAIN WAS the most remarkable example in modern Ireland of the writer *engagé*. His commitment, however, was such as one rarely encounters amongst writers of the major European literatures: because the main purpose of his life and work was that of rescuing the very language he was writing in – and therefore the nation it belonged to – from oblivion. His *Páipéir Bhána agus Páipéir Bhreaca*[1] a classic autobiographical lecture, comes both as apologia and as last will and testament of one who employed his extraordinary literary powers, and his unceasing turbulence of mind and heart, in the service of this cause.

The part of the Galway Gaeltacht where Ó Cadhain was reared – unlike some other Gaeltacht areas – had not a strong literary tradition. His natural heritage was rather the magnificent Irish oral literature. So much was this a part of his nature right up to his later years that on a trip to the USSR, as he tells us in this essay, he found himself instinctively identifying the Soviet Republic of Kirghizia with 'the well at the end of the world', and the horses of Genghis Khan with 'the slender brown steeds' from the stories related by his father and grandfather. One can better gauge how inextricably rooted in his own culture Ó Cadhain was when one considers that this same man, whose imagination was lit up to the end of his life by oral literature, spoke and read some half dozen European languages, and that the works of Shakespeare, Dante, Stendhal, Dostoyevsky, Mauriac, Chekhov, Joyce, Valéry, Gogol, Tolstoy, Balzac, De Chardin, Saunders Lewis, Swift, Eliot, Aristotle, Croce, Roman Jakobson, René Wellek – all referred to in this work – formed only a small part of his voracious and most meticulous reading.

Ó Cadhain wrote the most consciously-patterned and richly-textured prose that any Irishman has written in this century, except Beckett and Joyce. For all that, what seemed to give him greatest pleasure was not that he was widely regarded by Irish critics as a writer of stature but that parts of his writing, such as his novel *Cré na Cille*, were being avidly read by the ordinary people of his own district, Cois Fharraige. In his view, however (as against the view promulgated by An tAthair Peadar Ó Laoghaire and others at the beginning of the Irish revival), current idiomatic usage, even that of his own district, was no sacred cow. Colloquial speech was of course necessary in any dialogue purporting to represent native Irish speakers, but Ó Cadhain insists, quite rightly, that generally speaking it can only act as the necessary and fragile base of sophisticated writing. So it happened that it was he, above all other writers of modern Irish, who most sought and succeeded in making the language a flexible and compelling instrument of modern thought and feeling. Nobody in Ireland, of course, had a more complete and scholarly knowledge than him of his own dialect. He also had an overall knowledge of other Gaelic dialects, Scottish and Irish, and obviously had read practically everything worthwhile in Old, Middle, and Modern Irish. With help from all these sources he built up – sometimes skilfully, sometimes clumsily, always passionately – a prose style which (whatever its faults) has an undeniable sweep and grandeur.

Páipéir Bhána agus Páipéir Bhreaca has all the bite and style of Ó Cadhain's non-fictional writing (which is starker and, to me, frequently more impressive than his fictional work). He is much more sparing of imagery and circumlocution here than in his novels and short stories; and the images or metaphors which do appear are often more telling, more organically conceived. He can blend modern and ancient, homely and sophisticated elements in a most distinguished manner. On the one hand he can tell us in distilled folk style of the old people of his district 'in whose eyes the dead were more luminous than the living' (*go mba sholasaí in a súile an marbh ná an beo*); and on the other hand, in speaking some time later of the possible influence of a Dostoyevsky story on his work, can tell of its having, perhaps, remained 'refrigerated' (cuisnithe) in his mind, using unerringly here a classical Irish word to hit off a modern concept.

The quality of his thought and writing can only be properly experienced in the original, but a few passages in translation may help to give some indication of its pungency and lucidity:

> It frightens me when I hear a person declare that he wrote something to prove that one can deal with modern life in Irish. One can. But I know that it causes me the greatest distress to deal with even the most random thought that occurs to me, and I feel the case is similar for other

writers, or I hope it is. Words should be handled as carefully as eggs through which the unborn chicks are breaking [p. 19].

The kind of style I am endeavouring to cultivate is, perhaps, a little clumsy, but not as clumsy as it was. The new stories I am writing now are not at all concerned with my own district, or with Galway. . . . I am a longer period in Dublin now than I ever had been in my native place. I had to garner a very accurate knowledge of the city, a knowledge more accurate than many true Dubliners have, when I was an active member of the IRA. There are more of my near relations in Dublin than at home. Very many of my neighbours and people from my native district are living quite close to me. We are a kind of ghetto, perhaps. Kafka and Heine, to mention only two whose work I know, both came from ghettoes. As far as I can see Dublin consists entirely of ghettoes. One could not say that it has been a community since Joyce's day, when the town was very much smaller, more integrated, more dynamic. It was Joyce who wrote the first of Dublin's novels, and perhaps the last. Neither of them is a novel of conflict or action. *Ulysses* is of the picaresque type, a type which is not at all dissimilar to *Diarmaid agus Gráinne*. . . . I feel that a large labyrinth like Dublin lends itself easily to picaresque storytelling [p. 22].

In the suburbs of the cities, where there is neither city nor country, live the rich, industrialists who are not industrious, intelligent people, often, but with no intellectual curiosity. . . . Suburban luxury has perhaps by now spread over rural Ireland. It is quite certain that a Synge today would come on very little. At the same time it is in rural Ireland one finds the more established type of community, and I feel that a writer who has evolved from such a community is thrice blessed. But I feel also that my kind of person, who has spent the greater part of his life in Dublin, should not leave Dublin uncreated, a blank page [p. 23].

This style of writing – even when the author avails, as he sometimes does, of rather daring neologisms such as *Nollaicigh* (Decembrists), *Dionysiusach* (Dionysian), *niamhghlantóir* (purist), *eachtarmhúrach* (extra-mural), *nua-aosóir* (innovator) – is recognizibly in the tradition of the main corpus of Irish prose from the eighth to the twentieth century. Yet it also has emanated quite plainly from the world and feeling of a typical modern western European writer. In Ó Cadhain's prose, as in Seán Ó Ríordáin's poetry, Europe and Gaelic Ireland renew, in varying degrees, their age-old alliance.

Ó Cadhain did not begin writing seriously, he tells us, until he was interned in the Curragh Camp, 'the Siberia of Ireland', in the early period of the second world war. His crime was suspected membership of the IRA, a crime which had already led to his dismissal from his post as a national teacher. Amongst his meagre possessions on the day he was captured was a French translation of a short story by Maxim Gorky, the first literary work which persuaded him that this kind of writing was within his own compass. Prison was his university as it has been traditionally for generations of Irish patriots. He studied and read avidly, and taught Irish most successfully to many of his fellow-internees. He also wrote some of the most important of the short stories in *An Braon Broghach*. One readily believes him when he says that he was loath to leave prison. Soon after his release he managed – as did many ex-prisoners in Ireland – to secure a government job, in the parliamentary translation service. Finally, due to the most enlightened policy of Trinity College, he was invited to take up a post as lecturer in Modern Irish, and on the resignation of Professor David Greene, was appointed to the chair of Irish. His final apotheosis as professor of Irish in the oldest and most revered of the British colonial universities he accepted with great humility and the wryest good humour.

What we have of Máirtín Ó Cadhain's published work forms a moderately large opus, but, to judge by what he reveals in *Páipéir Bhána agus Páipéir Bhreaca* as much remains unpublished as has been published. At least two major fictional works should emerge posthumously, his prize-winning novel *Athnuachan*, and a further volume of short stories; and as well as these there is a keenly awaited critical work on modern Irish literature, and, doubtless, a collection of his essays and reviews.[2] His creative work, in particular, awaits refined and detailed literary analysis, and not least of the critical skills involved here will be a complete knowledge of the enormously rich Connaught dialect which acts as its underlying stylistic base.

One can say immediately, however, that all Ó Cadhain's fiction bears the seal of one who passionately wanted to interpret and understand life, whether in the Connemara Gaeltacht or in the Dublin Galltacht. His two early books of short stories *An Braon Broghach* and *Cois Caoláire* are possibly the most significant in this respect. In many of these he treats of the minds and moods of Gaeltacht women with especial tenderness. However these will finally be estimated as literature, it is indisputable that they have absolute authenticity. There can be no doubt but that these works, as well as his novel *Cré na Cille*, and a few of his later short stories, add up to a major revelation of Connemara Gaeltacht life.

One must not conclude, however, that Ó Cadhain thought of his writing as a means of setting down a realistic picture of people or communities. As he tells us in this essay, his understanding of literature is that which has always been most prevalent amongst poets and informed critics: that it is rather an extension of lived life, a new possibility for living – anchored securely, however, to the main framework of reality. In this sense one can surely say that Ó Cadhain's fantasy novel, *Cré na Cille*, is as valid a picture of the talk and mind processes of a Gaeltacht community, as Synge's phantasmagoria *The Playboy of the Western World* is of a facet of the Aran Island's psyche. But even in fantasy or phantasmagoria a writer has to work through characters who have basic affiliations with life as we know it, and he cannot but reveal and develop – at least at crucial junctures – their convoluted and often self-contradictory characteristics. It is here, I think, that Synge succeeds and Ó Cadhain, possibly, fails. His characters in *Cré na Cille* remain static, typed, underdeveloped, so that however valid a picture *in general* his novel is of a Connemara Gaeltacht, it is not in any way a deeply felt depiction of *personal* human life in detail as lived within that community. This is in essence Daniel Corkery's criticism of *Cré na Cille* to which Máirtín Ó Cadhain refers a little bewilderedly in this essay. Corkery pointed out that his characters were 'folklore' characters, in that they remained in the same state of development in the end as in the beginning, the interest lying in the events they encountered. One has to modify this opinion, however, by saying that in Ó Cadhain the superb dialogue of which he was a master more or less supplants the external wonders of the folktale. Folklore characters have never talked as do the characters in *Cré na Cille*.

In his short stories Máirtín Ó Cadhain sets out deliberately to avoid the folklore scaffolding of a set character enduring a series of events leading to a wonder ending. His stories are rather vast interior monologues, or detailed narrative or dialogue pieces concerning psychological states; or otherwise a circular-type comic tale much akin to some of Chekhov's short comedies. A few of these comic tales, such as the celebrated *Fios*, are brilliant. Many people, however, will find his more serious work, despite its authenticity, to be overloaded with not very felicitous imagery and metaphor. There is, in fact, a boring tendency to verbosity. For me, much of this turgidity and unsureness of style in his fiction is a result of his efforts to get away from the traditional storytelling form he had in his bones, and of his not having instinctively found another way of structuring his moods and themes in the manner of the most accomplished modern short-story writers. His technique often seems to be that of accumulation of detail or dialogue, in a way that does not help build up, or climax, his very powerful insights. I find, then, that he has rarely achieved fully satisfying form in his short-story work – and, having said that, am only too conscious that similar strictures were passed on Joyce and other pioneering artists in their day by academic critics who were eventually proved to be disastrously unperceptive in not recognizing the emergence of new and unfamiliar art-forms.

The style in his two later volumes of stories, *An tSraith ar Lár* and *An tSraith Dhá Tógáil*, is somewhat more assured, and in these Máirtín Ó Cadhain moves gradually away from his Gaeltacht material and endeavours to come to grips, in particular, with Dublin city life. He was convinced, as we have seen, that having spent more of his feeling life in Dublin than in the west, that he could as an artist deal with it in creative terms. Again one feels that he may have only partially succeeded. There are almost insuperable literary difficulties in dealing with modern urban life in a language which is not a current urban community language. Ó Cadhain certainly showed that most parts of this life could readily be *translated* into Irish. But in such translation one experiences only the denotative sense of language, rather than the connotative, so that it is quite dubious if Ó Cadhain ever manages to create verbally the mood of the city and its people for his readers. What does make an impact once more, however, is the author's gift for comic writing, for that kind of fantasy which could as easily be situated in a rural as in an urban milieu. Here Ó Cadhain is manifestly writing in the great Irish comic prose tradition of literary tale and folktale, from Mac Con Glinne down to Joyce. One foreign influence, however, in fantasies such as *An Eochair* must surely be Kafka. But the Irish tendency to mischievousness, to maliciousness, to absurdity supplants in Ó Cadhain the sense of threat and foreboding which Kafka so powerfully creates in his work.

Páipéir Bhána agus Páipéir Bhreaca touches tantalizingly then – and a little defensively – on the evolution of a unique writer and on the making of his books. The author may be unduly pessimistic or even wrongheaded from time to time about matters such as the future of writing in Irish or of writing in general (following as he does to some extent Edmund Wilson's lugubrious and obviously ill-founded prophecy about the demise of poetry in *Axel's Castle*). But this is an altogether absorbing and human document, wise, mischievous, gossipy, and startingly poetic by turns. Much is left unsaid, or said obliquely. We hear very little of the process by which this great cultural nationalist became an active revolutionary, and apparently, in time, a committed socialist. Sufficient is said, however, to help us understand how it was that Ó Cadhain in the last decade or so of his life was continually in the vanguard of the protesters who sought civil rights for Irish speakers and their language, thus causing acute embarrassment to a government which was nominally promoting the same cause. For Ó Cadhain, viewing the rapid liquidation of the Gaeltacht areas, such action had now become much more important even than his own writing. And in the final paragraph of this essay, for one short moment, he floods us in the depths of that feeling from which all his turbulence – and tenderness – emanated:

Irish is a new, though narrow medium, and it is to me a challenge. It is my own, and this I cannot say about any other medium. In the desolation of my heart I heard – I still hear:

> thc cry of the blackbird of Leiter Laoigh
> and the music made by the Dord Fiann.

I am as old as the Hag of Beara, as old as Brú na Bóinne, as old as the great deer. There are two thousand years of that stinking sow which is Ireland, revolving in my ears, my mouth, my eyes, my head, my dreams. Hugh Mac Diarmid, a minority language man, if indeed his language is a language at all, has said it better:

> The great rose of all the world is not for me
> For me the little white rose of Scotland
> That smells sweetly and breaks the heart.

Nobody, and in particular an Irish speaker, could read this passage unmoved. After all the polemic, the apologia, the literary gossip and argument, here suddenly and unashamedly is the revelation of a great heart breaking.

Máirtín Ó Cadhain died in Dublin on the 18th of October 1970. It is difficult to believe that he rests in peace.

[1972]

14

Synge and the Idea of a National Literature

T HE PROBLEM OF how to create an individual Irish literature in the English language began increasingly to exercise the minds of writers in Ireland in the second half of the nineteenth century. Yeats, following Ferguson and others, seems to have thought in his early years that such a literature could be achieved mainly by transposing the matter of Ireland into English. In a letter published in *United Ireland* in 1892 he said: 'Can we not build up . . . a national literature which shall be none the less Irish in spirit from being English in language? Can we not keep the continuity of the nation's life . . . by retelling in English which shall have an indefinable Irish quality of rhythm and style, all that is best of the ancient literature . . . until there has been made a golden bridge between the old and the new?' One wonders, however, if Yeats felt, even at that stage, that this was the complete answer.

In the last analysis, the continuing individuality of any national literature is primarily going to depend, not on the past artistic achievements of the nation, but on its present and enduring special pattern of life; on the nation's culture rather than on its Culture. Yeats, however, found himself unable to make any extensive contact with the more traditional Irish community mind. He was quite unable to master even the Hiberno-English he so often lauded. His advice to Synge then to go and live on the Aran Islands could be seen in the light of his own failure to respond adequately to a way of life not his own. One might even say that Synge, another member of the Anglo-Irish nation, was carrying out, on behalf of Yeats, a major step in the programme for building up a national Irish literature in the English language; a step, incidentally, which entailed using, not an 'indefinable Irish quality' of English, but an English so palpably, and so definably Irish, that one still feels somewhat disconcerted, even shocked, by it.

Synge, by his very nature, saw drama as emanating from the observable realities of known life, rather than, as Yeats saw it, from the life of myth. 'I do not believe,' he wrote to Stephen MacKenna, 'in the possibility of a purely fantastic unmodern ideal breezy springdayish Cuchulainoid National Theatre. We had the "Shadowy Waters" on the stage last week, and it was the most *distressing* failure the mind can imagine – a half-empty room with growling men and tittering females.'[1] The living Aran Irish-speaking community then was much more likely to be a source of drama for a person such as Synge than all the myth and literature of past centuries. Indeed so successfully did Synge allow his feelings to interact with those of this most traditional of Irish-speaking communities that it was he, and not Yeats, who shaped the future of the Abbey Theatre. So it was that our national theatre, in the process of being saved from becoming 'Cuchulainoid,' tended to become 'peasantoid' instead.

I am unaware that any detailed scholarly analysis has been made of the ascendancy culture to which Synge and other Anglo-Irish writers belong. On the surface, certainly, it would appear to have been the very antithesis of the peasant culture he came to identify with. It was traditionally middle-class urban or landed gentry; inheriting post-reformation ethics, enjoying formal educational and institutional buttresses, but not very deeply rooted outside its Dublin base. On the other hand the Aran world was rural, Catholic and tentacularly rooted, inheriting an oral learning and the widespread medieval type of Irish community life. It might seem rather improbable that a person of Synge's background could have made a successful emotional transition from the one world to the other.

This, however, is to speak of the two cultures – one rural-based, one Dublin-based – as if they had co-existed in Ireland, without change throughout some three centuries. The truth is that a complicated two-way assimilative process had been at work from quite early on. Swift, in the eighteenth century for instance, not alone spoke on behalf of the people of Ireland, but even learned some Irish. Later on in the nineteenth century, just as the mass of Irish people, under increasing pressure from the English political and economic machine, tended to become Anglicized, ironically enough there was a gradual withdrawal of the Anglo-Irish nation from its dependency on the English mother-culture, and an effort to identify with the older Irish culture. In the final decades of the nineteenth century there is real evidence for the mingling, in varying degrees, of the Irish and Anglo-Irish traditions. This tendency to merge the two traditions is more profoundly institutionalized, perhaps, in the Abbey Theatre, than in any other of the cultural or nationalistic societies which were founded at that time.

As a result of this assimilative process, it is more than possible that the Irish-speaking world Synge encountered in the Aran Islands, and elsewhere, was not as foreign to him as it might appear on the surface. Because, of course, the Aran Island community should not be thought of as being, in most essential ways, a special community in late nineteenth-century Ireland. Irish may have been its language, it may have had its local and regional customs and emphases, but fundamentally it shared the same value-system with the West Cork district where Synge's mother had been born, and with the Wicklow district where Synge's father had been born, where many of Synge's numerous childhood nurses must have come from, and where he himself had spent a good deal of his boyhood. One must postulate then that, long before Synge went to Aran, part, at least, of his psychological make-up responded to that special network of feelings and thinking which is characteristically Irish. Synge, in learning Irish and observing life in the islands was not only enhancing his previous intuitive knowledge of the traditional mind, he was building himself up immensely in the process as a responding and feeling person. Otherwise one cannot adequately explain how, as has been so justly remarked, a very minor poet became practically overnight a dramatist of major significance: in my opinion the one dramatist of enduring quality to come out of the early days of the Abbey Theatre.

Synge might, of course, have found Aran community life particularly appealing even on a purely personal plane, had he never been pre-conditioned culturally to understand it. Because of his own morbid obsession with death, the spectacle of human beings living fully, almost ritualistically, on the brink of death made a deep impression on him, as did the fact also that this simple, almost primeval people, articulated their life in a highly refined and poetic manner. However, this personal empathy with some features of the island way of life cannot in any real measure help us to understand why it is that Synge, in his very restricted opus, has captured more fully than any other Irish writer who has written in English, the deeper resonances of the traditional Irish mind: some of its basic attitudes to life and death, to religion and to heroism, to man–woman and mother–son relationships, to poetry, entertainment, work and a host of other values. Synge, then, is not to be reckoned as a dramatist who merely observed and reported with sympathy on a quasi-medieval way of life full of poetry, quaint customs and folkloric odds and ends. He is rather the Anglo-Irish writer *par excellence* who responded to the basic values underlying that life, and managed to recreate it unerringly in artistic form in two classic pieces, *Riders to the Sea* and *Playboy of the Western World*.

The culture which provided the basic material for the plays of Synge may in one sense be called a 'peasant' culture, but the term 'peasant', in the Irish context, needs more careful interpretation than usual. Obviously country people in Aran and elsewhere inherited what is usually thought of as a 'peasant' culture with all its restrictions and advantages. But they were also the inheritors of the remnants of a 'high Culture', an aristocratic tradition which lasted strongly in Ireland for practically two thousand years, down into the seventeenth century. The Irish aristocratic structure, as distinct from most other similar structures in western Europe, was rural and highly decentralized. The entire country, even in late medieval times, was a mosaic of some one hundred and fifty small kingdoms, each containing, on average, quite a small population. Aristocrats and peasants lived in close proximity to one another, and must have shared to a great extent the same world-view, the same primary attitudes to life in general.

One of these primary attitudes, firmly established throughout the whole historic Irish community, is the high status accorded to poetry, music, and storytelling. Quite clearly a large factor in preserving and disseminating this attitude was that in all the rural kingdoms special arrangements obtained for the provision of these arts. Each chieftain permanently employed professional poets and musicians and, doubtless, encouraged other professional and semi-professional artists to entertain himself and his people. Consequently, great numbers of people throughout rural Ireland were brought into constant contact with various levels of poetry, music and storytelling, unlike people in rural communities in countries such as England and France where the arts were mostly confined to the urban centralized centres of government. This more than anything else explains the esteem for poetry and music, the flair for fine talk and for storytelling, which still exists even in our rather characterless modern Ireland.

Synge, who has said that 'in a good play every speech should be as fully flavoured as a nut or apple', accepted quite naturally this basic community attitude. What is more significant still is that all his own work contains, in a quite uncontrived manner, many of the most typical and well-recognized traits of the two thousand-year-old native Irish literary tradition. One could argue, for instance, that the type of dramatic sequences or juxtaposition he employs, or his lyric changes of mood from situation to situation, owe more to the modes of Irish storytelling and the native dramatic monologue than to any established Anglo-Irish or foreign theatrical tradition. It is quite certain, however, that the concrete, sharp and dramatic quality of the best Irish verse is everywhere present in his work. Even the simplest speeches in *Riders to the Sea* have these characteristics:

Cathleen: . . . Give me a knife Nora; the string's perished with salt water, and there's a black knot on it you wouldn't loosen in a week. . . . Ah Nora, isn't it a bitter thing to think of him floating that way to the far north, and no one to keen him but the black hags that do be flying on the sea?[2]

One is inevitably reminded here of a score of poems in Irish where the same detailed and intense intimacy makes itself felt:

> A widow and a virgin
> I am left still so young,
> And go say to my people
> That my treasure was drowned;
> Had I been in the boat then
> And my two hands on the sheet
> Take my word, Mrs O'Reilly,
> I'd have cured all your grief.
>
> The eels have your eyes
> And the crabs have your mouth
> Your two shining bright hands
> Under sway of the salmon;
> I'd give five pounds to anyone
> Who would lighten my sorrow,
> A sad solitary woman
> Poor bright Nelly Sheridan.

> (Trans. Ó Riada and Lucy)

Una Ellis-Fermor has rightly remarked on the strange affinity between Synge's nature-passages and the nature-poetry of Irish monks from the ninth or tenth centuries. It is equally true that the Old Irish delicate and impressionistic reactions to natural phenomena – 'natural magic' was Matthew Arnold's description of this quality – must have remained a rooted characteristic of the Irish community mind. Several such passages in Synge are echoed again and again in Irish folksong, or in books such as *Allagar na hInise*, by Tomás Ó Criomhthain, the fisherman from the Blasket Islands. Compare these two passages for instance:

There's the sound of one of them twittering yellow birds do be coming in the spring-time from beyond the sea, and there'll be a fine warmth now in the sun, and a sweetness in the air, the way it'll be a grand thing to be sitting here quiet and easy, smelling the things growing up, and budding from the earth.[3]

It's in the white strand field I'm working. It's a sweet day . . . the sea
calm, curraghs coming and going, a single person in one of them - Seán
Léan, as stately in it as the Prince of Wales in his ornate coracle; the
fish showing their heads above water, the birds with their music, human
beings on dry land, dressed only in shirts, earthing potatoes; a crowd
coming from the two sides of the hill carrying handfuls of bracken,
another gang running eastwards across the hillside after school at mid-
day; smoke coming from every house just now - dinner is on, no
doubt.[4]

Not alone are such undoubted characteristic Irish literary traits to be
found in abundance in Synge, but his two major works seem to mirror,
respectively, the two main streams of the whole Irish literary tradition.
While Irish verse tends mostly to be concrete, and intense in quality, Irish
prose, from its very beginnings, inclines towards fantasy, burlesque or phan-
tasmagoria. This prose tradition remains mainly, down through the
centuries, a comic or satiric tradition finally manifesting itself indirectly.
and in an other language, in the works, say, of Stephens, Myles na gCopaleen
and the early Beckett. Synge's *Playboy* stems quite clearly from this prose
tradition, while his 'poetic' play *Riders to the Sea* remains firmly within
the main mode of the much more ascetic verse tradition, 'pared to the bone'.

Just as Synge's plays seem to be unusually in accord with the main Irish
literary tradition, so also do they contain basic insights not alone into
the psyche of Aran life, but by extension into the psyche of Irish life general-
ly. I will mention a few of what seem to me to be major points of creative
contact.

The attitude of the old woman, Maurya, in *Riders to the Sea*, worn out
by the attrition of the sea, finally and quietly accepting death - so long
as the requisite rituals are at hand to assuage its bitterness - is all of a
piece with anything similar I know of in Irish life or literature. Synge poses
no theories here about her death or about tragedy in general; while religious
consolations are used more as ritual than reality. In so far as one can deduce
a general statement from the play about death, it seems to say quite simp-
ly: 'having lived fully, using whatever props or illusions that are necessary,
death can be borne with some dignity'. As Maurya has used to the full
her six sons as props for her living, so also has Déirdre used to the full
her ideal love for Naisi, and can finally 'put away sorrow like a shoe that
is worn out and muddy', finding that 'in the grave we're safe surely'. These
words of Déirdre echo lines from the famous last speeches of Maurya;
and Maurya's last speeches, in turn, echo in their tone and in their in-
tensely subdued feeling a passage from Tomás Ó Criomhthain's biography,
An tOileánach, where in a short passage at the end of a chapter he describes
incidents in his personal family life which many other writers would have

made the main subject-matter of their memoirs:

> Ten children were born to us, but ill-luck dogged them, God help us.
> The first child of mine christened was seven or eight years of age when
> he fell down the cliff and was killed. From that time on as quickly as
> a child came, another went. Two of them died of the measles, and every
> disease that came swept some one from me. Donal was drowned trying
> to rescue the lady on the White Strand. I had another fine boy, growing
> up and helping. Shortly he was taken from me too. The sorrow of all
> these things affected their poor mother and she was taken from me. I
> was never blinded until then. . . . One boy only is with me now at home.
> Another boy in America. That is the end my children came to. God be
> with them - all of them who are dead - and with the poor woman whose
> spirit broke because of them.[5]

Compare this with:

> I've had a husband, and a husband's father, and six sons in this house
> . . . and some of them were found and some of them were not found,
> but they're gone now the lot of them. . . . There was Sheamus and his
> father, and his own father again, were lost in a dark night. . . . There
> was Patch after was drowned out of a curagh that turned over. . . . They're
> all together this time, and the end is come. May the Almighty God have
> mercy on Bartley's soul, and on Michael's soul . . . and may He have
> mercy on my soul, Nora, and on the soul of every one is left living in
> the world. . . . Michael has a clean burial in the far north, by the grace
> of the Almighty God. Bartley will have a fine coffin out of the white
> boards, and a deep grave surely. . . . What more can we want than that?
> No man at all can be living for ever, and we must be satisfied.[6]

This intense, near-fatalistic acceptance by the old of the brutal fact of
death - once the props had gone - did not mean at all that life before
death was futile. Life itself need not in any way be futile, because it could
always be transformed into poetry, fantasy, burlesque, anything one willed.
If myth, illusion or ritual helped one to master life so much the better.
Use it, Synge seems to say, in his comic interpretation of the Irish mind,
but do not depend on it. The Playboy grew in stature because he enjoyed
the illusion that he had killed 'his da'. This illusion was punctured, but
in the meantime he had mastered life (including his overbearing father)
and could live life in future more independently. Similarly Nora, in the
Shadow of the Glen, briefly enjoyed the illusion that her crusty old hus-
band had died. This illusion was again crudely shattered, but she seemed
in the meantime to have mustered up the courage - though dramatically
speaking, this is not at all rendered sufficiently credible - to risk a new

and fuller life with a man of the roads.

On the other hand, in *The Well of the Saints*, the two old blind beggars, have been living adequately, sometimes uproariously, with the illusion that if their sight were restored all should be well. Unfortunately for them their wish is granted, their illusion shattered; and because of their not being sufficiently equipped to deal with the raw reality of life, they choose rather pathetically to return to their former blind state. The comic vision cedes rather shakily here to the tragic vision, making the overall mood and effect of the play somewhat uncertain.

Synge uses anecdotes and folk stories as the basis for these plays, but he re-shapes his material in such a fashion that he leaves us in no doubt as to his own emotional involvement with this particular way of viewing life. Mastering life after all was of the most immediate importance to himself personally, given that this world was for him the only reality and afterlife a matter of lying in Mount Jerome graveyard 'with worms eternally'.

Some critics, notably Daniel Corkery, have argued that Synge fails to come to grips with the religious element in the Irish consciousness. It is, of course, true that what we have been used to think of as the traditional Catholic Ireland gets very little showing in his plays. One must say here, however, that, firstly, our concept of a traditional Catholic Ireland is to a large extent a nineteenth-century urban concept; and, secondly, that Synge's plays make no realistic attempt to reflect any section of life, in its particularity, as lived in the Aran Islands or anywhere else. Neither, of course, do Shakespeare's plays represent, in any detail, life in Elizabethan England. Synge possibly stays closer to lived life than does Shakespeare, but he still uses only the very basic elements.

Synge, no doubt, could have quite legitimately omitted the Catholic part of the Irish consciousness if he found it did not accord with his own temperament, or with his own particular artistic needs, thereby losing out somewhat on his claim to be a faithful interpreter of the traditional mind. One doubts, however, if this is the way to look at it. It seems to me that Synge, intuitively and by observation, felt that the pre-Christian sub-stratum of the Irish mind was still the more potent factor in the conduct of daily life. His description of a funeral in Aran makes this quite clear:

> After Mass this morning an old woman was buried. She lived in the cottage next mine, and more than once before noon I heard a faint echo of the keen. I did not go to the wake for fear my presence might jar upon the mourners, but all last evening I could hear the strokes of a hammer in the yard, where, in the middle of a little crowd of idlers the next of kin laboured slowly at the coffin. To-day, before the hour for the funeral, poteen was served to a number of men who stood about upon the road, and a portion was brought to me in my room. Then the coffin was carried,

sewn loosely in sailcloth, and held near the ground by three cross-poles lashed upon the top. As we moved down to the low eastern portion of the island, nearly all the men, and all the oldest women, wearing petticoats over their heads, came out and joined in the procession.

While the grave was being opened the women sat down among the flat tombstones, bordered with a pale fringe of early bracken, and began the wild keen, or crying for the dead. Each old woman, as she took her turn in the leading recitative, seemed possessed for the moment with a profound ecstacy of grief, swaying to and fro, and bending her forehead to the stone before her, while she called out to the dead with a perpetually recurring chant of sobs.

All round the graveyard other wrinkled women, looking out from under the deep red petticoats that cloaked them, rocked themselves with the same rhythm, and intoned the inarticulate chant that is sustained by all as an accompaniment.

The morning had been beautifully fine, but as they lowered the coffin into the grave, thunder rumbled overhead and hail-stones hissed among the bracken.

In Inishmaan one is forced to believe in a sympathy between man and nature, and at this moment when the thunder sounded a death peal of extraordinary grandeur above the voices of the women, I could see the faces near me stiff and drawn with emotion.

When the coffin was in the grave, and the thunder had rolled away across the hills of Clare, the keen broke out again more passionately than before.

This grief of the keen is no personal complaint for the death of one woman over eighty years, but seems to contain the whole passionate rage that lurks somewhere in every native of the island. In this cry of pain the inner consciousness of the people seems to lay itself bare for an instant, and to reveal the mood of beings who feel their isolation in the face of a universe that wars on them with winds and seas. They are usually silent, but in the presence of death all outward show of indifference or patience is forgotten, and they shriek with pitiable despair before the horror of the fate to which they are all doomed.

Before they covered the coffin an old man kneeled down by the grave and repeated a simple prayer for the dead.

There was an irony in these words of atonement and Catholic belief spoken by voices that were still hoarse with the cries of pagan desperation.

A little beyond the grave I saw a line of old women who had recited in the keen sitting in the shadow of a wall beside the roofless shell of the church. They were still sobbing and shaken with grief, yet they were beginning to talk again of the daily trifles that veil from them the terror of the world.

When we had all come out of the graveyard, and two men had re-built the hole in the wall through which the coffin had been carried in, we

walked back to the village, talking of anything and joking of anything
as if merely coming from the boat-slip, or the pier.[7]

Synge's viewpoint here, and elsewhere, that Christian dogmas and rituals
have been quite often a mechanical super-imposition on pagan attitudes
of mind, I find quite convincing; so much so that I consider him to have
been much more discerning than Anglo-Irish writers in general in plum-
bing the Irish religious consciousness.

A culture, anthropologists tell us, is a community's design for living,
handed down from generation to generation, refurbished, perhaps, from
time to time, but always retaining a certain structural permanency. The
community's language as a part of this design reflects and transmits a par-
ticular and evolving network of feeling, thinking and behaving. Theoretically,
no other language can in any satisfactory way express that culture, or
reproduce elements of it in that new extension or metamorphosis of life
(i.e. life as understood within that culture) which we call art.

Essentially then the main stylistic problem facing Synge as a dramatist,
who was expressing the elements of one culture in terms of a language
not expressly of that culture, was quite similar to that facing a writer
translating literature from one language to another. 'To translate well', Roger
Caillois writes, 'is to "invent" the text (vocabulary, syntax, and style) that
the translated author would have written if his native language had been
that of the translator, and not his own.'[8]

Synge, of course, did have the advantage here that a good deal of the
translation he required had been done for him by the country people of
Ireland in their nineteenth-century change-over from Irish to English. But
even at that Synge clearly had to 'invent': he took up the incipient Hiberno-
English dialect, elaborated on it, and shaped from it a fully-fashioned
diction, which I would say, had never been spoken at this consistency
by any community of people. He is, perhaps, the only widely-known writer
to build up an authentic and individual style based on the translation
of one language into another.

It must be stressed, however, that the Hiberno-English on which Synge
built is in many ways a very restricted dialect. It may have managed to
express adequately some or even all of the most basic attitudes and feel-
ings of a community which had historically been Irish-speaking, but it
was utterly defective as an instrument which would serve the same wide
range of linguistic functions as the Irish language did serve within such
a community – functions associated with a whole spectrum of formal,
semi-formal and informal speech (i.e. orations, sermons, story-telling,
various conversational tonalities, etc.). Synge's dialect, then, while it con-
tains some rather exotic elements, has little tonal subtlety, and cannot be

used effectively to reflect situations in any kind of realistic manner: it is very formalized 'peasant' diction, much more distanced from life and live situations than, one feels, has generally been realized. Moreover, this dialect is an isolated 'language in itself', having no conventional sociolinguistic relationship with a standard, or higher-class language, much as, say, a Yorkshire dialect would have with standard English.

Some consequences arise from these linguistic factors which are crucial both in the production and criticism of Synge's work. One of the most obvious of these is that Synge's style maintains credibility only in certain limited circumstances. In *Deirdre of the Sorrows*, for instance, despite its many very magnificent passages, the language is completely inadequate tonally to create a milieu in which kings and princes can operate. Here is Conchubar, the High King, speaking in turn to Déirdre's nurse and to Déirdre herself:

> Conchubar: . . . She's coming now, and let you walk in and keep Fergus till I speak with her a while.
> Lavarcham: . . . If I'm after vexing you itself, it'd be best you weren't taking her hasty or scolding her at all.
> Conchubar: . . . I've no call to. I'm well pleased she's light and airy. . . . The gods save you Deirdre . . .
> Deirdre: . . . The gods save you. . . . I have no wish to be a queen.
> Conchubar: . . . You'd wish to be dressing in your duns and grey, and you herding your geese or driving your calves to their shed . . . like the common lot scattered in the glens?[9]

The style here has become rustic fancy dress, it has not evolved in any way out of the various kinds of emotional and linguistic relationships existing between different strata of people. The High King cannot be distinguished stylistically from the 'common lot scattered in glen', and thereby loses dramatic credibility. One doubts very much, even had Synge lived long enough to rewrite it, that he could have made *Deirdre of the Sorrows* a true theatrical event.

On the other hand, the consequence for even the classic pieces such as *The Playboy of the Western World* and *Riders to the Sea* is that the style works only if the plays, in production, are sufficiently distanced from the life from which they have emanated. *The Playboy*, because of its being so patently in the realms of fantasy or phantasmagoria, is generally accorded an adequate treatment, from this point of view, in professional productions; *Riders to the Sea* never, or almost never, in my experience. The basic situation of this play is so familiar to people acquainted with the west coast of Ireland, that the tendency has been to produce it in a much more naturalistic manner than its formalized monotoned style allows.

Given this style one can see *Riders to the Sea* successfully produced only as a sort of ritual, where actors gesticulate most sparingly, where actions such as removing a cake from the fire become virtually sacramental acts, where the movements of girls crying together are stylized, yet natural, as in a Greek funeral *stele*. More particularly, the dialogue throughout needs to be spoken, simply, though ritualistically, and be seen as a part of a build-up for the last great litanies of Maurya, which should finally overwhelm us as surely as the sea has overwhelmed her.

Produced or interpreted at this sort of lyric-ritualistic level it can be shown, I think, that *Riders to the Sea* is functional in every line, full of the most intense dramatic action, one of the greatest works ever written in Ireland.

A host of considerations such as I have mentioned flow from Synge's highly successful attempt to recreate West of Ireland life in terms of Hiberno-English – an attempt which we have been looking at as an essential part of a programme to build up a national literature in the English language.

In this regard it must be remembered that Yeats and Joyce, as well as Synge, were also intensely concerned with the 'west', and all its implications. In their case, however, it became less and less an identifiable place, and more and more a territory or a tension of the mind. Yeats, on the evidence of his writings, spent his life working out in poetry and drama his tortured and ambivalent relationship with 'Connaught', his synonym for the older native Culture (or culture). But the poet who declared in his younger days 'Connaught for me is Ireland' was increasingly to renounce this concept until finally he felt he had nothing left to lean on but 'the foul rag-and-bone shop of the heart'.

Joyce, unlike the other two, being of native Catholic stock, and sensing, perhaps, more acutely the future cultural pattern of the country, had his own cunning answer to the east–west dilemma:

> He even ran away with hunself and became a farsoonerite, saying he would far sooner muddle through the hash of lentils in Europe than meddle with Irrland's split little pea.[10]

He did not run away, however, without having worked out his cultural problem also in terms of literature. *Ulysses* bears ample and complicated testimony to this; but *The Dead* is Joyce's most straightfonvard account of his situation. In this story Gabriel, the Dublin Palesman, having discovered an emotional chasm between himself and his Galway-born wife, seems to have resolved to 'journey westward'. Joyce himself, however, chose to go east. He must have felt finally that trying to assimilate 'Connaught' as Synge did, and as, after his own fashion, Yeats tried to do for a time, was at best a make-shift literary ploy. Absolutely revealing, however, in its depiction of his split-mindedness, is his account in *Portrait of the Artist* of an Irish-speaking old man a friend of his had encountered in the west of Ireland. Joyce declares with feverish clarity: 'I fear him. . . . It is with him I must struggle all through the night till day come, till he or I lie dead, gripping him by his sinewy throat till. . . . Till what? Till he yield to me? No, I mean no harm.'

For Joyce and Yeats, the conflict arising from the problem of whether to identify or not to identify with facets of Irish culture was clearly one of the most dynamic and productive factors in their whole work. For Synge, a much more monolithic character, the effort to identify never assumed the proportions of a problem: he merely went through the process simply, rigorously and successfully.

In either case the question of whether or not to identify could never have arisen had there not been a recognisable Irish culture, or pattern of life. Synge discerned this pattern of life, at its most elemental, on the west coast; and, as an artist, sensed that Hiberno-English was the only language which could successfully express it. Hiberno-English, however, has shown itself to be a very ephemeral dialect. It is quickly receding both as a spoken and a written tongue; so, of course, are many of the features of the more traditional Irish life. Synge's solution, then, is not a viable one.

Mention was made earlier in this essay of the rather ironic fact that, while the Anglo-Irish nation tended to identify increasingly with the native traditions right down through the nineteenth century, the older culture, at the same time, was being swiftly eroded by the English language and its traditions. Despite the establishment of an Irish state in the twentieth century, this assimilative process has continued inexorably. Indeed, it is more than probable that since the time of Synge the individuality of the whole of Irish life has diminished severely; and that this diminution has occurred not alone on the surface of life, but in that fundamental network of values and attitudes which is surely the basis on which the permanency of a culture depends.

In the early thirties, Daniel Corkery, in his book *Synge and Anglo-Irish Literature*, summed up the state of Irish culture thus: 'Everywhere in the mentality of Irish people are flux and uncertainty. Our national consciousness may be described, in a native phrase, as a quaking sod. It gives no footing. It is not English, nor Irish, nor Anglo–Irish . . .'. Numerous contemporary commentators – much less involved with traditional nationalism than Corkery – have been taking the view that our consciousness is, in fact, rapidly becoming less and less Irish or Anglo-Irish, and more and more provincial British. A foreign scholar, M.W. Heslinga, in his book *The Irish Border as a Cultural Divide*, finds that the whole country, north and south, shares by and large (except in the matter of religion) the one British culture. One feels, or at least hopes, that here the case has been overstated.

Corkery, in that controversial first chapter of his book on Synge – a book which, incidentally, still contains some of the best critical analysis of the plays – doubts if an eroded culture such as ours could, in the long term, produce an individual literature in English. The tone of this particular chapter is very much of its time, sharply polemical and rather condemnatory of Anglo-Irish writers in general. This is unfortunate: one cannot readily or generally condemn writers for being caught up willy-nilly in a complicated assimilative process. Corkery's main thesis, however, seems to me to have even more force today than at the time he stated it.

In this regard, the role attributed to a language by anthropologists in general, and by linguistic anthropologists in particular, in the formulation and transmission of a culture, has special relevance: 'The fact of the matter', says Edward Sapir, 'is that the "real world" is to a large extent unconsciously built upon the language habits of the group. No two languages are ever suffiently similar to be considered as representing the same social reality. The worlds in which different societies live are distinct worlds, not merely the same world with different labels attached. The understanding of a single poem, for instance, involves not merely an understanding of the single words in their average significance, but a full comprehension of the whole life of the community as it is mirrored in the words, or as it is suggested by their overtones. Even comparatively simple acts of perception are very much more at the mercy of the social patterns called words than we might suppose.'[11]

In the circumstances, then, that Hiberno-English has clearly lost ground, and that standard English is increasingly bringing with it, and imposing on us a 'world', a 'design for living', a 'value-system' at variance with our own, one cannot hope in the long term for a national literature in English, i.e. a literature which shall have an individual Irish way of seeing and expressing reality: a literature as specifically Irish *in its attitudes to life* as Synge's plays. Given what could be the present irreversible position, where the Irish 'experience' is so often an echo of the English 'experience', all one could visualize evolving finally in Ireland would be a British regional literature, containing, perhaps, a large residual element of 'Irishness' – remnants of Irish attitudes, customs and manners – but, in essence, growing gradually out of an overall British (or Anglo-American) way of viewing life. Whether one should call such a literature Irish (or even Anglo-Irish) is merely a matter of acceptable nomenclature, and almost irrelevant.

Whether one calls Languedoc cooking French, or Scottish sculpture British, is equally irrelevant.

Synge is possibly the only major writer of the Anglo-Irish nation to have achieved satisfactory identification with the historic Irish ethos. But the uniqueness, indeed the near-grotesqueness of his achievement, highlights the immense complexity of the task of any Irish writers of English in the future who feel they should have something to say which would recognizably grow out of the Irish way of encompassing reality.

[1972]

15

Daniel Corkery, Cultural Philosopher, Literary Critic: A Memoir

WHEN I WENT TO UCC (University College, Cork) in 1942 as a very young student, Daniel Corkery was approaching the age of retirement but was still a considerable influence on cultural affairs in Ireland. His name would have been frequently mentioned at the time in newspapers, amongst students and scholars, by my own parents. I understood him to be a national figure of near-mythic proportions. Consequently when I saw him – a small quite insignificant white-haired man – hobble into a lecture room in UCC dragging an emaciated leg behind him I was deeply dismayed; and still more dismayed when he spoke to us in a small hoarse croaking voice. Not but that he was quite attractive looking: trim, round faced, with a neat white moustache and a pink and white complexion – a ripe apple ready to fall from the bough.

When I finished with his courses three years later, all my perceptions of him had changed. The little white-haired man had become a luminous indestructible personage in my mind – the best teacher of literature I had met or would meet. In his classes, he fingered lovingly, as it were, the text of the poems or plays he discussed, taught you to appreciate the texture of words or images, helped you to see how the elements worked together in a successful piece of art. He was very much then a teacher who valued the poem as structure, long before the new critics and the structuralists advanced their notions. His observations on structure, of course, were mostly those of a practising writer concerned with the manner in which a literary artefact achieved its effect. And while he recognized, that to look on the poem as poem, play as play – structure in its own right – was the primary

234

function of a critic, he also understood that further insights could be gained by relating a poem/play to the period in which it was composed. I remember him saying, for instance, that in so far as one could distinguish, say, an Elizabethan love-lyric from a Restoration love-lyric, that the period of composition itself has to be seen as placing its own imprint on the texture of the poem. But I never saw him use literature as a social document, as a way to illustrate history. (I say this, in particular, because some modern historians who have been criticizing *The Hidden Ireland* have clearly misunderstood – as I will argue later – the *modus operandi* of the book.) Daniel Corkery was no historian then, but a literary critic and cultural philosopher who understood that the historical context was necessary for a fuller understanding of any literature.

As a teacher perhaps his greatest gift was to motivate his students to ask themselves the right questions. In the lecture room he was gentle, courteous, almost Victorian in his correctness; but one felt – I did at any rate – that the lid of one's mind was being gradually prised open by the manner in which he posed his questions and, more significantly, by the manner in which he got us to pose our questions. Finally, I ended up expressing ideas and perceptions about Shakespeare, Wordsworth, Shelley, Eliot, that I felt had always been my own – not his. In this way his influence could be, perhaps, too strong, and had to be guarded against. He rarely talked about anything else, however, but literary texts in his classes. I do not remember – and this will surprise people who imagine him to have been a consummate nationalist propagandist – that he ever talked in class about national/cultural or Irish language affairs. Indeed he scarcely ever gave a formal lecture on anything, except perhaps an introductory talk he would give in first year on 'What is Art'. His thesis was – as one would expect – that the primary function of art was to create precise moods or feelings or perceptions about various facets of life. He never seemed to think of literature as teaching anything in a doctrinaire sense.[1]

Outside the lecture hall, however, I found in the years I got to know him rather intimately – from 1945, say, until his death in 1964 – that he rarely discussed literature in any detail. In his later years – and he lived to the age of 86 – he was much more taken up, I guess, with the state of the country, cultural affairs, Irish language affairs, than he had been in his youth and middle-age. For him now the future of literature in this country had become a secondary problem to be solved within the framework of the cultural welfare of the country in general. The ideas he had expressed in *Synge and Anglo-Irish Literature* (1931) had been challenged in many quarters, and it is clear that he was worrying away at them, extending them, defending himself against his critics, just at the time I got to know him in college. His approach to the country's cultural future –

unlike his approach to literary texts – could be quite doctrinaire. He would wonder aloud for instance why certain (named) writers, who had a good knowledge of Irish, kept on writing in English. After all, one gathered from him (somewhat indirectly, admittedly), many people a generation before that had given their lives for the country's political freedom: could not writers – minor writers at that! – be expected to make a minimal sacrifice for the country's cultural freedom by turning from English to Irish as their creative medium?

I found some of this a little tiresome finally. But to the end he could be quietly amusing and perceptive about people, about places, even about new social and political departures.

This division I perceived between Corkery the *littérateur*, and Corkery the cultural philosopher is I think crucial for an understanding of Corkery's critical opus in general. He was not doctrinarie (as has been claimed) in matters which had to do with literature or literary theory, but he was (or at least became doctrinaire) in matters having to do with cultural philosophy.

The cultural philosophy espoused by Daniel Corkery was basically the traditional philosophy of the Gaelic League, as enunciated and developed by people such as Douglas Hyde, Eoin Mac Néill, Pádraig Pearse. A central tenet in this was that the Irish language would have to become again the predominantly written and spoken language of Ireland; the people of Ireland would then preserve and develop their own identity in a way they could not if the English language were to remain the major language of the country. The cultural conquest of the country by English colonial forces would cease; the Irish personality would flourish again. This was the kind of doctrine profoundly believed in by those who were centrally engaged in the fight for Irish freedom (1916–1922). Corkery in his writings would quote people like Mac Néill on these issues. Some ten years after his controversial book on Synge he quoted with approval what Mac Néill had written in 1909: 'In Ireland there is no possible foundation for a national culture except the national language. It can easily be shown that an attempt to base Irish culture on the English language can only result in provincializing Irish life'. Corkery remarks: 'That position is invulnerable'.[2]

Nowadays many of us concerned with Irish language policy have moved away somewhat from that 'invulnerable' position, by espousing a policy of flexible bilingualism rather than of monolithic monolingualism, and by proposing to offer people (somewhat optimistically some will say) a choice of either of the two languages as their main preferred one. Yet we today have no certainty that such a bilingual policy, or indeed any policy, will finally preserve the special cultural identity of the Irish people. It may well be that the Mac Néill–Corkery approach will be judged to have been the right one. Only time will tell. But in any case it should be borne in mind that if Corkery expressed opinions on these matters which today seem to us excessively doctrinaire, these opinions were perfectly reasonable and logical within the framework of the Gaelic League philosophy.

After the foundation of the state many responsible people in government and in public life began gradually, both consciously and unconsciously, to jettison a good deal of the philosophy (including the Gaelic League language philosophy) on which the state was founded. There is nothing new in such a situation. In a post-revolutionary era zeal diminishes; some of the revolutionary ideals begin to look too difficult, impracticable. Corkery was one of the few writers/intellectuals who did not jettison the language philosophy; indeed he was probably the only writer/intellectual who positively added to it. His thinking about the function of language in a culture was quite impressive for Ireland at that time. In 1943, for instance, he puts forward concepts which disciples of Lévi Strauss in the sixties and seventies would not have found strange or alien. Speaking of the link between culture and language he says, for example:

> Amongst them [the modes and forms of a culture] we may enumerate the language . . . all the arts, social customs, games etc. These modes and forms constitute a form of spiritual organism, the members of which are unequal in rank and great in variety. Any pair of them may at first view seem to be of disparate genera: actually they harmonise one with another, each with all, all with each – for the reason that the one mind has made each of them what it actually is. *They are organically coordinated.*
>
> Of those national pieties, the language is unique. It is the mother-form. It is the single form that every single individual in the community practices, day in day out, and for his whole life long. It feeds and sustains all the other forms.[3]

Some people, not adequately recognizing the staunch Gaelic League principles on which all his utterances are finally based, have attributed personal attitudes and prejudices to him which are quite unfounded. Even sympathetic Irish commentators are at fault here. For instance John A. Murphy has said that 'Corkery attributed to the Gaelic tradition a cultural and moral superiority over all other traditions in Ireland.'[4] Again Seán Lucy has written: '(For Corkery) the truly Irish was the truly Gaelic.'[5] All I can say is that I have never seen anything written by Corkery, or heard anything spoken by him, which would lend credence to such opinions. Corkery's stance was simply the Gaelic League stance that the language had to be restored as the main langage of communication in Ireland in order to halt the erosion of Irish identity; not because it was culturally or morally superior but because the Irish mind, the Irish personality – for good or ill – was so bound up with the language; was, in fact, as Corkery would say himself, the mother-form, the *matrix* of that mind and personality. And (*pace* Seán Lucy) even if Corkery did think that the only guarantee the Irish community had in the *long term* of remaining 'truly Irish' was to restore the Irish language, he did consider English speakers and English writers of his time in Ireland as 'truly Irish'; he considered himself 'truly Irish' and was inordinately proud that seven generations of his [English-speaking] ancestors had lived before him in Cork City. He believed that other writers like T.C. Murray and Pádraic Colum were 'truly Irish'.[6] He thought J.M. Synge had largely made the transition from being Anglo–Irish aristocratic Protestant to being 'truly Irish' in his English writings. Not only that but he has written that if it were possible to perpetuate Hiberno-English/Kiltartanese as the normal language of the country that a 'true Anglo-Irish' or even national literature in English might evolve in Ireland: 'If all our writers in English were to set up a Kiltartan League and by dint of propaganda to get this "dialect" adopted by the nation at large, and, then, rejecting English literary forms and condemning English syntax, were to write and publish all their books in the Kiltartanese, these works of theirs should have a fair claim to be called Anglo-Irish literature, even Irish literature, *for it would have developed a way of its own, and so become capable of dealing with universal literary material'.*[7] The concept of a Kiltartan League rather than a Gaelic League was, of course, a deliberate absurdity; but his final statement implying that if Ireland could develop 'a way of its own', an individual personality of its own through the English language, that there might be no pressing use for the restoration of the Irish language. This was completely consistent with his thinking as I knew it. At any rate it is not the statement of a person who is 'racist, narrow, exclusivist'[8] as John A. Murphy would have it; it is the logical position of a fundamental dogmatic thinker who wished Ireland to have and to continue to have 'a way of its own'. Of course he was reasonably certain that Hiberno-English would have no permanence in Ireland. On the other hand he was convinced that if we relied predominantly on English as our national language that our way of life, our literature, would become increasingly provincial British: 'There is therefore no means', he says, 'by which Ireland can come on a literature in English [i.e. a national literature in English] which shall have a way of its own.'[9] So he did fear, that without the re-establishment of Irish, fewer and fewer 'truly Irish' writers in the English language such as Murray, Colum, himself – and even J.M. Synge – would appear, as the years went by, writers who would be naturally in touch with the traditional values of the Irish mind. And it is not that their values were more noble or more spiritual – it was just that they were more fundamental. 'It is foundational,' as he said himself of the traditional Gaelic element, ' . . . coming on *Gaelachas* so understood we come on what is deepest even still in ourselves.'[10] He did then firmly believe that *in the long term* Ireland's daily life, Ireland's literature, would have to be predominantly in the Irish language; and to give the example himself he turned in old age from writing in English to writing in Irish, a language he did not speak or write with any great facility.

Now it is unlikely that many people today will find the basic Corkery/Gaelic League argument I have been outlining very acceptable. But I think it is only fair to ask that it be understood, at least, before being disagreed with. Much of the controversy resulting from this argument as presented in the notorious first chapter of *Synge and Anglo-Irish Literature* has come about, in my opinion, because of a misunderstanding of the basic tenets. It should be understood moreover that Corkery was not writing here in his primary role as *littérateur;* rather in his secondary role as cultural philosopher. His concern was not with good or bad literature, but with the role of literature in general in the long-term cultural future of the country. He obviously felt at the time that the probability was that our national literature finally had to be in Irish; and if it were to be for some time in English, it had to be 'truly Anglo-Irish'.

What he was mostly afraid of, no doubt, at that period (*c.*1930) was that the upperclass Irish Protestant ascendancy would dominate the future literature of Ireland for a long time to come, and thus stultify the effort of the new Irish state to preserve and develop an individual Irish culture. The literature of the Anglo-Irish Ascendancy – as represented in particular by Yeats – was his *bête noir.* (That is not to say, of course, that he did not appreciate it as literature; he did, and lectured well on it, but feared its consequence.) Attacking this literature was doubtless a grave mistake on his part. For one thing Ascendancy Anglo-Irish literature was rapidly losing ground as the class from which it originated became assimilated into the common Irish culture. (This may not have been apparent, of course, some sixty years ago.) Then again, it was not the fault of Yeats and others that historical circumstances had left them somewhat on the peripheries of things Irish: most of such writers were sincerely concerned with Ireland, and should not in any sense have been made to feel unwanted in any cultural plans for the future. This was at least a tactical mistake on Corkery's part, as was his effort to categorize Irish writers in English according as they were 'truly Irish' or not. This kind of 'geese and swans' methodology was guaranteed to bring the wrath of writers throughout Ireland on his head. And it did.

The final rift between Corkery and his disciples, O'Connor and Ó Faoláin, must have come about soon after his book on Synge. Corkery had been saying to O'Connor for some time before this – particularly since the death of Terence Mc Swiney in 1920 – that there were many things more important in life than literature. O'Connor's retort was typical: 'I knew there weren't, because if there were, I should be doing them.'[11]

Corkery was surely right that there are many things more important in life than literature; but he was surely wrong if he expected people such as O'Connor or Ó Faoláin to give adherence to a rather doctrinaire long-term cultural programme for the country in a way which would compromise their own immediate personal positions as creative writers in the English language.

At the same time I feel that Corkery's main argument in *Synge* – even given that it is doctrinaire – has been misrepresented (sometimes wilfully so). The grounds on which he made his distinction between writers in English who were 'truly Irish', and those who were not so, proved particularly irksome. Corkery, following Stopford Brooke, pointed to three basic elements in the Irish consciousness which he would expect to find reflected in any Irish literature calling itself a national literature, and by this criterion found many Irish writers, both contemporary writers of his and writers of the past, to have been colonial Ascendancy-type artists who did not 'belong'.

Whether Corkery was right in his identification of these basic elements – religion, nationality, land – in traditional Irish consciousness is, of course, debatable. Expert studies in the field of cultural anthropology may in the future help us here by giving us a clearer picture of our value-system. I feel from looking at traditional literature in Irish that Corkery was probably right in thinking that our value-system revolves to a great extent around these elements; but it is clear that a very flexible and sensitive interpretation of what is meant by these concepts, and how they operate, is needed before any attempt is made to apply them in any way. Corkery himself was quite wrong, I feel, in his own finding that Synge did not reflect traditional Irish religious values.[12]

What seems to have mostly disturbed O'Connor and other writers, however, about Corkery's incipient efforts in cultural anthropology was that it appeared to them to place restrictions on Irish writing in the future – that the Corkery doctrine took no account of the personal nature of creative writing, that it smacked of a programme which demanded that writers and artists treat of certain themes, represent certain situations and certain classes, have above all a rural orientation. While some of the phrases used by Corkery could in isolation be so understood, I fail to see that such an interpretation can fairly be read from Corkery's general argument. What he is in effect saying is, I take it, a commonplace nowadays in cultural anthropology: that where there is a special identifiable culture one finds a particular basic value-system, structured in a certain way or with a certain - though not static - permanency; and that writers and artists, as well as workers and managers, normally reflect that value-system in whatever they do (even sometimes by reacting or seeming to react against it). This may mean in the case of some writers that they deal directly with themes reflecting the basic value system; but it could also mean that the majority of writers, dealing as they will do with the whole spectrum of human life, would reflect it only very indirectly indeed in their work. This is clearly pointed out by Corkery himself in his comment on the element of nationality in Irish literature when he states: 'One may be sure we are come upon genuine Anglo-Irish literature when [nationality] . . . expresses itself almost in every page, no matter what the nature of the expression may be, direct or indirect, heroic or grotesque or perverse *but not alien-minded*.'[13]

As it happens most prominent Irish writers in English since Corkery's time - from Kavanagh to Heaney, from Joyce to McGahern - have dealt quite directly with the values Corkery identifies as basic in Irish culture. Corkery today would find it difficult indeed to deny the temporary emergence (at least) of a 'genuine Anglo-Irish literature'.

I regard the aspect of the controversy relating to the deleterious effect the Corkery doctrine might have on creative writing in Ireland to have been a polemical red herring. The real issue remained: whether Ireland - given its particular circumstances and cultural history - not alone can produce, but can keep producing in the long term an individual literature in the English language. (In so far as none of us will live long enough to find out, Corkery's belief that an individual Irish literature would finally have to be in the Irish language is, of course, unassailable!)

In *Synge and Anglo-Irish Literature*, Corkery did not seem ready to deal head on with an alternative proposition: that Ireland in the future could have two national languages, two national literatures? Later (in the 1940s) he was in no doubt: 'Ireland they say has literature in English and literature in Irish - and both are Irish literature. So that Ireland is like a two headed calf: it can cry out its hunger through two throats.'[14]

We today have mostly settled, at least temporarily, for the two-headed calf. We know that we have talented Irish writers who naturally reflect an Irish value system both in English and Irish. What the detailed long-term future shall or should be is not the kind of question we ask any more. *Solvitur ambulando* . . .

The controversy resulting from the cultural philosophy expounded in the first chapter of *Synge*, diverted attention almost completely from the rest of the book (217 pages out of 247!). This is regrettable, for his critque of the Synge plays was better than most others written in the following fifty years. There are judgements one would quarrel with – his denial of classic status to *The Playboy* – but there is evidence everywhere that the artist Synge was being interpreted by one who was a sensitive artist and dramatist in his own right. I have already referred to one major fault I would find with his critique of Synge's work: his conclusion that Synge had not succeeded in assimilating or reflecting the Catholic values of traditional Aran life. I have argued elsewhere that Synge was right and Corkery wrong:[15] that there is a marked ambivalence about Christian religion in traditional Gaelic literature; that pre-Christian values loom as authoritatively if not more authoritatively than Christian values in the traditional consciousness; that what is understood as 'traditional Irish Catholicism' is largely an invention of the nineteenth century.

Many commentators find that particular criticism of Synge by Corkery to be typical of one who would stipulate that all Irish literature should be Catholic (as well as Gaelic). All I will say here in that regard is that there was grave doubt in the minds of some of his friends as to whether he was in any real sense a Catholic himself. The sculptor Séamus Murphy, a lifelong friend, has said that Corkery was an unbeliever, even refusing at the end to have the ordinary Christian iconography on the head-stone over his grave. Whether this is true or not, I think Corkery's assumption – the assumption of all Gaelic Leaguers – that Irish traditional life was deeply Catholic led him astray in his analysis of the religious element in Synge (and in Irish literature). I see no evidence, however, in anything he wrote or said that he personally wished Irish literature to be overwhelmingly Catholic in the future. What he did obviously personally wish is that there should be, as in all cultural matters, natural continuity and development in the Irish religious and ethical tradition – whatever it was.

If it was the ideological first chapter of *Synge* which mostly raised the hackles of *littérateurs* fifty years ago, it is, ironically enough, the first chapter of *The Hidden Ireland* which has mostly been raising the hackles of historians in recent years. This time, however, it is not Corkery's vision of the future which is being questioned but his vision of the past. His picture of eighteenth-century Ireland is considered by some social historians to lurch from the highly romantic to the plainly erroneous. I am one of those who first questioned the accuracy of Corkery's perceptions about life in the eighteenth century;[16] but I am also one of those who believe *The Hidden Ireland* to be one of the few really important books written in Ireland in this century. The fact that some of the social history is seen through the eyes of an ardent early twentieth-century nationalist gives it a special slant undoubtedly. But if he had not been just that, this book would never have been written, by him or by anybody else.

Many people I know who have read *The Hidden Ireland*, even in recent years, find it an inspirational book. The feeling of inspiration or excitement which the book can arouse and has aroused, is mostly, of course, a reflection of Corkery's own exhilaration when he began to discover the literary heritage of Ireland at the beginning of this century. It has to be remembered that literature in Irish, while carefully preserved in manuscripts, by and large had not been published in book form until from *c.* 1900 onwards. In the years 1900-1920, during Corkery's prime, the poetry of Aogán Ó Rathaille, of Eoghan Rua Ó Súilleabháin, of Brian Merriman, and so on, began to appear and to be read. In 1925 in *The Hidden Ireland* Corkery describes and analyses the effect this hidden heritage had on him.

Corkery, in conversation, has said that he never really understood that the Irish language existed when he was growing up in Cork City (say 1878-1900); and that he was about thirty years of age before he managed to get to grips, in any serious way, with the language. The fact that a vast and exciting literature was being written in Irish all over Ireland a mere hundred years before his birth, and for a good thousand years before that again, must have astounded him. In *The Hidden Ireland* he set out to depict for his own generation the great wealth and quality of that literature, and the sensibility of the community from which it emanated. If I were asked to summarize his intention in that book I would probably say it was to give an interpretation of the poetry and sensibility of Gaelic Ireland in the eighteenth century, as revealed in the work of the (then published) Munster poets.

The historians will not have it thus, however. They insist on treating the book not primarily as an analysis of literary work, but as an analysis of eighteenth-century social history. Louis Cullen in his paper 'The Hidden Ireland: Reassessment of a Concept' says: 'The concept of a "hidden Ireland" is now long established as an aspect of the interpretation of the eighteenth century economic and social history of Ireland'.[17] Even if that is true, the hidden Ireland of the social historians is not Corkery's hidden Ireland. Corkery says quite clearly in his book: 'In these pages only one aspect of the Hidden Ireland is delineated; the literary side'; or again: 'This book is a study of some of the Munster Gaelic poets of the eighteenth century'.[18] He says quite clearly, in fact, that he is making no attempt to engage in social or economic history: all he is doing is giving a resumé of what historians such as Lecky have written. His treatment of history he says 'will be only a glance; for the historians, Lecky especially, have made their own of it, and their books are there for the reading'.[19] The approach Corkery is engaged in is, in fact, the same approach he used in literary classes when discussing 'The Elizabethan Love-Lyric', or 'the Restoration Love-Lyric', or 'The Romantic Poets': he is trying to place literary work in its historic context, so as to give us a deeper appreciation of the literature itself.

It has to be repeated then that his primary concern was to portray a literature, not to write a social history. Historians keep on assuming, as Louis Cullen assumes, that Corkery is engaged in 'the use of literary material as historical evidence',[20] whereas he is quite clearly engaged in the use of historical material as a context for a literature and a sensibility. It is apparent that the historians have not understood the methodology of a *littérateur,* and this is never more obvious than when Louis Cullen inexplicably imagines that 'the Hidden Ireland' should in fact be identifiable (not as a unique literary heritage, as most of us would have it) but as a certain place or region in eighteenth-century Ireland![21]

Having said that, one has to agree that the historical landscape Corkery depicts is, as was quite common up to twenty or thirty years ago, seen through romantic nationalistic-tinted glasses. Eighteenth-century Ireland, in his view, was uniformly poor, miserable, ground down by Penal laws: there is no sense of the teeming life, the sense of humour, the community vitality, which must have been widespread and is readily apparent from sources such as the diary written by Amhlaoibh Ó Súilleabháin as late as the early nineteenth century. In particular there is no real sense of Irish speakers, including Irish poets, being anything more than peasants doomed to live in 'hovels'. Yet among the very poets Corkery speaks of, Eibhlín Dhubh Ní Chonaill lived in a fine large house (still standing) near Macroom, County Cork, and sent two sons to be educated in Paris; Seán Clárach Mac Dónaill owned a large farm and mill near Ráth Luirc; Piaras Mac Gearailt's house where Courts of Poetry were held was a large beautiful Georgian mansion which still stands . . . and so on. Corkery didn't quite see eighteenth-century Ireland, or indeed eighteenth-century poetry, in all its extraordinary diversity. But, of course, most of the evidence for this diversity only came to light many years after the publication of *The Hidden Ireland.* And, doubtless, further evidence will keep on coming to light, so that the views of present-day historians of the eighteenth century will in turn be challenged and discounted.

Corkery achieved triumphantly, however, the main objective of his book, which was 'to see [the poetry] against the dark world that threw it up'.[22] That world may not have been as dark as he, following nationalistic historians in the first quarter of the twentieth century, painted it. On the other hand it was quite dark enough to justify his astonishment at the flourishing of such a poetry in such a context and in such a time. Because no matter how much we modify the eighteenth-century picture, this literature *is* the literature of a subject population who saw their native educational, legal, economic and religious institutions demolished before their eyes, so that more and more people (including the poets), isolated within a repressive foreign system, died in despair or abject poverty; so that, indeed, the Great Famine holocaust in the next century was to be the logical conclusion of the continuing English conquest. Against all that, Corkery's celebration of eighteenth-century poetry, his declaration of being 'astonished' at its quality, is not out of place in any way.

The author's *modus operandi* in the book was tailored to the needs of people who in the early twentieth century knew little of their hidden literary heritage. Chapter I was a general resumé of eighteenth-century social history as understood by nationalist historians; chapter II a resumé of the role of the Irish big house; chapter III of the bardic past; chapter IV of the eighteenth-century courts of poetry; chapter V of the *aisling* genre. All this resumé work was absolutely necessary for general readers at the time but contained little or nothing that was new to Irish scholars working in these various fields. What was new was his handling of the material and the general excellence of the writing (albeit over-mannered in places). And it should be said that scholars of Irish literature over fifty years later find very little to quarrel with in his general picture of our literary history.

It is in the second half of the book (chapters VI–X) that Corkery speaks out of his own particular expertise, that of critic and writer (except that his restricted knowledge of the Irish language caused him to be less footsure than he would have been dealing with poetry in English). Here, however, he tackles the extremely difficult poetry of Ó Rathaille, Merriman, Eoghan Rua Ó Súilleabháin and others with a certain assuredness which comes from a deep acquaintance with the process of creative writing. And I should say that I have not detected anywhere that his romantic/nationalistic view of history has affected his assessment of any particular poem or of any particular poet.

His assessment of O'Rahilly was a masterful piece of work for its time. It was an assessment that persuaded many people that the eighteenth-century Irish-speaking community of Sliabh Luachra had produced a poet that could possibly be spoken of in the same breath as Yeats. O'Rahilly's anguished aristocratic spirit had a special appeal for Corkery (as it had indeed for Yeats who helped Frank O'Connor in his translations of O'Rahilly).

Corkery's evaluation of Merriman was also quite perceptive, but slightly begrudging (as in the case of Synge's *Playboy*). The Corkman's somewhat genteel Victorian disposition took fright a little at the explicitly sexual content of *The Midnight Court*. At the same time it must be remembered that even in the highly puritanical Ireland of the 1920s he rates the poet as one of the three major poets of the eighteenth century, and the poem as one of the most remarkable ever written in Ireland.

On the other hand, I feel he grossly overrated the work of Eoghan Rua Ó Súilleabháin (as he did the work of some of the other minor poets).[23] He spoke enthusiastically of some poems by Ó Súilleabháin, for instance as 'perfect lyrics', whereas nowadays most of us who teach these poems would look on the majority of them as pieces of overblown virtuosity. Corkery was probably led astray here by his lack of natural feeling for the Irish language but he was mostly led astray I think by his perception as critic that if Eoghan Rua's poems had survived (as they had) on people's lips for some 150 years, they had to have in them the enduring stuff of literature. These poems certainly had survived; but they had survived, I would submit, as lyrics for music, rather than as poems to be read or listened to. Eoghan Rua had the sagacity to write his poems to the finest of the classic Irish airs; so that his songs are still reckoned high amongst our Irish *Lieder* (*Cois na Siúire, Ceo Draíochta, Im Aonar Seal, Ag Taisteal na Blárnan,* etc.).

Corkery's greatest literary achievement in *The Hidden Ireland*, however, is not, in my view, his appraisal of the work of the different poets. It is rather his formulation of the critical viewpoint that the nature of Irish language poetry – its conventions, its diction, its values – is quite different to that of the nature of the central tradition of English poetry. Irish/Gaelic poetry of the seventeenth and eighteenth centuries inclined more to the modes of medieval European poetry; and as this was so, Corkery felt that critical approaches proper to an evaluation of English post-Renaissance poetry were not always the approaches appropriate to a consideration of Irish poetry. Consequently in *The Hidden Ireland* he began his probe into the special nature of Irish poetry, a probe he was to elaborate on later in other articles and essays.

I will not attempt here to describe in any detail what he was to discover for himself about the nature of traditional Irish poetry.[24] In general, however, he found it much closer to the spirit of certain medieval work such as that of Villon; or on the other hand to the work of poets in countries such as Russia which were never heavily influenced by the Renaissance. He liked to quote, in particular, this passage from a book on Russian literature by Maurice Baring:

> Russian poetry does not only cling close to the solid earth, but is based on and saturated with common sense, with a curious matter of fact quality. And the common sense which the greatest poet, Pushkin, is so thoroughly impregnated with is as foreign to German *Schwärmerei* as it is to French rhetoric or the imaginative exuberance of England. What the Russian poets did . . . was to extract poetry from the daily life they saw about them and to express it in forms of incomparable beauty.

Corkery's comment on this was (and I translate from an essay of his written in Irish in the 1950s): 'There is scarcely a word in that which doesn't fit our own poetry. . . . As for myself I can say that before coming on our own poetry I just could not understand that poetry of the kind Maurice Baring describes could exist.'[25]

This then was the Hidden Ireland, the hidden literature, he came on fortuitously; and the excitement it generated in him he still manages to communicate with us. Some sections in his book we may find today over-mannered or a little rhetorical. On the other hand there are very many marvellous well-wrought passages. In general the book remains a monument to his own 'dazzlement'; to his astonishment of having come on such a unique literature in English-speaking, English-reading, English-leaning, Cork City at the turn of the century. However much scholarly historians continue to amend his historical viewpoint (which I stress again was not his own viewpoint but the viewpoint of historians of his day), nothing can diminish this sense of wonder; and very little can be altered I think in his general assessment of the nature of Irish poetry in general.

Daniel Corkery was not endowed with enormous mental agility or brilliance; he was rather an original meditative highly-perceptive man. In addition he had an extraordinarily refined and wide-ranging flair for artistic work of various kinds. Frank O'Connor, having castigated him roundly in the 1930s for his cultural philosophy, could still say of him a quarter of a century later: 'The greatest artist of his generation, I still feel.'[26] O'Connor was referring, in particular, I take it, to Corkery's three influential books of short stories and his one novel. Corkery also happened to be a watercolourist of distinction (especially after his retiral, at the age of seventy), a musician who could play Mozart on the violin, a woodworker who (inheriting the craft instincts of his English-speaking Cork ancestors) could make a workmanlike chair or bookcase. I am convinced that this many-sided unique man has not yet received half the attention he deserves. In the last few decades, in particular, he has become an undeserving casualty of ideological warfare.

[1988]

16

Celebration of Place
in Irish Writing

A T THE BEGINNING of this century a little-known poet, Pádraig Ó hÉigeartaigh, writing in the United States of the drowning of his son Donncha, complains that his child has been buried in foreign ground:

> My sorrow, Donncha, my thousand-cherished under this sod stretched,
> this mean sod lying on your little body – my utter fright . . .
> if this sleep were on you in Cill na Dromad or some grave in the West
> it would ease my sorrow, though great the affliction and I'd not complain.
>
> (D, p. 261)

Few Irish people will question the poet's notion of the foreign soil being mean or hostile. Nor will very many wonder unduly about the whereabouts of Cill na Dromad, where he would wish his son's body to lie. We all know Ó hÉigeartaigh is speaking here of the centre of his universe, the beloved home-place/parish/territory; the burial place pre-ordained for his people through countless centuries.

This emotional response to home-place has become a cliché, of course, in much of Ireland's literature. It is not, of course, unique to Ireland. One will probably find a reverential feeling for home-place in every country – and in every literature – throughout the world. Some poets, in particular, tend to regard the place where they spent their childhood as a kind of paradise; a paradise which they keep on trying to retrieve during their adult life.

248

It is unlikely, however, that feeling for place (including feeling for home-place) is found so deeply rooted, and so widely celebrated, in any western European culture as it is in Irish culture. It seems to have made its presence felt in Irish literature at every level and in every era from early historic times to the present day. By and large the places revered, or identified with in traditional Irish literature, are rural places - the townland of Cill na Dromad rather than the town of Tralee, the parish of Iveleary rather than the city of Cork. And while over half of the population of the Irish Republic lives today in cities and large towns, considerable numbers of our urban dwellers still appear to look to the ancient rural home-places. Máirtín O Direáin (1910-1988), amongst modern Irish language poets, is a classic example: much of his work centres on his feeling of being an exile, uprooted in 'the deceitful city'.[1] Even Seamus Heaney speaks of 'the empty city'.[2]

Cities and towns - particularly on the east coast - have historically been the creations and preserves of invading colonists, and the consequent sense of alienation of the native population may help to explain some of the difficulty many Irish people still have in identifying fully with urban life. The main reason for this difficulty, however, must stem from the special decentralized and rural nature of Irish society itself, from pre-historic times down to the recent past. Eoin Mac Néill has said: 'We find the ancient Greeks organised like the Irish in small political communities, but these [Greek communities] . . . are based in each case on a walled town. The Irish state remained a rural city, a city of the fields'.[3] The land of Ireland in pre-Elizabethan times was divided into anything from one hundred to two hundred of such 'rural cities' all autonomous or semi-autonomous kingdoms. The chieftain-kings of these territories - and often, doubtless, the sub-chieftains of even smaller territories - were imagined from ancient times as being wedded to their land. Inauguration ceremonies of an archaic pre-Christian form, symbolizing the nuptial ties between chieftain and place, were enacted down to the seventeenth century. Even in the late eighteenth century when Eibhlín Dhubh Ní Chonaill made her famous lament for her husband, Art Ó Laoghaire, it was clearly still the norm to think of the ancestral kingdom as blazing up in grief for the death of its aristocratic spouse.

Generally speaking, families clearly identified with particular places did not move outside the territorial limits. And it is quite surprising, despite all our wars and plantations, how many of the descendants of our aristocratic families still live on today in the old beloved territories - the McCarthys and the O'Learys in their Cork territories, the O'Dohertys in Donegal, the O'Neills in Tyrone, the O'Byrnes in Wicklow, the O'Flahertys in Galway, the O'Donoghues in Kerry.

It seems then that it is the sacred wedding of territory to chieftain – and by extension of territory to kin – which lies near the heart of the passion for place in Irish life and literature. Parallel with this bonding, of course, was the bonding of each free family group with its own particular inherited land. Down to our own day each field, hill and hillock was named with affection.

The feeling for place has been acutely intensified, of course, by events following on the English conquest (1600–   ): plantations, evictions, enforced exile. There is scarcely one of the many scores of literary poets writing in Irish in the seventeenth, eighteenth, and nineteenth centuries – from Haicéad and Mac Cuarta down to Máire Bhuí Ní Laoghaire and Raftery – whose poems do not focus in some way on his/her feeling for home or ancestral land. A great number of folk-poems tell of the pain of exile from home. Some other poems, both literary and folk, tell of the destruction of famous houses on home territory. The folksong *Kilcash*, in particular, which laments the destruction of a great house owned by a Catholic branch of the Anglo-Irish Butlers, hovers on the edge of heartbreak:

> What shall we do for timber?
>   The last of the woods is down.
> Kilcash and the house of its glory
>   And the bell of the house are gone,
> The spot where that lady waited
>   Who shamed all women for grace
> When earls came sailing to greet her
>   And Mass was said in the place.
>
> My grief and my affliction
>   Your gates are taken away,
> Your avenue needs attention,
>   Goats in the garden stray.
> The courtyard's filled with water
>   And the great earls where are they?
> The earls, the lady, the people
>   Beaten into the clay.
>
> No sound of duck or geese there,
>   Hawk's cry or eagle's call,
> No humming of the bees there
>   That brought honey and wax for all,
> Nor even the song of the birds there
>   When the sun goes down in the west,
> No cuckoo on top of the boughs there,
>   Singing the world to rest.

There's mist there tumbling from branches,
   Unstirred by night and by day,
And darkness falling from heaven,
   For our fortune has ebbed away,
There's no holly nor hazel nor ash there,
   The pasture's rock and stone,
The crown of the forest has withered,
   And the last of its game is gone.

I beseech of Mary and Jesus
   That the great come home again
With long dances danced in the garden,
   Fiddle music and mirth among men,
That Kilcash the home of our fathers
   Be lifted on high again,
And from that to the deluge of waters
   In bounty and peace remain.[4]

The traditional treatment of home-place and territory in literature survived in good measure the linguistic changeover in the nineteenth century from Irish to English. In the case, however, of a great number of English-language ballads – and some Irish language songs – of beloved places and counties, a blurred maudlin tone often asserts itself. But the old values continue to be reflected with dignity and perception in the verse of poets such as Kavanagh, Montague, Kinsella, Heaney, and in prose-works such as Behan's *Borstal Boy*. There is no doubting, for instance, that place (with its special connotation of stability) fuels real passion in the poetry of Patrick Kavanagh. In his poem on the black hills of Shancoduff 'eternally' looking 'north towards Armagh', he clearly identifies the heart of his own universe:

> These are my Alps and I have climbed the Matterhorn
> With a sheaf of hay for three perishing calves
> In the field under the Big Forth of Rocksavage.[5]

Seamus Heaney points to a certain lack of dimension in Kavanagh's use of place in his work. 'Kavanagh's place-names,' he says, 'are there to stake out a personal landscape, they declare one man's experience, they are denuded of tribal or etymological implications. Mucker, Dundalk, Inniskeen, provide no frisson beyond the starkness of their own daunting, consonantal noise.'[6]

This perceptive comment alerts us to the fact that one would never guess from Kavanagh's poetry that he spent his youth in a territory where the gods and godesses of the Ulster sagas once played out their complicated games of love and war; where every townland once echoed with the memory of heroic deeds. At the same time it may not be quite accurate for Heaney to say that the poet's use of placenames declares 'one man's experience'. Kavanagh obviously shared in the traditional communal feeling that the home-place or territory was indeed the stable centre of the universe, that the surrounding hills were 'eternal', and that some gods – whose names he does not know – preside over the local scene. 'I have lived in important places', Kavanagh declares in the well-known poem where he has Homer assuring him that local rows and heroics are not to be minimized: I made the Iliad/from such a local row. Gods make their own/importance.' It is clear that the absence of a sanctioning mythology was at least a matter of passionate concern to him in his exploration of the poetry of place. In that way he reflects a traditional concern.

It can be said then that while *passion for place* remains an integral part of the work of Patrick Kavanagh and of the work of a large number of other Irish writers in English, that *sense of place* – the sense of all the historical, mythological, environmental and familial associations previously mentioned – tends to fade away. In the nineteenth-century linguistic change-over from Irish to English, the passion has been cut off to some extent from its primal Irish source, and remains somewhat under-developed, unarticulated. And some writers, W.B. Yeats for instance, deploy place-names coldly in a formal, rhetorical fashion to establish a certain tone of voice or to achieve the sought after verse pattern.

On the other hand, Máirtín Ó Direáin, a modern poet writing in Irish, has no great difficulty in fitting his own long lyric obsession with the island of Aran into the complete traditional framework – even though his evocation of Aran as the paradise of his childhood takes absolute precedence over all other elements of his sense of place. Again a much younger poet, Nuala Ní Dhomhnaill, has made unique creative use of her sense of place in a remarkable series of poems written on her return from Turkey to live in West Kerry. In one of these poems, *I mBaile an tSléibhe*, she identifies with the places and the flora of her ancestral district, and moves easily in a short space from personal and family involvement to an awareness of the folklore and mythology associated with named places such as Mount Eagle and the ancient aristocratic habitation of Cathair Léith (where, tradition has it, even the spancels of sheep were made of silk):

> In Baile an tSléibhe
> is Cathair Léith
> and below it
> the house of the Dunleavies;
> from here the poet Seán

went into the Great Blasket
and from here the red hair
and gift of poetry came down to me
through four generations.

Beside the road
there is a stream
covered over with fuchsias
and the wild flag
yellow
from the end of April
to mid-June,
and in the yard there is a scent
of pine-apple mayweed or camomile
as it is commonly known in the
    surrounding countryside,
in Cill Uru and in Com an Liaig
in Ballinchouta and in Cathairbuilg.

And one day
in Cathair Léith
a white trout leapt
out of the river
and into the bucket
of a woman
who had led her cow
to water there;
a time
when three ships came sailing
into the bay
the eagle was still nesting
on the top of the hill
and the sheep of Cathair
had spancels of silk.[7]

(H, pp. 152–53)

I am unaware, however, that any poet or writer of Irish has managed to evoke this kind of identification with the city or town in which he or she was reared. The idea of an Irish city or town being the loved home-place is, one feels, of more recent origin. Not, perhaps, until James Joyce wrote *Ulysses* did a whole Irish city figure unreservedly in serious literature as one man's revered universe. Seán O'Casey and Brendan Behan are among those who have since added significantly to the sense of Dublin city as home. It is worth recalling, for instance, Behan's beautifully cadenced identification of freedom with Dublin's 'high-places' at the end of the *Borstal Boy*, when he is about to step off the ship, home from exile and prison:

> The next morning I stood on the deck while the boat came into Dún Laoghaire, and looked at the sun struggling up over the hills; and the city all round the bay.

> >   . . . and I will make my journey,
> >   If life and health but stand,
> >   Unto that pleasant country,
> >   That fresh and fragrant strand,
> >   And leave your boasted braveries,
> >   Your wealth and high command,
> >   For the fair hills of Holy Ireland....

> There they were, as if I'd never left them; in their sweet and stately order round the bay – Bray Head, the Sugarloaf, the Two Rock, the Three Rock, Kippure, the king of them all, rising his threatening head behind and over their shoulders till they sloped down to the city. I counted the spires, from Rathmines' fat dome on the one side to St George's spire on the north, and in the centre, Christchurch. Among the smaller ones, just on the docks, I could pick out, even in the haze of morning, the ones I knew best, St Laurence O'Toole's and St Barnabas; I had them all counted, present and correct and the chimneys of the Pigeon House, and the framing circle of the road along the edge of the Bay, Dún Laoghaire, Blackrock, Sandymount Tower, Ringsend and the city; then the other half circle, Fairview, Marino, Clontarf, Raheny, Kilbarrack, Baldoyle, to the height of Howth Head.

> I couldn't really see Kilbarrack or Baldoyle, but it was only that I knew they were there. So many belonging to me lay buried in Kilbarrack, the healthiest graveyard in Ireland, they said, because it was so near the sea, and I thought I could see the tricolour waving over Dan Head's grave, which I could not from ten miles over the Bay. And I could see Baldoyle there, because it was the races.

> 'Passport, travel permit or identity document, please,' said the immigration man beside me.

> I handed him the expulsion order.

> He read it, looked at it and handed it back to me. He had a long educated countryman's sad face, like a teacher, and took my hand.

> 'Céad míle fáilte abhaile romhat.'

> A hundred thousand welcomes home to you.

> I smiled and said, 'Go raibh maith agat.'

> Thanks.

> He looked very serious, and tenderly enquired, 'Caithfidh go bhfuil

sé go hiontach bheith saor.'
  'Caithfidh go bhfuil.'
  'It must be wonderful to be free.'
  'It must,' said I, walked down the gangway, past a detective, and got
on the train for Dublin.

Brendan Behan, of course, was one of our writers in English who also
wrote in Irish, and was quite conscious of the Irish language literary tradi-
tion. He would have read Merriman and Donncha Rua Mac Conmara (as
verse quoted in the passage above reveals), and almost certainly some songs
of Raftery. Merriman spoke of the healing nature of the home landscape
– the hills in particular. For Raftery the home territory was a kind of Land
of Youth/Tír na nÓg ('If I were found standing amidst my own people/Old
age would drop from me and I'd regain my youth'). It is quite probable
then that his acquaintance with the Gaelic literary tradition heightened
Behan's awareness of his own community's feeling for the city in which
he was born and bred.

And it is to be noted that in the midst of the circle of hills, spires, and
'high-places', Behan also identifies with the *cill*/graveyard of Kilbarrack where
so many belonging to him lay buried.

The homeplace is not, of course, the only place to merit special recogni-
tion in traditional Irish literature. Historic places – places, in particular,
which were associated with the deeds of mythological and heroic figures
of the Irish sagas – were also specially revered; as were hilly places of
wild beauty where wild animals and birds of prey were hunted.

Wordsworth in one of his poems complained that England, unlike Greece,
lacked hills or mountains 'by the celestial muses glorified'.[8] Ireland, like
Greece, had scarce a hill or tract of land which was not invested in some
way with mythological glory. All this was given special recognition in early
medieval Ireland in the form of a branch of learning called *Dinnshean-
chas*; the lore of places, in particular 'high-places'. No professional poet
was accounted educated if he were not fully acquainted with this discipline.
Place-names, as a consequence, became a part of the resonance of some
of the finest Irish literary works of medieval times – *Agallamh na Seanórach*
(The Colloquoy of the Ancients), *Buile Shuibhne* (translated as *Sweeney
Astray* by Seamus Heaney), the lays and lyrics of the Fianna.

In a paper on 'Place-names and Mythology in Irish Tradition',[9] Proin-
sias Mac Cana says: 'The conceptual framework of the Dinnsheanchas is
thoroughly and consciously pre-christian'; and he goes on to discuss, inter
alia, the special religious status given in pre-Christian times to natural
features such as hills and springs. It is likely indeed that substantial

fragments of such pre-Christian values still lie deep in the Irish con-
sciousness, preserved and consolidated in various communities in lore
and oral literature.

One of the great agents of transmission would have been the literature
of the Fianna, which from being a high literary concern of learned men
in the later middle ages was mostly known as the chief popular entertain-
ment of a majority of Irish people in the eighteenth and nineteenth
centuries. In this literature which was still being listened to in our
Gaeltachtaí with both reverence and glee down to the twentieth century,
Oisín son of Fionn keeps on persuading St Patrick of the pre-eminence
of the old pre-Christian life. In the lays of the Fianna, in particular, freedom
and scope and virtue is associated with hills; the *cill* (kill/church graveyard)
is deemed hostile. 'Hill' connotes all wild nature; 'cill' connotes the bells,
rules, and beliefs of Christianity. The lays recount innocently and openly
the attempts of St Patrick to convert Oisín to an acceptance of Christian
dogma, and especially of a Christian eternity. Oisín demurs and speaks
of the beauty and the music which existed during the time of the Fianna,
a warrior-group who 'loved the hills, not hermit-cells'; and as part of his
argument Oisín creates a litany of names of places[10] and wildlife which
existed long before the time of Christ:

> Throat-song of the blackbird of Doire an Chairn
>   and the stag's call from Aill na gCaor
> were Fionn's music, sleeping at morn,
>   and the ducks from Loch na dTrí gCaol,
>
> the grouse at Cruachan, seat of Conn,
>   otters whistling at Druim Dá Loch,
> eagle cry in Gleann na bhFuath,
>   cuckoos' murmur on Cnoc na Scoth,
>
> dogs' voices in Gleann Caoin,
>   cry of the half-blind hunting eagle,
> patter of hounds, on their way early
>   in from Tráigh na gCloch nDearg.
>
> When Fionn and the Fianna lived
>   they loved the hills, not hermit-cells.
> Blackbird speech is what they loved
>   – not the sound, unlovely, of your bells.
>
>   (*D*, p.43)

Karl Popper has remarked that when a culture is under severe strain
it either completely rejects existing society or looks for a utopia in the

past or in the future. There is much evidence to suggest – especially in the sagas – that the deeply-rooted archaic Irish society, put under strain by the advent of Christianity sought its utopia in the old pagan past. It is not at all surprising that Oisín would name for St Patrick, lovingly and lyrically, the names of places in his own eternal utopia on the pagan land of Ireland.

Some places were more revered than others, of course, in the Irish utopia. Places where druidic worship or celebration of nature took place, for instance, would have been most highly regarded. Although we know very little about our pre-Christian religious ceremonies, it can be confidently said that two type of sites would clearly have been treated as 'holy' in ancient Ireland: certain hill-tops and, by and large, sites where the Christian *cill* (cell/church) was established. The *cill* was generally placed, it seems, in the vicinity of holy wells, graveyards or other basic locations of pagan worship. The sites named in memory of the local god/goddess would have been later named in honour of the local Christian saint.

It is widely accepted that church authorities made Trojan efforts from earliest historic times in Ireland to transform the holy druidic sites into places of Christian worship. (Even the author of that marvellous prose-compendium *The Colloquoy of the Ancients* (*c.* 1200) endeavoured to present an acceptable Christian version of Fianna lore, a version, let it be said, which never made an impact on the populace at large.) Innumerable monastic *cill*-type churches sprung up all over the country. The patron saints of the *cill*-sites ousted to a large extent the patron gods/goddesses of the pagan sites. Yet a substantial part of the public continued to perform rites, which were manifestly un-Christian, in honour of the *cill* patron. As late as the nineteenth century, Catholic bishops published edicts condemning riotous behaviour of various sorts on the patron's name-day, at the site of the *cill*. And in our own time, indeed, while riotous behaviour has been eliminated, some of the pre-Christian rites still mingle freely with the more orthodox rites, at the yearly 'pattern'. It is probable that the mingling of two religions, two loyalties, only served to magnify the importance of the *cill*-site as the principal 'holy' site in the district. It was after all the place where the patron of the territory (whoever he was) was laid to rest, the patron under whose protection the people of the territory would prepare for entry into eternity. The ambivalence of it all is highlighted by the Armagh poet Art Mac Cumhaigh who, having yielded to the wiles of his fairy lover, is willing in a decidedly non-christian manner, to abandon his wife – on the strict understanding that his body be finally buried in his home-graveyard, *Úir-Chill an Chreagáin*: 'though I die by the Sionainn, in Man, or in mighty Egypt/bury me under this sod with Creagán's sweet Gaels' (*D*, p. 181). So it is that when Pádraig Ó hÉigeartaigh speaks, in this century, of *Cill na Dromad* (the church/graveyard of Dromad), he is, one thinks, speaking as much of the graveyard site as he is of his home-place.

It is probable that certain social circumstances in the nineteenth century – emigration to the USA, migration from rural to urban areas – intensified the importance of the ancestral graveyard. Since that time Irish prose-writers, in particular, have explored its central importance in people's lives. The moving story of an elderly woman in Cork City whose last wish is to be buried in the rural family graveyard is told by Frank O'Connor in *The Long Road to Ummera*;[11] the traditional conflict as to which cemetery the body of a young married woman should be laid in is powerfully describ-ed by Donncha Ó Céileachair in *Sochraid Neil Chonchubhair Dubh*;[12] Seumas O'Kelly's *tour de force, The Weaver's Grave*,[13] treats of a woman who is obsessed not alone with burying her husband in the right cemetery but in the exact ancestral plot; the comic frustration of Caitríona Pháidín who feels she has been buried in a cheap plot is the central theme of Máirtín Ó Cadhain's *Cré na Cille*. The literary work in which I find the most sensitive artistic expression of the general theme is a poem in Scots Gaelic by Sorley Maclean where the poet laments his brother Calum who had died far from home.[14] This remarkable poem is full of the place-names of the Scottish Gaeltacht all played against each other like a series of war-pipe variations on a single theme. Maclean's hypnotic concentration throughout the whole poem is centred on what earth, what district, which clan would most willingly and most reverentially, give sanctuary to his brother's ashes. Nowhere in the poem – nor indeed in the stories by our Irish writers – is there much concern for the welfare of the soul in a Christian afterlife.

Despite the underlay of non-Christian feeling and behaviour associated with the *cill*, since early times it has remained formally an important part of the Christian presence throughout the country. Not so 'the hill' (which the Fianna loved); the hill, by and large, remained 'pagan'.

In *The Festival of Lughnasa*, an authoritive study of hill-top fertility ceremonies in Ireland at the time of Lúnasa, Máire MacNeill concludes that the number of sites where such ceremonies were held must have been at least one hundred and ninety five; and of the ceremonies for which she has some detailed descriptions only seventeen (out of ninety five) show any signs of having been Christianized. (Among the Christianized sites, St Patrick's Reek, of course, is the most notable example.) Máire MacNeill comments: 'A remarkable feature of these Lughnasa celebrations is that so many survived into the nineteenth and twentieth centuries without hav-ing been taken over by Christianity'.[15]

Curiously, the religious mystique of the hills does not seem to have been a major emotional focus for our creative writers; in particular for those writing in Irish. In popular songs and ballads, however, there is much mention, both in Irish and English, of the hills of the home place – from *The Hills of Donegal* to *Sliabh Geal gCua* – so that one is tempted to assume that the feeling of the Fianna for the freedom, beauty and stability of high places lived on strongly as a community value. Indeed some of our English language writers seem to mirror the ancient community opposition between Christian *cill* and pagan hill. Can it be fortuitous, for instance, that Behan speaks reverentially of the high places around Dublin while he somewhat facetiously points to his people's graveyard as 'the healthiest graveyard in Ireland'? Can it be fortuitous that Patrick Kavanagh's black pagan hills are looking 'eternally' north to Armagh – the principal *cill* of Christendom in Ireland? Despite Yeats's unfamiliarity with the sense of place in Irish tradition, can it be fortuitous that he also has linked *cill* and 'hill' together in some of his last lines?:

> Under bare Ben Bulben's head
> In Drumcliff churchyard Yeats is laid.

And it is, probably, not fanciful to suggest that Derek Mahon – while missing out on the *cill* – links freedom, stability and a sense of home with the timeless hills of Belfast:

> But the hills are still the same
> Grey-blue above Belfast
> Perhaps if I'd stayed behind
> And lived it bomb by bomb
> I might have grown up at last
> And learnt what is meant by home.[16]

It seems to me that reverence for homeplace and for the 'holy' sites in the homeplace – the *cill*, the hill, the *lios*, the well, etc. – does not make the same impact on novelists and short-story writers as it does on poets. Writers of fiction – especially novelists at home and abroad – tend to link their creative impulses with a region rather than with a single beloved place. Thus one associates Hardy with 'Wessex', Mauriac with Les Landes, Marquez with 'Macondo', Máirtín Ó Cadhain with Cois Fharraige. A basic requirement for many novelists is a large multi-layered cohesive community on which they can base their fiction. In this sense community for them is a substitute for place. Novelists, however, may frequently display a frustrated affection – rather than reverence – for their chosen community.

The American novelist, Louise Erdrich, has said: 'Through the close study of a place, its people and character, its crops, products, paranoias, dialects and failures, we come closer to our own reality. . . . Truly knowing a place provides a link between details and meaning. *Location, whether it is to abandon it or draw it sharply, is where we start*.[17] This could well be a description of Máirtín Ó Cadhain's short story opus – even of his efforts to substitute the city of Dublin for the region of *Cois Fharraige* in his later work; while the idea of abandoning a specific location in one's fiction and yet be completely dominated by a hidden sense of place or region applies, one thinks, to most of Beckett's novels and plays. As Elizabeth Bowen puts it: *Nothing can happen nowhere. The locale of the happening always colours the happening and often, to a degree shapes it.*[18] On the other hand some writers, poets as well as writers of fiction, reveal a distaste for – or at least an active disatisfaction with the place or region which fate has ordained for them. Some cultural obstacle or tension causes them to feel at odds with their home-place. Displaced, they often search for some other location where they can feel at ease, feel fulfilment. Among writers of this kind I would include Synge, Brian Moore, Derek Mahon, Seosamh Mac Grianna (probably), Seán Ó Ríordáin. Synge abandons genteel landlord life in Wicklow and reaches out for primitive Aran; Moore and Mahon reach out for everywhere else except Belfast; Seosamh Mac Grianna from Donegal chooses the coal valleys of Wales; Seán Ó Ríordáin chooses the Dún Chaoin Gaeltacht in preference to his birthplace, Ballyvourney.

Ó Ríordáin's case is instructive for those concerned with the Irish language. Dismayed by the manner in which the English language and culture had made inroads into the life of the former Gaeltacht of Ballyvourney, he seeks his 'house' and 'tribe' elsewhere. (Nor does he even mention the famous *cill* of the district, Cill Ghobnatan, where he himself is now buried.) He will find fulfilment in the rich traditional Gaeltacht of Dún Chaoin:

> Leave Gleann na nGealt and head back west,
> Renege on the contemporary in your blood,
> Shut your mind to what has happened
> Since Kinsale was fought and lost.
> And since the load is heavy
> And the road is long
> Rid your spirit
> Of the civilized yoke of English,
> Of Shelley, Keats and Shakespeare.
> Reclaim your patrimony,
> Cleanse your mind, and cleanse
> Your tongue bewildered by syntax
> At variance with your nature.

Confess and make your peace
With your own house
And your own people
And do not forsake them.
No man should forsake his tribe or habitation.
Take the cliff-edge west some sunny evening to
      Corca Dhuibhne
And you will find there shoaling on the horizon
The subjunctive and the dual number
And the vocative case on the lips of people.
That's your door,
Dún Chaoin in the evening sun.
Knock and you will find opening
The core of your mind and feeling.[19]

It is probably true to say that there is generally a strong connection bet-
ween a community's view of the otherworld and their view of this world.
The community, for instance, which provided Máirtín Ó Cadhain with
material for his early fiction, gave special homage not alone to the usual
'holy' places in their territory – the *cill*, the *lios*, the well, the boundary
fence in which unbaptized children were buried – but also treated with
reverence much of their daily material environment. Eoghan Ó Tuairisc,
in his splendid foreword to *The Road to Brightcity* (a volume of transla-
tions from the early Ó Cadhain opus) describes how close the interaction
can be between the material and the spiritual:

> The real difficulty of the tongue, and its prime attraction for a modern
> writer, is its unique mixture of the muck-and-tangle of earth existence
> with a cosmic view and a sense of 'otherworld'. This otherworld sense
> as Ó Cadhain presents it is a very complex combination of a fundamen-
> talist Christianity, emphasising the Fall of Man, with a large share of the
> old pagan nature religion. 'Ghost', 'phantom', 'fairy', 'the dead', 'the changel-
> ing' are practically identical terms, and all of them, along with the living
> are implicated in a conflict of good and evil, light and dark. Such a
> worldview is the opposite of romantic, for in it almost all aspects of wild
> nature – not only sea and storm, but the blue sky, the butterfly, the fine-
> weather sparkles on the water, the hazelnuts – are felt as hostile, always
> inhuman, at times malicious. Among the few friendly forces are eggs,
> fire, greying hair and, oddly enough, hendirt.
>   In this milieu many things are 'alive' – the thornbush, the filling tide,
> the wind through the telegraph wires. This Irish double view, a two-light
> of the mind, is most readily seen in the images, some extended into epic
> similes which are mini-stories in themselves, as when Bríd in *The Road
> to Brightcity* sees the dusky moon, adulterated in some primordial tragedy,

declining over the sea as a dying Cleopatra. Often these images are contracted into short phrases which express many areas of experience and
intuition in one - for instance, the afterlife, the grim graveyard, and the
little stonewalled garths of their daily struggle, are all apprehended in
the witty image 'na críocha déanacha', the final fields.[20]

Any community in which this continuous interaction occurs must have
a very unusual kind of cultural awareness; it is this whole community
culture of Cois Fharraige, rather than the specific locations within it, which
ignites the Ó Cadhain passion. So for him - as indeed for many other
writers - the importance of community supplants the importance of place;
or to put it in another way, place becomes community, community place.

The Cois Fharraige community culture is not in any special way unique
in Ireland for its underlay of non-Christian values and beliefs. Traditional
Irish literature - that part of it which is not overtly religious - reveals that
Christian values rarely left a strong imprint on its imaginative content.
Neither the numerous elegies or eulogies, love lyrics or love songs, of even
the Modern Irish period, show many signs of having been shaped in a
Christian society. Referring to Irish society in the period when most of
this literature was composed, a historian comments: '[An] amalgam of
paganism and Catholicism runs through life.'[21]

The concept of the Christian afterlife seems to be one of the values which,
to judge by Gaelic literature, made little impact. In the popular keens for
the dead where one might particularly expect an emotional acceptance
of the Christian eternity, there is generally little or, no hope expressed
of any kind of afterlife. In her turbulent keen for Art O'Leary, for instance,
Eibhlín Dhubh Ní Chonaill does not anywhere reveal even the most timid
expectation that she could still share eternal bliss with her husband. The
afterlife for her seems tantamount to propping up 'clay and stones'.

Likewise in the poem attributed to Aogán Ó Rathaille on his deathbed,
there is no sense of an eternal life; his expectation is rather of an eternity
spent under the earth in the company of those McCarthy kings whom
his 'people served before the death of Christ'. Interestingly enough, while
neither Aogán Ó Rathaille in his deathbed poem, or Eibhlín Ní Chonaill
in her lament, makes reference to an eternal God of creation, both poets
most meticulously mention the *cill* in which the dead body will lie.

There is, of course, a multitude of formal references to a belief in the
Christian God, and a Christian eternity, not alone in our substantial
religious literature, but in our still more substantial secular literature. But
even in our best religious literature, while there is a fundamentalist
adherence to Catholic dogma, there is very little feeling for a number of
Christian concepts including that of eternal bliss. The notion does not

seem to awaken any real imaginative response. One feels that Synge may have revealed the heart of the matter in his description of the keening of an old woman in the Aran Islands:

> This grief of the keen is no personal complaint for the death of one woman over eighty years, but seems to contain the whole passionate rage that lurks somewhere in every native of the island. In this cry of pain the inner consciousness of the people seems to lay itself bare for an instant, and to reveal the mood of beings who feel their isolation in the face of a universe that wars on them with winds and seas. They are usually silent, but in the presence of death all outward shows of indifference or patience is forgotten, and they shriek with pitiable despair before the horror of the fate to which they are all doomed. Before they covered the coffin an old man kneeled down by the grave and repeated a simple prayer for the dead. There was an irony in these words of atonement and Catholic belief spoken by voices that were still hoarse with the cries of pagan desperation.[22]

Whatever weight is to be finally attached to the various Christian and non-Christian elements in our culture, it is more than likely that the constant conflict between them has led to a deep ambivalence within the Irish psyche. The world/community/place depicted by Máirtín Ó Cadhain is indeed a true manifestation of the divided – and half-concealed – traditional Irish mind.

It may be significant, in relation to our traditional ambivalence towards the notion of an afterlife presided over by a Creator/God, that Irish/Celtic pre-Christian mythology seems not to contain any perception of a pagan God/Creator. While versions of an eternal life on earth are clearly imagined – from life underground in the *lios* to life overground in *Tír na nÓg* – there is no concept (so far as I understand from scholars of mythology) of a God or of Gods who fashioned it all. In short, there seems to be no Irish/Celtic creation story.

This absence of a sense of God/Creator seems most marked in the Old and Middle Irish nature lyrics (600–1200) – work admittedly, in which I cannot claim any expertise. The devout and religious lyrics of the same period do certainly proclaim the Christian message, but the nature lyrics (which are widely held to mirror a pre-Christian tradition) proclaim a contrary feeling. Things are seen and heard meticulously in the here and now, and responded to with a sort of impressionistic elation; as in these lines recording a blackbird call over Belfast Lough:

> A little bird
> has whistled now
> from a beak-tip
> brightly yellow –
> a blackbird's call
> over Belfast Lough
> tossed from bushes
> tufted yellow.

But, as far as I know, in none of the poems of this tradition is there a sense of a God who has created this beauty, this joy. The voice of a Creator does not sing for us in the song of the blackbird; nor does any super-natural spirit speak to us either within or without the material world of nature (as happens, say, in work so diverse as the poetry of Wordsworth or the poetry and lore of the American Indians). But what one does feel in most of this early nature poetry is the utter stability of this ever-changing world; and sometimes a hint of a *Fiannaíocht*-type conflict between the stable natural world and the concept of an eternal afterlife (as symboliz-ed by the hermit and his bell):

> Ah blackbird it is well for you,
> nesting somewhere in the bushes:
> hermit that clangs no bell,
> sweet soft peaceful is your whistle.

Can it be then that the half-concealed pre-Christian perception which lies deeply in the Irish subconscious is that the natural world is itself eternal; that there is no personal Creator, no transcendental afterlife? The Greeks – whose mythology also lacked a creation story – subscribed to this view. 'They believed,' says Stephen Hawking '. . . that the human race and the world around it had existed, and would exist for ever'.[23] Hawking himself is perhaps the best-known of the many contemporary physicists who are concerned about the concept of 'a beginning', a Creator. 'Hawking is at-tempting,' says one commentator, '. . . to understand the mind of God. And this makes all the more unexpected the conclusion of the effort at least so far: a universe with no edge in space, no beginning or end in time, and nothing for a Creator to do.'[24]

Any people, Greek or Irish, who would have sensed that this world was without end – or at any rate that this was the only world they would ever experience – were likely to identify in an intense fashion with it, and with special and beloved places on it. And if, of course, some sort of eternity was envisaged by them, on or under the earth of a world without end, the place of burial itself, the *cill*, would be seen as the necessary local en-trance through which one passed into eternity.

Referring specifically to Irish folk perceptions of an afterlife, Gearóid Ó Crualaoich has remarked on this connection between the local and the eternal: 'By contrast with the unfathomable or transcendent Christian afterlife the ancestral/fairy otherworld was envisaged as being located underground in the locality of the Community.'[25]

Thus the named local burial place tends to become the most revered of all places. And conversely, of course, the presence of the bodies of ancestors and relations in the family graveyard, magnifies greatly the bonding of the living with the family territory. A character in *One Hundred Years of Solitude* declares: 'A person does not belong to a place until there is someone dead under the ground.'[26]

From the seventeenth and eighteenth century onwards stern efforts were spasmodically made by a small band of Catholic clergy (aided at times by British legal measures) to root out non-Christian beliefs and practices in Ireland. Judging by the main body of literature in Irish, acceptance of these post-Tridentine reforms came very slowly indeed; but that some gains were made is clear from the work of a few religious poets and by the corpus of devotional stories and poems which survived in folk memory. Not until the nineteenth century perhaps were many of the beliefs, devotions, and practices, now imagined to be the essence of Irish Catholicism, propagated successfully. But that some of the reforms proposed were reluctantly accepted is evidenced for instance, by the constant stream of episcopal directives regarding the behaviour proper to people celebrating a central event in the Catholic calender – the feast day in the *cill* of the local patron saint.

The new amalgam of post-Tridentine Catholicism and British Victorianism, perpetuated (in parallel with the Irish-to-English language change) by the British educational system in the nineteenth century, made its greatest impact in cities and urban areas. Large tracts of rural Ireland, however, seem to have solidly preserved their traditional ambivalence regarding Christian values. To read of nineteenth century behavioural patterns in County Kilkenny as described in the diaries of Amhlaoibh Ó Súilleabháin,[27] or of life in County Tyrone as described by Carleton – or, as we have already noted, to discover twentieth century Connemara through the eyes of Máirtín Ó Cadhain – is to be convinced of that.

On the other hand, James Joyce, citizen of east coast Dublin, was heavily burdened during his schooldays with the dogmatic Irish Victorian version of Catholicism. His considered reaction was 'non serviam' – in effect the answer given by Oisín to St Patrick in the late medieval lays of the Fianna. He may have been somewhat ambivalent for a time regarding Catholic values, but there is no question but that he dissented finally from all Christian beliefs and found psychological stability in identifying only with the cities, rivers, and eternal places (both 'high' and low) of this world, rather than of the next; with Dublin rather than with God. In all this his values are much closer to those of the pagan Irish *dinnsheanchas* tradition than has generally been supposed. 'Almost no other writers in English,' says a British critic, 'have attempted anything like the same identification with place.'[28] In that respect, at least, James Joyce is the most traditional of all Irish writers, either in English or in Irish.

[1992]

17

Three Lyrics
I Like

I SOMETIMES FEEL that one can gain an added understanding of the nature of art by treating it as just another of the life games which help people – in particular, the artist himself – to 'survive'. Nobody, of course, survives finally; I use the word merely to indicate some *pro tem* resolution of emotional disturbance which enables a person to come provisionally to terms with the hurt or the ecstasy of life.

A good number of the life-games I have in mind – *Games People Play*[1] – are light routines which enable people to handle normal daily events with a minimum of discomfort. These tend to have a recognizable game-structure. This is particularly evident in the conversational element associated with many of them – from the typical conversational *duo* at breakfast time to the typical conversational *duo* in a barber's shop, from the dialogue of neighbours on a wet day to their completely different 'dry day' dialogue.

Games dealing with events which stir the human heart more deeply, the *rites de passage*, for instance, are commonly linked with religious rituals which give a special dimension to their structure. I am not aware of any civilization which does not ordain special rituals (i.e. games) in relation to birth, marriage and death. The Irish rituals dealing with death, in particular, have been widely noticed. From the numerous descriptions of our death rituals – one need only read Synge's account of keening on the Aran Islands – it is quite clear that they were used predominantly to help the living to 'survive'.

It appears, however, that the popular games or rituals do not always fulfil the needs of everybody – of artists, in particular, who tend to be more vulnerable, more emotionally volatile, than the norm. The traditional public keen or wake-ritual, for instance, has not been sufficient to assuage the grief of a number of our poets – from Muiríoch Albanach Ó Dálaigh (*c.*1200) to Seán Ó Ríordáin (*c.*1945) – who were endeavouring to 'survive' the death of a loved one. The game of poetry became their survival weapon. To 'survive' each had to develop a personal insight into his own special disturbance.

The raw material available to any poet who attempts to gain an insight into his/her feelings (which often lie partially concealed from consciousness) are words. The poet's poem then is a construct, a game of words, within which the development of an insight occurs. It is not a matter of the poet presenting a statement (*insint*/reporting, as Ó Ríordáin has it),[2] but of creating a construct in a way which communicates at different levels with his/her readers. In poems of quality I believe that evidence for the process of individual creation is present throughout the text.

Every poet goes about the task of creation, playing his/her own personal art-game – which quite often is found to be unconsciously modelled, to some degree or other, on traditional patterns.

I

It is not a very helpful exercise, generally, to attempt a minute analysis of a lyric as slight and simple as *Dínit an Bhróin* (*Grief's Dignity*) by Máirtín Ó Direáin. It is, however, instructive to note that the poem contains within it four distinct structured steps – from 'reporting' to 'creation' – in the art-game the poet (probably unconsciously) devises for us:

> I once had a glimpse
> Of grief's great dignity
> When I saw two women
> Emerge from a crowd
> In dark funereal garb
> Neither uttering a word:
> Dignity departed with them
> From the large and noisy crowd.
>
> A tender was in
> From a liner in the roadstead,
> Everyone was scurrying around
> Hubbub and loud chatter;
> But the silent couple
> Who emerged on their own

In dark funeral garb
Dignity departed with them

(trans. Mac Síomóin and Sealy)[3]

In the first section of his poem (the first six lines), the poet sets down a general 'report' regarding an occasion when he felt that some great dignity was linked with the grief of death. The level of these six lines differs little from the level of prose-writing most professional writers could aspire to; the main function of the section is to set the general theme (mentioned in line two) in context. The artistry of the first section, indeed, lies more in the ordering of the lines than in anything else. It is no accident, in particular that the last of the six lines is 'neither uttering a word' - thus enabling the poet (in section 2) to proceed to a more specific perception of the dignity of grief which he now sees leaving the noisy gathering in the company of two *silent* women. It is clear that Ó Direáin's emerging insight into the dignity of grief has much to do with the silent isolation in which it leaves the grief-stricken.

In the next section of the poem (section 3), Ó Direáin paints a fuller, more vibrant, picture of the noisy crowd. A liner, we hear, is moored out at sea: there is 'scurrying', 'hubbub', and 'loud chatter'. Having managed to create for us the feeling of quayside turmoil, the poet is now in a position (in section 4) to create for us, by contrast, the silent isolation of grief:

But the *silent* couple
Who emerged on their own
In dark funereal garb
Dignity departed with them.

We are finally persuaded *creatively* that the dignity of grief has indeed - in measured steps one thinks - departed from the gathering.

It can scarcely be claimed that Ó Direáin's insight into the grief of death is unusually profound or revealing, but the perception he creates here he creates with assurance and grace. Throughout the poem (in the original, at any rate), there is a sense of poetic integrity; the voice, from the beginning, is authoritative; the articulation of the insight is so fluid, indeed so naïve, that one could easily underestimate the degree of stylistic refinement needed to produce such a work.

To read the poem through as one unit, leaving aside any consideration of the various structured steps, is to be convinced that it contains just one simple created poetic perception.

II

A folk-lyric, to my knowledge, is rarely submitted to critical analysis. There is no reason at all why this should be so; there are many folk-lyrics – in Irish, at any rate – which merit a much sharper literary analysis than has yet been accorded them. Literary scholars, however, are slow to deal with folk-lyrics in the manner they deal with more 'literary' lyrics because they cannot talk about a settled authoritative text, or a known author, and so on. The literary critic, however, who is mainly concerned with the aesthetic experience provided by poetry ought not allow himself be disconcerted by such considerations; his main business should be to interpret the poetic insight emerging from the best text available for his purpose.

As it happens, I know of only one version of the folk-lyric *Mo bhrón ar an bhfarraige* (*My grief on the ocean*),[4] a version collected by Douglas Hyde from an old woman living in a bogland area of County Roscommon. As far as I am aware, this version is not linked with any traditional song-tune, nor can its composition be dated. The version below is probably a late nineteenth-century version; it is highly unlikely, for instance, that the reference made to emigrating to America would have been made before that time. Yet one cannot rule out the real possibility that the original lyric had been composed two or three centuries previous to that (the reference to America being inserted later).

The dating factor, however, is not of crucial importance. No matter what process of reworking of the basic text was carried out in community, the version we have today is an extremely sensitive work of art in which one can identify a genuine creative inner structure:

> My grief on the ocean
> it is surely wide
> stretched between me
> and my dearest love.
>
> I am left behind
> to make lament
> – not expected for ever
> beyond the sea.
>
> My sorrow I'm not
> with my fond fair man
> in the province of Leinster[5]
> or County Clare.

My grief I am not
with my dearest love
on board of a ship
for America bound.

On a bed of rushes
I lay last night,
and I shook it out
in the heat of the day.

My love came near
up to my side
shoulder to shoulder
and mouth on mouth.

(*D*, p. 287)

The main theme – the vastness of the sea-divide between the poet and her lover – is introduced immediately. The space between the lovers is magnified (in verse 2) by her understanding that she is doomed to remain at home, never to cross the sea.

Then suddenly a turn-about occurs (in verse 3 and 4). Perspectives begin to narrow: she begins to cut down the space between them. She names places in Ireland where she can imagine herself in his company – in the province of Leinster, or County Clare, or the Irish port from which they could sail to America. Finally she imagines (dreams?) that her lover has come to her during the night and slept with her on a bed of rushes 'shoulder to shoulder/and mouth to mouth': the space between them could not be less. When she wakes in the morning, however, she finds it all a delusion, and throws out the bed of rushes in despair. Her imagined closeness with her lover has left her in isolation, increased the sea-divide between them. For the first time we grasp something of what the rather naïve opening lines signify: 'My grief on the ocean/*it is surely wide*'.

My grief on the ocean, is a moving, sophisticated lyric. Most of the thematic material in it corresponds closely to that found in the international type of abandoned woman's love-song, but it is transformed here into a new refined sort of structure. The principal artistic device used by the poet is that of dramatic contrast so that the poem's final effect on us is to persuade us that the closer the poet imagines herself and her lover to be, the wider the ocean becomes between them.

III

Claustrophia by Seán Ó Ríordáin, which I have already looked at,[6] is worth looking at again in the context of the present discussion:

Beside the wine
there is a candle and terror,
The image of my Lord
Seems to have no power,
The rest of the night
Is like crowds without,
Night reigns
Outside the window;
If my candle goes out
In spite of me now
Night will leap
Right into my lung,
My mind will be overcome
And terror created for me,
I shall be turned into night
To be a living darkness:
   But if my candle lives on
   For one night alone
   I shall be a republic of light
   Till daylight comes.

(James Gleasure, T, p. 47)

Ó Ríordáin's general theme 'the terror of darkness *versus* the light of a candle' is stated in the opening lines. Traditional religious symbols associated with (sacrificial) altars are to the fore here – wine, a lighted candle, an image of the Lord. Even the image of the Lord is not affording him any protection from terror.

The terror (for which religious belief or ritual offers no antidote) is now more sharply defined. It emanates from the forces of darkness, well ordered and marshalled (*rialtas* na hoíche/the government of night, in the original Irish) outside his window: they are plotting to quench his candle, puncture his lungs – leaving the poet to take his place amongst the evil forces of darkness; to become himself a part of the 'living darkness'.

This feeling of active evil or darkness trying to eliminate him is a recurrent motif in Ó Ríordáin's work. The specific element of it which surfaces in the main body of this poem (lines 5 to 12) is terror of suffocation. (The title *Claustrophobia*, does not seem to me to describe the main mood). As soon as this terror is created for us – in nervous, palpitating lines – the poet returns unexpectedly to the candle which is still lighting. He had imagined the forces of darkness as being some sort of ruthless fascist government; as long as his candle lasts, he says now (with a wry grin), he will be a free independent 'republic of light/till daylight comes'.

The solitary lighted candle is commonly found in different cultures to symbolize steadfast hope of resurrection or survival. It is a much-favoured symbol in Ó Ríordáin's work but in *Claustrophobia* it signals only a very temporary relief, hope 'till daylight comes'. The more we sense this hope to be temporary, of course, the more it communicates to us the permanence of the threat of final suffocation.

I suggested at the beginning of this discussion that art-games bring for the most part only *pro-tem* resolutions of emotional conflict. One could scarcely imagine any resolution of the terror of death so temporary as the resolution offered in *Claustrophobia*, i.e., the hope of survival from night until the following morning. This was frequently, we know, the only kind of resolution Ó Ríordáin could hold out for himself. It is not at all far from the resolution arrived at by one of Beckett's characters: 'I can't go on, I'll go on.'

Of the three lyrics discussed, I suspect that *Claustrophobia* would make most impact on present-day readers. It communicates a palpable sense of the abyss (typical of the *zeitgheist* of most of the twentieth century) and in doing so avails of imagery which both encapsulates the poets feeling and connects vividly with the deepest reaches of the reader's subconscious.

Yet there are fundamental similarities in the creative pattern of *Claustrophobia* and the other two lyrics. Notwithstanding the fact that each of the three poets has his own individual voice, a common perception that he is addressing an audience of listeners (rather than readers) seems to emerge. More significantly, the main theme of each poem is stated immediately (in line 2 precisely), and then a more specific build-up of the main theme occurs in gradual recognizable steps so that a *dénoument* is achieved through the establishment of a basic dramatic contrast (noise/silence; space/closeness; darkness/light). It is interesting to note also that the substance of all three lyrics deal, to some degree or other, with the more serious events of life which are commonly dealt with by the *rites de passage*. Nor should it go unremarked that the simple metrical form used by the anonymous composer of *Mo bhrón ar an bhfarraige* is the basis on which Ó Ríordáin builds his own verse pattern.

It can be shown, I feel, that strong creative structural elements – though not always those discussed here – are present in a significant body of traditional Irish poetry, no matter what compositional conventions were observed by the poets and what their own conception of poetry was. I have attempted myself to point to these structures in work as diverse as the medieval literary love-poems, modern Irish folksong, the poetry of Aogán Ó Rathaille (d. 1729), the lament for Art Ó Laoghaire (c.1773), *The Midnight Court* (c.1780), the poetry of Seán Ó Ríordáin (d. 1977). From this experience it is clear to me that various types of dramatic structures were highly favoured in the Irish literary tradition.

[1990]

Notes to Chapters

1: Background

(Based on my preface to *Coiscéim na hAoise seo*, Ó Tuama and de Paor, Dublin 1991, and on the translation of parts of the preface by A. Mac Póilín in *Krino*, summer 1991.)

2: Seán Ó Ríordáin, Modern Poet

(Based on 'Seán Ó Ríordáin agus an Nuafhilíocht' in *Filí faoi Sceimhle*, Dublin 1978, pp. 1-80.)

1   From a typewritten copy in my possession.
2   From a typewritten copy in my possession.
3   From a typewritten copy in my possession.
4   Seán Dunne (ed.), *Poets of Munster*, Dingle 1985, p. 49.
5   Edmund Wilson, *Axel's Castle*, London 1961, p. 12.
6   See, for instance, M. White (ed.), *The Age of Analysis*, London 1955, pp. 65-81, 100-15.
7   See J.B. Leishman, *Rilke Selected Poems*, London 1964, p. 16.
8   John Gross comments: 'An epiphany means a "showing forth", and Joyce believed that if he transcribed a moment of revelation, however outwardly commonplace, with sufficient care, he could make it yield up its full spiritual value.' (*Joyce*, London 1971, p. 34).
9   F. Ponge, *Le Grand Recueil*, Paris 1961.
10 D. Donoghue, *Yeats*, London 1971, p. 71.
11 S. Burnshaw, *The Poem itself*, London 1964, p. 178.
12 Baudelaire, *Oeuvres complètes*, Paris 1961, p. 49.
13 C. Rycroft ed., *Psychoanalysis Observed*, London 1968, p. 74.
14 For his reading see Nic Ghearailt, *Seán Ó Ríordáin agus 'An Striapach Allúrach'*, 1988.
15 Rycroft, op. cit., p. 121.

16 For a commentary on *Fill Arís* see below pp. 260–61.
17 See Nic Ghearailt, op. cit. pp. 58-86.
18 D. Kiberd and G. Fitzmaurice, *An Crann Faoi Bhláth*, Dublin 1991, pp. 23-24.
19 E. Keeley and P. Sherrard (eds), *Four Greek Poets*, London 1966, p. 57.
20 Kiberd & Fitzmaurice, op. cit., p. 55.
21 Ó Ríordáin, *Tar éis mo Bháis*, Dublin 1978, p. 29.

3: 'The Loving and Terrible Mother,' in the Early Poetry of Nuala Ní Dhomhnaill

(Based on a lecture published in *Léachtaí Cholm Cille*, 17, 1987, and on a revised version in Ó Tuama, *Cúirt, Tuath agus Bruachbhaile*, 1990, pp. 159-76.)

1 Original text in *DD*, p. 39.
2 *Selected Poems*, London 1972, p. 158.
3 A translation of this poem is discussed below on pp. 252-53.
4 C. G. Jung, *The Archetypes and the Collective Unconscious* (*The Collected Works*, Vol. 9, part I, trans. R.F.C. Hull, Princeton 1980, p. 77).
5 E. G. Gose, *The World of the Irish Wonder Tale*, Dingle 1985. See p. 39.
6 Original text in *FS*, p. 32.
7 Original text in *FS*, p. 11.
8 See *FS*, p. 57.
9 *FS*, p. 65.
10 *FS*, p. 72.
11 Conor Cruise O'Brien, *The Irish Times*, 7 August 1984.
12 *H*, p. 79.
13 *H*, p. 123.
14 James Hillman, *The Dream and the Underworld*, New York and London 1975, p. 29.
15 Original in *FS*, p. 110.
16 Valéry, *Oeuvres*, Paris 1957, Vol. II, p. 787.
17 *H*, pp. 87-89.
18 *H*, p. 85.
19 *Ph*, p. 59.
20 *Ph*, p. 149.
21 *Ph*, p. 57.
22 *H*, p. 137.
23 *Ph*, p. 95-97.
24 G. G. Jung, op. cit., p. 188.

4: Background

(From *An Duanaire, Poems of the Dispossessed*, Portlaoise 1981, pp. xix-xxvi.)

1 *D*, no. 58.
2 *D*, no. 68.
3 *D*, nos. 34, 35.
4 *D*, no. 36.
5 *D*, no. 42.
6 *D*, nos. 45, 52, 53.
7 *D*, nos. 49, 50, 51.
8 *D*, no. 51.
9 *D*, nos. 28, 29.
10 *D*, nos. 40, 41.
11 *D*, no. 43.
12 *D*, no. 48.
13 *D*, nos. 62, 63.
14 *D*, nos. 76-83.
15 *D*, nos. 69-75.
16 *D*, nos. 23, 26.
17 *D*, no. 22.
18 *D*, no. 44.
19 *D*, no. 59.

5: Brian Merriman and his *Court*

(Published in *Irish University Review*, 1981, pp. 148-164.)

1 For a detailed comparison between *The Midnight Court* and various medieval works of the Court of Love genre see my essay 'Cúirt an Mheán Oíche', *Studia Hibernica*, Dublin 1964, pp. 7-27; also my later essay on the same subject in *Cúirt, Tuath agus Bruachbhaile*, Dublin 1990, pp. 7-37.
2 Máirín Ní Mhuirgheasa, *Feasta*, May 1951.
3 W. A. Neilson, *The Origin and Sources of the Court of Love*, Boston 1899, p. 214.
4 Nina Epton, *Love and the English*, Harmondsworth 1964, p. 102.
5 Ibid., p. 103.
6 See *Grá*, p. 38, note.
7 This speculation reverses a former suggestion of mine in 'Cúirt an Mheán Oíche', *Studia Hibernica*, p. 19, that the Court of Love genre might have existed already in the fifteenth or sixteenth-century Gaelic literary tradition.
8 For various viewpoints see R.A. Fraser, *The Court of Venus*, Durham N.C. 1955, and C. A. Huttar, 'Wyatt and the several editions of the Court of Venus', *Studies in Bibliography*, xix, 1966, pp. 181-95.
9 Ó Tuama, 'Cúirt an Mheán Oíche', op. cit., p. 23.
10 Johan Huizanga, *The Waning of the Middle Ages*, Harmondsworth 1955, pp. 110-12.

11 Frank O'Connor, *The Midnight Court*, London 1945, p. 10.
12 Cecile O'Rahilly, *Five Seventeenth-Century Political Poems*, Dublin 1952, p. 73.

6: The Lament for Art O'Leary

(Published under title 'The Lament for Art O'Leary and the popular keening tradition' in Alluin and Escarbelt (eds), *Mythe et Folklore Celtiques*, Lille 1987, pp. 103-125.)

1 S. Ní Chinnéide, 'A new view of eighteenth-century life in Kerry' in *The Journal of the Kerry Archaeological and Historical Society*, 1973, p. 92.
2 Peter Levi, *The Lamentation of the Dead*, London, 1984, p. 18. It is curious, however, that Peter Levi would make such a judgement on the basis of a translation of merely one poem from the vast Gaelic (and Welsh) literatures. Eilís Dillon gave me permission to use her translation of *The Lament for Art O'Leary*.
3 S. J. Connolly, *Priests and People in Pre-Famine Ireland*, Dublin 1982, pp. 148-49.
4 Vivian Mercier, *The Irish Comic Tradition,* Oxford 1969, p. 50.
5 B. Ó Madagáin (ed.), *Gnéithe den Chaointeoireacht*, Dublin 1978, pp. 26-28.
6 Ann Cornelisen, *Torregreca*, 1971, pp. 125-26.
7 Ibid., p. 249..
8 Françoise Gilot, *Life with Picasso*, London and New York 1965.
9 It has now been pointed out by L. M. Cullen that Morris was not High Sherriff at the time of the killing of Art O'Leary. See 'Caoineadh Airt Uí Laoghaire', *History Ireland*, Winter 1993, pp. 23-27.
10 Ó Tuama, *Caoineadh Airt Uí Laoghaire,* Dublin 1961.
11 Shán Ó Cuív, *Caoine Airt Uí Laoghaire*, Dublin 1923.
12 The translation of the last two lines is problematic.
13 Various themes and formulistic phrases common to keens in Ireland and Scotland (and to older literary texts) have been noted in *The Lament for Art O'Leary*. Oscar Wilde's comment is relevant here: 'The originality I mean, which we ask from the artist is originality of treatment, not of subject. The true artist is known by the use he makes of what he annexes, and he annexes everything'. See R. Ellman, *Oscar Wilde,* London 1987, p. 358.

7: The World of Aogán Ó Rathaille

(Based on 'Aogán Ó Rathaille' in *Filí faoi Sceimhle*, 1979, pp. 83-187, pp. 193-202.)

1 For a detailed discussion of these probable links see F, pp. 181-85.
2 *AOR*, pp. 181-83.

3 Mary A. Hickson (ed.), *Selections from Old Kerry Records*, II, London 1784, p. 187.

4 Ó Rathaille's status after dispossession from the Sliabh Luachra district wuld almost certainly be that of landless labourer, possessing at most a cabin / hovel, an acre of land and a cow (or two); and when he returned to Sliabh Luachra this was clearly his status still (see below p. 115).

It has been suggested to me that the use of the word 'hovel' may lead to an overdramatic interpretation of the wretched conditions under which Ó Rathaille lived at the time. It should be noted, however, that cabin / hovel were interchangeable terms used by English travellers in the eighteenth and nineteenth centuries, and describe the standard type of housing available to the mass of Irish people. See, for instance: E. Wakefield, *An Account of Ireland*, London 1812, vol. i, pp. 257-308, vol. ii, pp. 731, 735, 742, 745; Anon., *Journal of a Tour in Ireland*, London 1806, p. 18; John Forbes, *Memorandum made in Ireland in the autumn of 1852*, pp. 16, 40, 63; A. Young, *A Tour in Ireland*, Dublin 1780, vol. I, p. 97, vol. II, p. 83; H. D. Inglis, *Journey throughout Ireland*, London 1836, pp. 18-19, 22-23, 34, 38, 44-45, 56, 120-21; T. Campbell, *A Philosophical Survey of the South of Ireland*, London 1777, pp. 145-47; Anon., *A Tour through Ireland by two English Gentlemen*, London 1748, p. 147; J. Bush, *Hibernia Curiosa*, London 1764, pp. 29-31.

5 Mary A. Hickson (ed.), *Selections from old Kerry Records*, II, London 1874, p. 147.

6 P. Ronsard, *Oeuvres Complètes*, II, Paris 1950, pp. 550-59. For the related Pastourelle and Reverdie-type love formula, see below pp. 145-58, 156.

7 E. Mac Lysaght, *The Kenmare Manuscripts*, 1970, pp. 92-138.

8 Ibid., p. 112.

9 Ibid., p. 109.

10 There is no clear evidence as to what political event or situation caused this to happen. For a discussion see G. Ó Cléirigh, 'Cérbh é Mac an Cheannaí', *Irisleabhar Mhá Nuad*, 1983, pp. 7-34.

11 Hickson, op. cit., p. 182.

8: Gaelic Culture in Crisis: The Literary Response (1600-1850)

(Published in *Irish Studies: A General Introduction*, ed. Bartlett et al., Dublin 1988, pp. 28-43.)

1 B. Ó Cuív, 'The Irish language and political history', *A New History of Ireland*, III, Moody *et al* (eds), Oxford 1976, p. 509.

2 J.T. Leersen, *Mere Irish and Fíor-Ghael*, Amsterdam 1986, pp. 40-53; also, T. Ó Fiaich 'The language and political history', *A View of the Irish Language*, Ó Cuív (ed.), Dublin 1969, pp. 104-05.

3 A. Bliss, 'The English language in early modern Ireland', *A New History*

of Ireland III, op. cit., pp. 346-47.

4 *D*, nos. 25, 34.

5 Leersen, *Mere Irish and Fíor-Ghael*, op. cit., pp. 320-21.

6 P. J. Corish, *The Catholic Community in the Seventeenth and Eighteenth Centuries*, Dublin 1981, pp. 1-17; S. Ó Tuama 'Stability and ambivalence: aspects of the sense of place and religion in Irish literature', *Ireland, Towards a Sense of Place*, J. J. Lee (ed.), Cork 1985, pp. 29-32.

7 Ó Cuív, 510.

8 J. J. Silke, 'The Irish abroad, 1534-1691', *A New History of Ireland* III, op. cit., pp. 587-633.

9 *D*, no. 23.

10 *D*, nos. 35, 38, 45, 52, 53.

11 Ó Tuama, pp. 21-28.

12 A. Chambers, *Eleanor, Countess of Desmond*, Dublin 1986, p. 147.

13 *D*, no. 90.

14 *D*, no. 45.

15 *D*, nos. 49, 50, 51.

16 *D*, no. 52.

17 *D*, no. 53.

18 *D*, no. 50.

19 *D*, no. 46.

20 *D*, no. 54.

21 *D*, no. 56.

22 *D*, no. 57.

23 *D*, no. 58.

24 *D*, no. 62.

25 *D*, no. 55.

26 *D*, no. 48.

27 S. Ó Dufaigh and B. Rainey, *Comhairle Mhic Clamha*, Lille 1981, pp. 13-17.

28 Ibid., pp. 67-69.

29 D. Corkery, *The Hidden Ireland*, Dublin 1941, pp. 90-125.

30 Leersen, op. cit., p. 286.

31 L. de Paor, 'The rebel mind: republican and loyalist', *The Irish Mind*, R. Kearney (ed.), Dublin 1985, p. 175.

32 J. F. Nagy, *The Wisdom of the Outlaw*, London and San Francisco 1985, p. 13.

33 Ibid., pp. 17-40.

34 Ibid., p. 42.

35 Ibid., p. 42.

36 Ibid., p. 46.

37 Ibid., p. 48.

38 Ibid., p. 52.

39 *D*, no. 59.

40 See, for example, *D*, nos. 64-83.

41 Ó Cuív, p. 533.

42 S. J. Connolly, 'Marriage in pre-famine Ireland', *Marriage in Ireland*, A. Cosgrove (ed.), op. cit., pp. 78-98.
43 A. Cosgrove, 'Marriage in Medieval Ireland', op. cit., pp. 78-98.
44 *D*, no. 60.
45 *D*, nos. 40, 42, 43, 44, 63.
46 T. de Bhaldraithe, *The Diary of Humphrey O'Sullivan*, Cork 1979.
47 M. Wall, 'The Decline of the Irish Language', *A View of the Irish Language*, Ó Cuív (ed.), op. cit.

9: Love in Irish Folksong

(Based on my book *An Grá in Amhráin na nDaoine*, Dublin 1960, xv and 348 pages.)

1 W. P. Ker, *Form and Style in Poetry*, London 1928, p. 22.
2 P. Dronke, *Medieval Latin and the Rise of European Love-Lyric*, Oxford 1965-6, vol. I, p. 33.
3 J. T. Gilbert, *Facsimiles of National MSS of Ireland*, London 1879, vol. III and app. II.
4 *Grá*, p. 208. For a more detailed account of the history of the carole in Ireland (with appropriate references) see *Grá* pp. 203-17; for aspects of the musical structures employed see Joan Rimmer 'Carole, Rondeau and Branle in Ireland 1300-1800' in *The Journal of the Society for Dance Research*, vol. VII, no. 1, Spring 1989.
5 *Miscellany of the Celtic Society*, Dublin 1849, p. 97.
6 E. MacLysaght, *Irish Life in the Seventeenth Century*, Cork and Oxford 1950, p. 36.
7 R. Greene, *The Early English Carols*, Oxford 1935, p. cxli.
8 'The spoken languages of medieval Ireland', *Studies* 1919, pp. 237-38.
9 For a detailed account of the history of the English carol see R. Greene, op. cit.
10 For a detailed account (with appropriate references) see *Grá* pp. 220-49.
11 R. Green, op. cit., no. 445.
12 Ibid., p. xlvii, note 7.
13 *Grá*, p. 243, note 107.
14 Alexander Krappe, *The Science of Folklore*, London 1930, pp. 154-55.
15 J. M. Cohen, *A History of Western Literature*, Penguin 1956, p. 13.
16 For a detailed analysis and appropriate references see *Grá*, pp. 104-73.
17 G. L. Brook, *The Harley Lyrics*, Manchester 1948, p. 11.
18 C. Dawson, *Medieval Religion and other Essays*, London 1935, p. 142.
19 See Douglas Hyde, *Love Songs of Connacht*, 1909, p. 60.
20 For a detailed analysis and appropriate references see *Grá*, pp. 15-22. The classic source for the French origins of the Pastourelle and other medieval love-genres is A. Jeanroy, *Les Origines de la poésie lyrique en France au moyen âge*, Paris 1925.

21 *Grá*, p. 30.
22 For a detailed analysis and appropriate references see *Grá*, pp. 31-47.
23 *Grá*, p. 31.
24 A. Jeanroy, op. cit., pp. 150, 157, 334-6.
25 J. B. Entwistle, *European Balladry*, Oxford 1939, p. 133.
26 Margaret Dean Smith, *A Guide to English Folk-song Collections*, Liverpool 1954, p. 21.
27 *Grá*, p. 88-89.
28 See my essay 'Three Lyrics I Like', pp. 267-73 below.
29 *D*, pp. 312, 316.
30 *Grá*, pp. 48-75.
31 See below p. 168.

10: Background

1 Katherine Simms, *From Kings to Warlords*, Suffolk 1987, p. 4.
2 Osborn Bergin in D. Greene and F. Kelly (ed.), *Irish Bardic Poetry*, Dublin 1970, p. 4.

11: Love in the Medieval Irish Literary Lyric

(Based on my monograph *An Grá i bhFilíocht na nUaisle*, Dublin 1988, 93 pages.)

1 Frank O'Connor, *A Book of Ireland*, p. 257.
2 Frank O'Connor, *Kings, Lords and Commons*, London 1962, pp. 51-2.
3 Cross and Slover, *Ancient Irish Tales*, pp. 93-4.
4 Roger Boase, *The Origin and Meaning of Courtly Love*, Manchester 1977, pp. 129-30.
5 George Duby, *The Knight, the Lady and the Priest*, New York 1983, p. 217.
6 Jean Frappier, *Romania*, 1972, p. 188.
7 Robin Flower, *The Irish Tradition*, Oxford 1947, p. 143.
8 A. Young, *Love Poems*, London 1975, no. 18.
9 Frank O'Connor, *Kings, Lords and Commons*, pp. 69-70.
10 H. W. Simon, *The Complete Sonnets, Songs and Poems of William Shakespeare*, New York 1951, no. cxxxix.
11 See pp. 185-89 below.
12 Flower, *The Irish Tradition*, p. 148.
13 J. Stevens, *Music and Poetry in the Early Tudor Court*, London 1961, p. 228, note 33.
14 Pierre Bec, *Burlesque et Obscénité chez Les Troubadours*, Paris 1984, p. 7.
15 F. L. Utley, *The Crooked Rib*, Columbus, Ohio 1944, p. 45.
16 R. H. Robbins, *Secular Lyics of the xivth and xvth Centuries*, Oxford 1952, no. 37.
17 *U*, p. 76, note 70.

18 O'Connor, *Kings, Lords and Commons*, pp. 65-66.
19 *U*, p. 65.
20 *U*, p. 84.
21 K. Nicholls, *Gaelic and Gaelicised Ireland in the Middle Ages*, Dublin 1972, p. 73.
22 Canice Mooney, 'The Irish Church in the Sixteenth Century', *The Irish Ecclesiastical Record*, Dublin Feb. 1963, p. 106.
23 *U*, pp. 86-87, note 110.
24 J. M. Cohen, *A History of Western Literature*, Harmondsworth 1956, p. 26.
25 *U*, p. 19.
26 Frank Kermode, *Romantic Image*, London 1971, p. 121.
27 *U*, pp. 71-73, notes 32 and 33.

12: Some Highlights of Modern Fiction in Irish

(Based on my essay 'The other tradition' in *The Irish Novel in our Time*, Rafroidi and Harmon (eds), Lille 1975, pp. 31-47.)

 1 Original in M. Ó Droighneáin, *Taighde i gComhair Stair Litridheachta na Nua-Ghaeilge*, Dublin 1936.
 2 See T. C. McLuhan, *Touch the Earth*, New York, 1971, for a useful bibliography.
 3 Translation by Robin Flower, Oxford 1951. Translations from *An tOileánach* are by myself.
 4 Translation by Bryan McMahon, Dublin 1973, under title *Peig*.
 5 Translation by M. L. Davies and George Thomson, London and New York, 1933.
 6 Ibid., p. 14.
 7 See p. 16 of *An tOileánach*, first edition, for original.
 8 See p. 163 of *An tOileánach*, first edition, for original.
 9 Translated under title *An Irish Navvy*, by Valentine Iremonger, London 1964.
10 The discussion of Ó Cadhain which follows is largely based on a general review of his work by me, with particular reference to his autobiographical essay *Páipéir Bhána agus Páipéir Bhreaca*, in *Ériu*, xxii, 1972.
11 Ó Cadhain, *Páipéir Bhána agus Páipéir Bhreaca*, Dublin 1969.
12 Ibid., p. 19.
13 Ibid., p. 22.
14 Ibid., p. 42.

13: A Writer's Testament

(Based on 'A Writer's Testament', *Ériu*, xxii, 1972, pp. 242-48.)

 1 Dublin 1969.

2 See A. Titley, *Máirtín Ó Cadhain: Clár Saothair*, 1975, for a comprehensive bibliography.

14: Synge and the Idea of a National Literature

(Reprinted from M. Harmon (ed.), *J. M. Synge Centenary Papers*, 1972, pp. 1-17.)

1 Robin Skelton and David R. Clark (eds), *Irish Renaissance*, Dublin 1965, p. 57.
2 *Collected Works* III, pp. 15-17.
3 J. M. Synge, 'The Well of the Saints', *Collected Works*, III, p. 131.
4 Tomás Ó Criomhthain, *Allagar na hInise*, Dublin 1928, p. 66; trans.
5 Ó Criomhthain, *An tOileánach*, Dublin 1929, p. 163; trans.
6 Synge, 'Riders to the Sea', *Collected Works*, III, pp. 21-27.
7 Synge, *Collected Works*, II, pp. 74-75.
8 Roger Caillois, *Times Literary Supplement*, 25 September, 1970..
9 Synge, 'Deirdre of the Sorrows', *Collected Works*, IV, pp. 189-91.
10 James Joyce, *Finnegans Wake*, London 1939, p. 171.
11 See 'The status of linguistics as a science' in *Selected Writings of Edward Sapir*, D. G. Mandelbaum (ed.), Berkeley 1963, p. 162.

15: Daniel Corkery, Cultural Philosopher, Literary Critic: a Memoir

(Published in *Anglo-Irish and Irish literature*, B. Bramsbäch and M. Croghan (eds), Uppsala 1988, pp. 117-30.)

1 This general view of Corkery as teacher is borne out by other students of his. See P. Maume, *Life that is Exile*, Belfast 1993, pp. 122-23, p. 60 note 7.
2 Corkery, *What's this about the Gaelic League*, Dublin 1942, p. 15. Hereafter, *GL*.
3 Corkery, *The Philosophy of the Gaelic League*, Dublin 1943, p. 4. Hereafter, *P*..
4 John A. Murphy, *Cork Examiner*, 6 March 1978.
5 Seán Lucy, *The Canadian Journal of Irish Studies*, 3: 2, p. 6.
6 Corkery, *Synge and Anglo-Irish Literature*, Dublin 1931, p. 14. Hereafter *Synge*.
7 *P*, p. 10.
8 John A. Murphy, *Cork Examiner*, 6 March 1978.
9 *P*, p. 10.
10 *GL*, p. 21.
11 Frank O'Connor, *An Only Child*, London 1970, p. 161.
12 *Synge*, pp. 104-05.
13 Ibid., p. 21.
14 *P*, p. 24.

15 See my essay in *J.M. Synge Centenary Papers*, M. Harmon (ed.), Dublin 1972, pp. 9-11; and my 'Stability and Ambivalence', in *Ireland, Towards a Sense of Place*, ed. J. J. Lee, Cork 1985, pp. 21-33.

16 See my edition of *Caoineadh Airt Uí Laoghaire*, Dublin 1961, and my essay 'Dónal Ó Corcora and Filíocht na Gaeilge', *Studia Hibernica*, 5 (1965), pp. 29-41.

17 Louis Cullen, 'The Hidden Ireland: Re-assessment of a Concept', *Studia Hibernica*, 9 (1969), p. 7.

18 Corkery, *The Hidden Ireland*, Dublin 1941, pp. xxix and v. Hereafter, *HI*.

19 Ibid., p. 5.

20 Louis Cullen, *Studia Hibernica*, op. cit., p. 10.

21 Ibid. Louis Cullen writes: 'An immediately obvious limitation in Corkery's concept is that the location of the hidden Ireland appears to be curiously elusive'.

22 *HI*, p. 159.

23 I discuss this aspect of Corkery's criticism in *Studia Hibernica*, 5 (1965), pp. 32-35.

24 Ibid., pp. 35-41.

25 For Baring quotation, ibid., pp. 36-37.

26 See Frank O'Connor in *The Irish Theatre*, L. Robinson (ed.), London 1939, p. 52.

16: Celebration of Place in Irish Writing

(Based on my essay 'Ómós áite: a rian ar scríbhneoirí in Éirinn', *Comhar*, Bealtaine 1992, pp. 176-185; and on 'Stability and Ambivalence' in *Ireland, Towards a Sense of Place*, ed. J. J. Lee, Cork 1985, pp. 21-33.)

1 Máirtín Ó Direáin, *Selected Poems*, T. Mac Síomóin and D. Sealy (trans.), The Curragh 1984, p. 75.

2 Seamus Heaney, *Station Island*, London 1984, p. 37.

3 Eoin Mac Néill, *Early Irish Laws and Institutions*, 1935, pp. 99-100.

4 O'Connor, *Kings, Lords and Commons*, pp. 100-101.

5 Patrick Kavangh, *Collected Poems*, Martin Brian and O'Keefe, London 1964, p. 30.

6 Séamus Heaney, *Preoccupations*, 1980, p. 140.

7 *H*, pp. 152-53.

8 William Wordsworth, *Poetical works*, T. Hutchinson (ed.), 1974, p. 200.

9 Gordon W. MacLennan (ed.), *Proceedings of the 1st North American Congress of Celtic Studies*, Ottawa 1986, pp. 319-42.

10 Some scholars doubt if many of the places named in the Fiannaíocht ever existed. Perhaps their function was to establish the feeling of the fantasy-land of pre-Christian Ireland.

11 Frank O'Connor, *The Stories of Frank O'Connor*, London 1953, pp. 128-37.

12   See *T*, pp. 49-55.
13   Seumas O'Kelly, *The Weaver's Grave*, Dublin 1989, pp. 15-69.
14   Sorley Maclean, *Selected Poems 1932-72*, Edinburgh 1985, pp. 166-81.
15   Máire Mac Neill, *The Festival of Lughnasa*, vol. I, Dublin 1982, p. 68.
16   Derek Mahon, *Selected Poems*, Oldcastle, Co. Meath 1991, p. 51.
17   Louise Erdrich, 'Where I ought to be', *The New York Times Book Review*, July 28, 1985, p. 1.
18   G. Tindall, *Countries of the Mind*, London 1991, p. 2.
19   See Seán Ó Ríordáin, *Brosna*, Dublin 1964, p. 41.
20   Eoghan Ó Tuairisc (trans.), *The Road to Bright City*, Dublin 1981, pp. 10-11.
21   P. J. Corish, *The Catholic Community in the Seventeenth and Eighteenth Centuries*, Dublin 1981, p. 11.
22   Synge, *Collected Works* II, pp. 74-5.
23   Stephen Hawking, *A Brief History of Time*, London 1988, p. 7.
24   Ibid., p. x.
25   Gearóid Ó Crualaoich, *Cosmos*, vol. 6, Edinburgh 1990, p. 148.
26   G. Marquez, *One Hundred Years of Solitude*, London 1975, p. 19.
27   M. MacCraith (ed./trans.), *Cinn Lae Amhlaoibh Uí Shúilleabháin*, ITS London, 1928-37.
28   G. Tindall, op. cit., p. 6.

17: Three Lyrics I Like

(Based on 'Trí Liric a thaitníonn liom' in *Cúirt, Tuath agus Bruachbhaile*, 1990, pp. 184-92.)

1   See book of this title, E. Berne, New York 1978.
2   See introduction to *Eireaball Spideoige*, 1952.
3   M. Ó Direáin, *Selected Poems*, trans. Mac Síomóin and Sealy, The Curragh 1984, p. 5.
4   *D*, pp. 286-87.
5   'Munster' (rather than 'Leinster') appears by error in the translated text in *An Duanaire*.
6   See pp. 20-21 above for further discussion.

Index